excellence in

Services
Procurement

How to how to optimise costs
and add value

excellence in
Services
Procurement

How to how to optimise costs and add value

Barry Crocker, David Moore & Stuart Emmett

First edition published by Cambridge Academic, The Studio, High Green, Gt. Shelford, Cambridge CB2 5EG.

ISBN 1-903-499-53-4
978-1-903499-53-5

Printed and bound in the United Kingdom by
4edge Ltd, 7a Eldon Way Industrial Estate, Hockley, Essex, SS5 4AD.

Contents

About this book

This book compliments the other **Excellence in...** titles, for example, on Procurement, Supplier Management, Supply Chain Management, and also titles on Inventory, Freight Transport and Warehouse Management.

Why then a new title on Services Procurement? The authors have, for many years, observed that most books on Procurement cover mostly the procurement of material products and goods and give little attention to services. Whilst of course much of the process is the same, as noted by the Aberdeen Group *"services purchases represent one of the largest and largely untapped opportunities for cost savings within organisations."* The cost for services compared to products is high, simply because most services require the use of individual people with no opportunity for production economies of scale.

Indeed whilst preparing this book we saw the publication called **Central Government's Management of Service Contracts** by the National Audit Office (December 2008). Whilst this specifically covers Government public sector organisations, it also contains clear messages for all private sector organisations. The Key Findings are as follows, with the stated Central Government being bracketed here, to emphasise, the wider organisational aspects for non government service buyers:

- (Central government) organisations are not always according contract management the priority it deserves.
- (Central government) organisations do not always allocate appropriate skills and resources to the management of their service contracts.
- There are weaknesses in key performance indicators and limited use of financial incentives to drive supplier performance
- Despite the critical nature of the contracts in our survey, many did not have in place some or all elements of good practice risk management processes
- Value for Money testing can result in significant savings but the extent to which (central government) organisations tests the Value for Money of ongoing services and contract changes is variable
- In general, both (central government) organisations and their suppliers are positive about working relationships, though less than half of organisations had implemented a supplier relationship management programme despite what appear to be clear benefits.

We therefore cover these aspects and others in this and other books in the **Excellence in...** series.

In writing this book, we have endeavoured not to include anything that if used, would be injurious or cause financial loss to the user. The user is however strongly recommended before applying or using any of the contents, to check and verify their own organisation policy/requirements. No liability will be accepted by the authors for the use of any of the contents.

It can also happen in a lifetime of learning and meeting people, that the original source of an idea or information has been forgotten. If we have actually omitted in this book to give anyone credit they are due, we apologise and hope they will make contact so we can correct the omission in future editions.

About the authors

Barry Crocker

I am a lecturer in the Salford Business School at the University of Salford and am currently the Programme Leader for the MSc Procurement, Logistics and MSc Supply Chain Management. Previously, I had many years industrial experience in various management positions in the field of transport, warehousing and physical distribution.

I have also been an assistant chief examiner for the professional stage of the CIPS Diploma; an external examiner for several universities, and am currently external examiner for Leeds Metropolitan University.

My previous publications include, as co-author with Stuart, The Relationship Driven Supply Chain (2006), Excellence in Procurement (2008), Excellence in Supplier Management (2009) and with Bailey, Farmer, Jessop and Jones Procurement Principles and Management (2008). I have conducted many training sessions for multinationals in Africa, the Middle East, the Far East and Russia in the field of Procurement, Logistics and Supply Chain Management. Many of these were undertaken with co-authors, David and Stuart.

I would like to give special thanks to my lady, the lovely Rosalind, without whom this book would not have been possible.

David Moore

Having gained considerable experience in purchasing, logistics and supply chain management within public sector and commercial organisations, I entered academia with a view to 'put something back' into the procurement world. I never thought that I would be as well rewarded as I have been (not financially!) but by through the development of others and the pleasure of assisting others in moving forward with their careers.

At the University of Glamorgan, I developed and delivered Chartered Institute of Purchasing and Supply (CIPS) courses for organisations such as British Airways, London Underground and the Civil Service College. These were followed by the development and leadership of the MBA full time and part time programmes, as well as the MBA 'by Directed Learning in Bahrain.' In 1996, I joined Cranfield University where I initiated the BSc (Hons) Management and Logistics course and then the MSc Defence Logistics Management.

More recently I designed, developed and delivered the MSc Defence Acquisition Management course. Such has been the growth and development of education to enable effective procurement, logistics and supply chain management within the defence environment that I am now Director of the Centre for Defence Acquisition for Cranfield University at the Defence Academy of the United Kingdom.

I have undertaken extensive education, training, and consultancy assignments in the UK, USA, Europe, Middle East and Far East for many multinationals. I have also spoken at conferences around the world.

I am currently an External Examiner for Procurement Undergraduate and Masters level programmes at Strathclyde University and the University of Glamorgan. Particular interests include outsourcing, the use of contractors for service provision, management of relationships, humanitarian logistics and developing effectiveness through professionalism. I have written a number of books and book chapters plus conference and journal papers. I served in the RLC (TA) until 1999 and held both staff and CO appointments as Lt Colonel.

I have been married since 1974 to Sandy and we have two children of whom we are very proud, AJ who having gained a BA in Marketing is a radio presenter and Disc Jockey, and Charlie who, having very successfully completed her BA in French and Italian, is now attending Bristol University, where she is undertaking a teaching qualification.

Stuart Emmett

After spending over 30 years in commercial private sector service industries, working in the UK and in Nigeria, I then moved in Training. This was associated with the, then, Institute of Logistics and Distribution Management (now the Chartered Institute of Logistics and Transport).

After being a Director of Training for nine years, I then choose to become a freelance independent mentor/coach, trainer and consultant. This built on my past operational and strategic experience and my particular interest in the "people issues" of management processes.

Trading under the name of Learn and Change Limited, I now enjoy working all over the UK and on five other continents, principally in Africa and the Middle East, but also in the Far East and North and South America.

Additional to undertaking training, I also am involved with one to one coaching /mentoring, consulting, writing, assessing and examining for professional institutes' qualifications. This has included being Chief Examiner on the Graduate Diploma of the Chartered Institute of Procurement and Supply and as an external university examiner for an MSc in Procurement and Logistics.

My previous publications include, as co-author with Barry, The Relationship Driven Supply Chain (2006), Excellence in Procurement (2008) and Excellence in Supplier Management (2009). Other titles include, Improving Learning & for Individuals & Organisations (2002), Supply Chain in 90 minutes (2005) , Excellence in Warehouse Management (2005) , Excellence in Inventory Management (2007, co written with David Granville) , Excellence in Supply Chain Management; (2008) ; Excellence in Freight Transport" (2009) and a series of seven Business Improvement Toolkits (2008) with individual titles on motivation, learning, personal development, customer service, communications, systems thinking and teams. Whilst these toolkits are written for a general audience, the case studies and examples have many supply chain applications.

I am married to the lovely Christine and with two adult cute children, Jill and James; James is married to Mairead, who is also cute. We are additionally the proud grandparents of three girls (the totally gorgeous twins Megan and Molly and their younger sister, Niamh).

I can be contacted at stuart@learnandchange.com or by visiting www.learnandchange.com. I do welcome any comments.

1: Procurement Objectives

In this part of the book we give an overview of what procurement is and how it functions, along with discussions of the methods that are used in the procurement process. These aspects can be seen as being essential and foundational, and they will be amplified in later parts of the book when we consider some of the more specific service contexts and drill down into the some of the appropriate detail.

Procurement Evolution

Procurement is steadily evolving and changing through the following stages:

- **Stage one:** Product centred procurement that was concerned with tangible products and outcomes.
- **Stage two:** Process centred procurement that has moved beyond stage one into process measurement.
- **Stage three:** Relational procurement that has expanded into purchaser/ supplier relationships.
- **Stage four:** Performance centred procurement that focuses on best product/ service management and integrates relationships, processes and outcomes, which are jointly resourced with suppliers.

To undertake this evolution, procurement needs to be integrated through all of the strategic, tactical and operational levels in organisations, for example to:

- Acquire and procure what the organisation needs, by spending money externally, to satisfy the needs of internal customers/users or external customers.
- Follow up on the performance of suppliers.
- Provide information and services to internal customers.
- Liaise, integrate and coordinate the internal supply chain.

Procurement and the Internal Offer

In many organisations Procurement does occupy a role that:

- recognises that buying gives both Value for Money and cost reduction.
- takes whole/holistic views over the longer term.

- uses a more integrative process approach.
- builds internal and external relationships.
- coordinates with suppliers so as to meet the requirements of the users/ customers.

Many organisations, however, actually operate their procurement activities sub-optimally and in a silo. This is because suppliers, organisations and internal business are not integrated in any meaningful way.

Whilst such issues have been fully covered in *Excellence in Supplier Management* (Crocker and Emmett 2009), when it comes to services, this can be an especially difficult issue; it is not unusual to find many internal users are involved with buying services directly with suppliers with little or no procurement department involvement.

Procurement should therefore be part of the corporate strategy of an organisation which involves aspects such as value, risk, cost, service etc. and recognises that these are all involved in a complex series of trade-offs that attempts to optimise the "whole" business/supply chain.

Strategic and Corporate Procurement

Corporate Strategy

Corporate strategy links down to business strategy which in turn links to functional strategy, for example of the procurement function. The following points can be noted on the links and connections between strategies:

- Strategy is long term, broad in scope and can be determined at corporate, business or functional levels.
- Strategy is best applied by establishing a mission or goals, assessing the organisation, assessing the environment, identifying strategic options, implementing strategy to achieve the chosen option(s).
- Continuous improvement will be needed to gain competitive advantage in times of dynamic change in global markets, shortened product life cycles and more demanding customers.
- Value is essentially what is perceived by the customer and is something they are prepared to pay for.

Corporate strategy is therefore a concept of an organisation's business, which provides a unifying theme for all its activities by asking three basic questions:

- What is the mission: what will we do and for whom will we do it (what business are we in?).
- What objectives do we want to achieve (what are the goals?).
- How will we manage the activities to achieve the chosen objectives?

Strategic Management of Procurement

Strategic management of procurement will need to include the following:

- Reviewing existing suppliers related to potential supply risks for the business and the spend levels.
- Identifying a number of potentially strategic suppliers.
- Examining existing activities to see if they can be outsourced.
- Developing strategic alliances, collaborations and partnerships.
- Developing strategic performance criteria.

The strategic management of procurement will need to be related to the corporate strategy and the needs of the business. For example, a local public sector authority will need to demonstrate public accountability.

Taking a more strategic view of procurement involves the following differences:

Operational procurement	Strategic procurement
Transactional order placers	Value added facilitators
Short term	Long term
Cost focus	Customer/user focus
Internal view	External views
Performance statistics	Benchmarking
Technical processes	Business process

Procurement Objectives and the 5 Rights

In examining the objectives of the procurement process, let us make the important point that these objectives do not necessarily equate to only one functional department in an organisation.

A classic definition of procurement is the Five Rights:

"Securing supplies, materials, and services of the right quality in the right quantity at the right time from the right place (source) at the right cost."

It should be appreciated that the Five Rights (quality, quantity, time, place and price) are inter-related and not mutually exclusive. Using them, however, ensures that all aspects have been considered and the priority by which the rights are applied can also be dictated by organisational strategy and the requirements of the business. It is these requirements to satisfy needs that are the driver for procuring.

It is important to note here, that these requirements are not those of the procurement department but rather those of the business; the procurement department being an internal service provider that works towards meeting such ends.

Meanwhile another aim for procurement is:

"To obtain bought in goods/services at the lowest acquisition cost."

The Total Acquisition Cost (TAC) concept emphasising that more than the cost price is involved, and we shall be examining this important price concept soon, but let's first look at each of the Five Rights.

Again, it should be appreciated that these Five Rights apply for the business, additionally, as we will explain; the Five Rights also become critical in determining key performance indicators for the procurement process.

The Right Quality

Quality is the degree of level of excellence as perceived by the customer; it may also be viewed as the product or service being "fit for purpose" and also "performing right first time every time". These involve:

- Meeting requirements.
- Fitness for purpose.
- Minimum variance.
- Elimination of waste.
- Continuous improvement culture.

The right quality should be agreed by the buyer with their customer. Whilst their customer may be restricted by design, performance or safety factors, the buyer may be restricted by costs and market competition. From the buyer's perspective, the quality agreed should also allow for and facilitate fair competition between suppliers.

The Right Quantity

The right quantity to be ordered by the buyer and being sold by the supplier, will attempt to balance the requirements of both parties. When taking a wider procurement/supply chain management view, then, possibly, collaboration or partnership methods may well be used in the supplier/customer relationship to better balance the requirements.

The Right Time (to buy and to deliver)

The right time to buy will be influenced by the following factors:

- Availability.
- Market conditions.
- Competition.
- Procurement policies.
- Customer Demand.

The right time to deliver will be influenced by:

- Supply lead time, which includes the supplier's lead time.
- Organisational requirements.
- Customer demand.

The Right Place

Buyers need to ensure that the products or services are bought from the right supplier. Once the source has been identified, the market conditions will need to be assessed and a formal supplier appraisal may be needed, depending on spend, volume and risk. It is also often the responsibility of the buyer to ensure that the services are delivered to the right place.

The Right Price

Information on prices should be gathered to allow full analysis of market prices. For example, raw material prices could be monitored as such prices may affect the cost of services that are being bought, for example, the fuel costs in third party transport logistics.

Total acquisition cost (TAC) is a concept that can be used to cover the Price Paid plus all of the other costs that are involved or result from the purchase, for example, with services:

• Quality	e.g. errors, defects, returns
• Delivery	e.g. transport modes, timescales
• Delivery Performance	e.g. non availability, unreliability
• Lead Time	e.g. cost of waiting
• New Supplier	e.g. start-ups, assessments
• Administration	e.g. order processing

The question to be answered is: exactly what are all these costs, beyond the price paid?

The importance of TAC is that it goes beyond looking only at the cost price and emphasises that there is more involved than just the lowest cost price.

Factors affecting the immediate cost of acquisition are as follows:

- initial price.
- cost of financing.
- terms of payment.
- performance and technical guarantees.
- liquidated damages.
- conformance with programme.
- after-sales service/support.

The 5 Rights and Supplier/Buyers

The Five Rights actually connect customer/internal users, buyers and suppliers. The following commonalities can be identified.

Quality

Clarity with suppliers will better enable the meeting of quality requirements. Customers who are very clear on their specific requirements may generate a response from their suppliers that gives them some alternative options. Sharing of requirements is therefore useful; after all, suppliers "do not know what they do not know." Suppliers can then deliver the appropriate quality required in accordance with a negotiated "right price."

Quality needs to be designed into services before they are supplied and those organisations working collaboratively with suppliers can more easily ensure that this is the case.

Quantity

It is the placing of an order quantity that triggers the ongoing buyer/supplier relationship. Order size differences between the parties will require discussion. It may be that allowing suppliers access to demand information and forecasts will enable them to plan better, and enable them to better match the buyer's requirements for more instant service.

Time

In the total supply lead time, the supplier's lead time only starts after the all of customer's internal processes have been completed. If therefore, buyers/customers are reporting supply lead time delays or variations in the supply lead times, then it may not be always the "fault" of the actual supplier. An examination of lead times will therefore indicate all the process involved in the lead time "chain." Supply lead time is a critical aspect of procurement and has been examined in *Excellence in Procurement* (and is discussed more fully, for products, in *Excellence in Inventory Management*).

Place and delivery

It should also be appreciated that delivery has common Key Performance Indicators (KPIs) for both the supplier (on the outbound delivery) and the customer (on the inbound delivery), for example deliveries being, on time, in full. If both parties are able to record these on a per transaction basis and then share such measurements openly and periodically, they will find that this enables better communications and understanding.

Cost/price

If total cost approaches are used, then there is really little to stop the sharing of the results with suppliers. Again, this can mean that they may be able to better suggest alternatives and options. It will also show fairness, which is what many suppliers look for.

Costs on services have some classic signs of cost saving opportunities, and opportunities to determine whether potential for price reductions exist. The following are some of these signs:

- there are many suppliers in different locations for a nationally consistent service.

- use of a single, non-competitive source, yet there is a competitive supply market waiting to be contacted.
- no written contracts.
- existing contracts are old and are automatically renewed.
- multiple contracts with the same supplier.
- paper intensive ordering/approval process.
- no real ordering/approval process.
- price for similar services are varied and are not in line with market benchmarks

The 5 Rights and Key Performance Indicators (KPIs)

Key performance indicators (KPIs) must be determined, and are discussed more fully in part 3 of *Excellence in Procurement*.

Suffice to note here that the determining and handing over of KPIs to be used in monitoring the following service performance delivery, follows on from the order stage. The order stage therefore "scene sets" how the subsequent contract and orders should be handled. Accordingly, time spent now in determining and agreeing KPIs with all the relevant players is time well spent to prevent subsequent confusion and disputes. This may well involve determining service level agreements.

Service Level Agreements (SLAs)

These can be defined as the following:

"A contract that defines the relationship between a supplier and a customer."

"A negotiated agreement designed to create a common understanding about service."

SLAs therefore set objective targets that prioritise needs and wants, by defining what is acceptable for both supplier and customer. SLAs attempt to clarify the following:

- What is expected?
- What the supplier will supply/deliver?
- How often will it be supplied?
- To what quality standards will it be supplied?
- At what price?

- What are the supplier's obligations?
- What is the recourse for both parties if things go wrong?

Typical clauses in SLAs are as follows:

- Service description.
- Service levels.
- Duration.
- Reporting levels.
- Level monitoring.
- Performance standards.
- Review meetings/frequency.
- Dispute resolution.
- Termination.

We will return to the importance of SLAs later in the book.

Procurement of Products and Services

There are some important differences between products and services and, whilst this book is totally about services, it is useful early on to look at these differences.

Services procurement is viewed by some as being indirect procurement, whereas direct procurement covers products, goods and materials. The following differences can be seen:

5 Rights	Products	Services
Quality	Tangible so testing is possible	Intangible therefore difficult to access
Quantity	Large to low orders	Often low quantity
Time	Regular frequency	Irregular frequency
Place	Sourcing can have global origins	Locally dependency is paramount
Cost	Low to high	Usually high

Services have many unique attributes that require a different approach from a standard product procurement solution. The following can be noted on services procurement:

Needs are often unique.
Business processes and sourcing options will differ by service context/category, part 5 of this book looks at such differences. For example, it will show that the eventual price charging will often depend less upon service level milestones or upon the user's own measures of service satisfaction.

Spending control is decentralised.
Different business units and departments are usually buying different services. Centralised buying, as used with standardised product contracts, is not usually an automatic option for services. The view here is that the standard workflows have to fit in with specific individual local requirements and that such local knowledge must be available so that new users, categories and suppliers, can all be easily and readily served on a local basis.

Subjective factors come into play with services buying.
Buyers purchasing services will, generally, have to give more emphasis on subjective factors; these being things such as skills, knowledge, experience, references and sometimes the specific identification of individuals.

Services are also more complex and difficult to price than goods; buying marketing services for example, involves many intangible activities, such as how to price the creativity involved in coming up with an excellent advertising slogan. Investment and spend on consultancy services may be extremely worthwhile, but how do you measure the value or the success?

The total process must be tracked rather than just the order delivery management.
Unlike goods purchases, the value obtained from the services doesn't always happen with the receipt/usage of the service; full value can be only found when the service people have delivered the service and left. It is therefore much more difficult to manage a services contract than a product supply contract. Thus, the total process engagement must be tracked to ensure that the expected value was delivered, for example:

- Did the temporary worker show up each day, as promised?
- Did the contractor do all the work that was expected?
- Did the consultant complete the project on time and in full?
- Did the contractor meet the service level agreements (SLAs)?

Therefore, someone must track the whole performance of the service provider/supplier to make sure that the expected value was delivered; for example, supplier invoices must not be paid without checking the applied rates or verification of the value delivered. Whilst it may not be the procurement department's job to do this, someone must.

Procurement may actually only place the order and then wave it goodbye, leaving someone else to ensure the total service delivery is in accordance with criteria/expectations; a theme very fully explored in our book *Excellence in Supplier Management.*

Who undertakes the end-to-end management review of services is, to say the least, important. It this is not done properly, then *caveat emptor,* "let the buyer beware" – the buying organisation is most clearly placing itself at risk.

Services procurement is more locally dependent.
Unlike goods and materials procurement, which can be specified centrally, nearly every office in an organisation is actively buying and receiving services. Yet in many countries and each region there are often differing laws or regulations governing labour, taxation, audit ability and data privacy. Moreover, language requirements and supplier networks are often regionally dependent.

Product characteristics.
For some absolute differences between products and serves, we can see that products are those things bought and owned, that will satisfy a want or need. Product characteristics are as follows:

- Goods are tangible.
- They can be specified in quantifiable terms such as dimensions, weight, colour, conformance to a standard of workmanship and the required reliability standard.
- There is usually a time gap between production and consumption.
- Has features; those characteristics beyond the product's basic functioning
- The performance is the designed output levels that may have been engineered into the product to give a specific level of reliability for given operating conditions.
- Has an expected operating life.
- Reliability; the probability that a product will not malfunction or fail within a specified period of time.

- Reparability; the ease of fixing a product that malfunctions or fails.
- Style; how well the product looks and feels to the buyer.

Services characteristics

Services are also bought to satisfy needs and can be defined as:

"The performance or act from one to another that does not result in ownership".

Services are an intangible exchange that may or may not be connected to a physical product; they are thus perishable and cannot be stored.

Compared to products, the performance of services may be often highly variable and unreliable, as whilst products can be engineered and certified/tested to give a standard and known reliable performance, services will nearly always rely on the performance of people.

With regard to services, whilst the products and goods (like the plant, equipment, hardware) have a real part to play on the service performance, ultimately it is the people delivering the service that will give the value/satisfaction.

Services have the following characteristics:

- Are intangible:
    - cannot really be seen, tested, touched, felt etc.
    - have to be experienced/bought.
- Are produced and consumed at the same time.
- May have a variable performance.
- Are perishable and cannot be stored.
- Often the success in delivery of services appears to be due more to qualitative factors such as the human interactions between the user and provider; rather than the terms of the supply contract.

Services can however, also be directly involved with products as follows:

- Installing; the work done to make a product or service operational in its planned location.
- Training; ensuring the customer's employees can use products properly and efficiently.

- Consulting; data, information systems and advising services that the seller offers.
- Repairing; describes the quality of repair service available to buyers of the organisations product.
- Delivering; how well the product and supportive service has been delivered/received/used.

Procurement by the Strategic Requirements of the Service

As we have shown, Procurement departments have a strategic role. They should therefore arrange procurement according to the strategic requirements of the business, or simply by what is the most important for the organisation.

For example, once a need has been identified, next is to determine the importance which is applied to the service that is required. ABC/Pareto analysis, or the 80-20 rule, provides a basis to identify where spends are the greatest and where, therefore, most effort should be directed to reduce costs.

Pareto analysis can also be most usefully run separately for both product procurement spend and for service procurement spend – the 80/20 rule here noting that in most cases, 80% of the procurement spend is concentrated with 20% of the suppliers used.

Additionally, risk and other factors are involved and these can be viewed from high to low, against the following criteria:

- Experience with the service (high risk for a new, untried services to a lower risk for repeats).
- Supply/demand balance (short supply/excess capacity).
- Supply chain complexity (many parties involved to "direct" purchases).
- Financial aspects of supply disruption (high to negligible costs).
- Safety consequences of disruption (high to low hazards).
- Design maturity (new to established services).
- Service complexity (complex to simple).

The other factors can also be rated from high to low against the following criteria:

- Market structure (many sources to a monopoly supplier).
- Value of spend (high to low spending).

- Supply/demand balance (spare to no capacity).
- Efficiency of buying process (identical for all, to tailored buying).
- Development of buying process in the organisation (users agree specifications to cross functional reviews).
- Knowledge of supplier's pricing (cost plus to market based pricing?).

To account for both spend and risk; based on the work of Kraljic, purchases can be broken down into four categories:

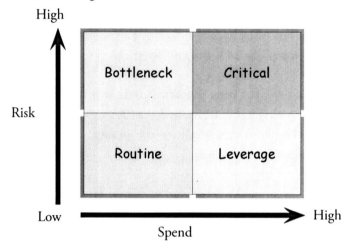

This indicates that different purchases have different strategic requirements to a business. It also can give a broad indication of how buying and the supplier relationships can be conducted.

Some examples of different services, from the oil and gas sector, for each of these four categories are as follows:

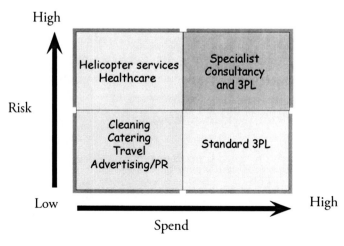

Clearly in different organisations the above examples would differ, but in general terms the following will be involved:

Leverage; Low risk, high spend items
*   Leverage items are those where a high volume is purchased with a high level of supplier numbers giving competition. Here the lowest cost can easily be found. There would be a need to create competition in the marketplace for these items to drive down price. The supply market is however a competitive one, with many available sources, hence buyers are able to leverage by maximising economies of scale and by offering large spends in return for lower prices.

Routine; Low risk, low spend items
*   Routine buying of standard services, needing efficiency. Minimal effort is needed for sourcing these items due to the relatively low impact procurement can make to reducing purchase costs. Therefore acquisition costs are targeted by the use of credit cards, internet ordering and call-offs, with users directed to place orders direct with the selected supplier; who then reports on the usage.

Critical; High risk, high spend items
*   Critical items require closer supplier relationships to ensure they are always available. Additionally the service required maybe a specialised one and will involve usually longer term relationships and partnering approaches with suppliers. These items rank high in the Pareto analysis of spend but can also be difficult to source due to low numbers of suppliers. Close supplier relations are needed with possible use of joint working and multi-functional teams.

Bottleneck; High risk, low spend items
*   The need here is to ensure the supply and reduce the risk of non-supply and disruption to the business. Suppliers are often few in numbers, for example, a monopoly supplier of helicopter services. These items would not rate as important when analysing spend alone, but due to difficulties in-sourcing there would need to be concentrated effort to secure supply of these items as the supplier often has the power.

Levels of risks

Risk is the impact of uncertainty and results from:

- an unexpected event, for example, a "wildcat" strike.
- false assumptions, for example, on supplier performance.
- human failure, for example, misinterpretations of requirements.

The sources of risk can be as follows:

- poor planning.
- not enough competent resources.
- unrealistic timescales.
- evolving technology.
- poor communication.
- insufficient task definition.
- financial restrictions.
- legislative requirements.

The level of risk will depend on a variety of factors, such as those already covered above; the strategic requirements of the product, the spend and the usage. The acceptable level of risk will therefore vary from contract to contract.

Risk can rarely be eliminated, but it can be managed or transferred to another party; the key principle is that risk should be allocated to whichever party can best manage it. Of course risk must always be managed; merely "dumping" the risk on a supplier is likely to create an eventual failure, during which the buyer's organisation will also be directly affected.

In conducting business, commercial risks will often need to be taken and, specifically for procurement, the following are examples of commercial risks:

- supplier liquidation.
- poor performance.
- supplier failure to meet environmental requirements.
- cost and/or price inflation.
- changes in law.

Risk factors must be identified and then the probability of each risk occurring should be estimated. Risks can then be placed in rank order and the likely impacts of each risk on success factors are determined.

The risk assessment process therefore has the following four stages:

- identify potential problems and causal factors.
- consider possibility of problems arising.
- weight factors and assess impact.
- devise strategies to control risk.

Procurement Strategy

As noted earlier, many organisations actually operate procurement sub-optimally and we also noted that the value, risk, cost, service etc. are involved in a complex series of trade-offs and suggested that these must be examined with all relevant parties to optimise the "whole" business/supply chain.

Therefore suppliers, customers and the internal business must be integrated in a meaningful way. Many organisations therefore need aligning to their core business drivers, such as customers' "needs."

This in turn impacts on the core business competences and capacity. It will also require internal integration and the removal of functional silos, or "win the home games first" as described more fully in *The Supply Chain in 90 Minutes*.

Externally, this will mean developing a clear strategic view and fit of suppliers using, for example, the above Kraljic procurement portfolio analysis.

The following ideal-typical view presents an overview and outline strategy for procurement. As with all ideal-typical views, it is not "absolute", but is intended to demonstrate the alternative methods available and that "one size does not fit all."

Aspect	Bottleneck Items	Critical Items	Routine Items	Leverage Items
Supplier numbers/availability	Fewer specialist monopoly/oligopoly suppliers	Few to More suppliers	Many suppliers	Many competing suppliers
Power	With supplier	Interdependent	Independence	With buyer
Alternatives	None to few	Few to none	Many	Many
Costs of disruption	High	High to medium	Low	Medium to low
Relationships	Close with the preferred suppliers. Long term. Supply agreements.	Long term "partnerships" and collaborate with selected trustworthy and reliable suppliers.	Short term and often "distant" and "arms length."	Short term "deals" with possible long term buying consortiums, alliances, groups to concentrate buying power.
Buyers Needs	Need security and certainty of supply. Then find alternative sources.	Need security and continuity of supply.	Need to simplify product variety and the ordering/supply process.	Need low cost supplies.
Service quality	Critical	Critical	Marginal	Marginal
Procurement Staffing	Hi level buyers with market knowledge and contingency plans.	Top level buyers in the start up, implementation and monitoring.	Low level buyers, procurement maybe actually contracted out.	Medium level buyers.
Sourcing methods	Elemental questionnaires. RFI/RFQ	Comprehensive questionnaires. Competitor analysis can be used. Agreements for shared risk and responsibility.	RFI/RFQ with possible ITT / competitive bidding.	Elemental questionnaires with some RFI/RFQs. ITT and competitive bidding with reverse/e-auctions.
Terms/Inquiries	Negotiate. Availability and Supply "Rules." Term contracts.	Open book with "Partnership"/ blanket agreements.	Direct Negotiations. Price and Availability "Rule". Price agreements.	Wide negotiations. "Price rules" with "wheeler dealing." Multi-sourcing.
Orders	Standard POs. Framework agreements, medium term contracts. Quick responses.	Possible framework agreements with call offs and vendor managed inventory.	User direct call offs with agreements; otherwise spot buys/self managed with P cards/web ordering.	Standard POs.

An important aspect to consider here is how the different strategies line up and if they are really being consistently applied in the organisation.

For example, an organisation may proclaim that "quality is number one in our business", but then they select suppliers based on the lowest price. They may also say that partnership approaches are preferred, but it is actually adversary buying methods that rule.

The point here of course, as with any strategy: it is the implementation and application that is critical; the design is the easiest part. Merely trying to implement by the planners and strategists "waving the wand" is damaging, wrong and can be fatal. It is a pity that more strategists in organisations (and in politics) do not recognise this simple and eternal truth.

The Procurement Process Cycle

This cycle is that of the overall procurement process involved, and should not be viewed as being the total of what every procurement department does. For some organisations the procurement department may be involved in everything from the "start" to the "finish" of the cycle, but for many organisations, the procurement department will only have some partial involvement in the total process, for example, from taking over the need and working on the specification with the user through to placing the order.

Meanwhile the overall procurement process has the following stages:

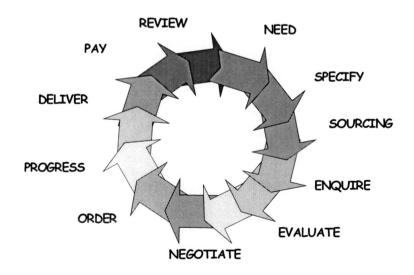

This procurement process cycle can be broken down into the following three main stages:

The Pre-Order stage: Need/Requirements – Specify - Sourcing – Enquiry – Evaluation – Negotiation/Selecting/Contracting.

The Order stage: Ordering – Progressing/Expediting – Delivery/receipt.

The Post order stage: Payment /Invoice verification – Reviewing of performance.

All of these stages have been already fully covered in *Excellence in Procurement* so this detail will not be covered here. However, so that we can highlight aspects for Service Procurement purposes, we will briefly mention some of the relevant aspects from the Pre-Order stage.

Needs

As explained in *Excellence in Procurement*, an initial requisition is used to identify the user or customer needs. This may range from a simple requisition covering a standard service requirement, right through to a complex project where a more thorough analysis will be carried out prior to making the final requests for services.

The need is what has to be satisfied, it represents the demand that "kickstarts" the process.

Specifications

Specifications are a description of what a customer/user wants and therefore communicate what is required to meet the needs. They are a statement of need from internal sources that is to be satisfied by the procurement of external resources. They can rightly be seen as the cornerstone of the whole procurement process, as everything that happens after the specification will be dependant on and results from the specification, including, as we will see, legal aspects in contracts.

Specifications therefore do need to be clear and to communicate properly; they may take the form of industry used standards. Standards differ from specifications. Whilst every standard is specification, not every specification is a standard, as standards are all about obtaining the expected performance or the expected output from the use of a product or service.

Standards have also often been originated by organisations such as The British Standards Institution (BSI) and The International Standards Organisation (ISO). Where such standards are found, it will usually imply that there are many supply sources; it can however also mean that the use of such a standard may preclude other suppliers, which in turn, may be against legislation on preventing competition. Where standards are a part of specifications, it is useful to check that the current version is being used as standards are often regularly updated.

The use of the BSI 5750/ISO 9000 standards for services does not necessarily guarantee that it is a "good" service. For example, IS 9002 and its forerunner BS 5750 part 2, cover the procedures that have to be followed to give the service standard required. They make no comment whatsoever about the service that is required, as it is for the organisation holding the standard to determine what these service levels are.

Accordingly, for service supply, whilst IS 9002 tells you that the organisation has procedures to ensure the compliance with a standard, it tells you nothing about "goodness" of the standard. IS 9002 therefore accredits the means, not the end.

Determine the specification types
Specifications should comply with the following criteria:

- Are the requirements stated clearly, unambiguously and with only the essential characteristics stated?
- Will it enable suppliers to decide and cost their offer?
- Will the suppliers offer be able to be evaluated against the specification?
- Does the specification enable opportunity for all suppliers to make an offer?
- Does it include any legal requirements?

The development of specifications will usually require liaison between users, procurement and maybe potential suppliers. Trade associations and other users can also help, as can independent people who can check and verify the final draft specifications.

Specifications may take various forms as follows. It will be seen that many of these find a better fit for products rather than services:

- Technical specifications: such as a highly detailed description; e.g. especially with engineering products.

- Sample specifications: such as to assess the suitability of chemicals or fabric on products.
- Brand specifications: such as a specific brand which may denote the customer's preference; it is also actually identifying a standard, as the acceptance of a brand will limit the supplier options, and any such use will need to be specially justified.
- Design specifications: such as to identify dimensions and outlines.
- Form specifications: such as the shape and appearance.
- Functional specifications: such as to ensure the product or service performs as 'fit for purpose' or what it has to achieve.
- Performance specifications: such as the output range within which the item must function; these, as will be seen next, are very useful for services.

Performance specifications/contracts

Performance is the output(s) required from the product or service; the aim here is to provide a clear and objective view of the expected output. Therefore the nature of the product/service being procured may determine that a performance-related specification is required, perhaps becoming part of the formal final contract.

The following questions can be asked, and the answers will assist in determining objective performance outcomes:

- Clarity; what has to be done? This must be very clear, along with who is accountable with clear levels of responsibility and authority.
- Competence; do the knowledge and skills exist?
- Consequences; why is it being done? These must be clear.
- Competition; what other tasks are there to do? Prioritising may be needed.
- Co-operation; who else is to be involved?
- Control; how is it known that a desired and satisfactory end has been reached?
- Commitment; do the suppliers have the confidence to do it willingly and well?
- Context; are the right surroundings and support available?

On performance specifications, the UK public sector has used performance contracts widely in recent years, for example, in the provision of services such as ambulance, police, hospitals and fire rescue. The aim here is also to ensure that government objectives can be maximised by the setting of targets to be achieved that will also bring improved performance.

These expected conditions can however fail to materialise when, for example, managers with information and bargaining power and with no strong incentive to "comply", can manipulate targets to ensure performance is judged satisfactorily.

For performance specifications to work correctly, objectives must be explicitly stated, with assigned weighting and priorities translated into clear and agreed performance improvement targets, perhaps also with clear incentives and disincentives about compliance.

Differences between Technical and Performance Specification

The following shows the important differences between the two types of specifications:

	Technical specifications	Performance specifications
Supplier	Receives an exact and clear specification.	Responds to the outcomes required in the customers required operating conditions and environment
Buyer	Has certainty of what is being bought. However these may not the "best", as other options that may satisfy the need are excluded	Must very clearly specify the requirements and outcomes needed
Technical risk	With the buyer	With the supplier
Supplier Innovation	Low/little	Highly likely
Examples	Simple and branded products	Services and complex projects

It should be noted that the above technical specifications and the subsequent, so-called technical assessment in the evaluation process, are not the same.

The technical assessment looks at things such as compliance with the specification (and this is either the technical or the performance specification) and also looks at the performance parameters of the specification.

Performance contracts

It is important also to appreciate the link between specification and contracts. Performance contracts are an enforceable agreement between suppliers and buyers as they link incentives and disincentives to the contractual performance outputs. The supplier is required to provide guarantees, for example, a timely completion, and for the achievement of performance specifications, for example on quality and cost.

Liquated damages may be a part of such contracts; this is a pre-determined estimate of loss by the buyer and payable by the supplier in the event of failure to meet agreements. Liquated damages for delays are determined by a time scale (e.g. daily) and normally will equate to the buyer's financial loss. Liquated damages for failure to meet performance are normally based on an amount for each percentage point the failure falls below the guaranteed performance level. We will look at contracts later on.

Role of Procurement with Specifications

From the user's specifications, procurement is then better able to:

* Provide information on available supply.
* Provide a supplier appraisal.
* Identify risks on suppliers and products.
* Identify where the business able to standardise.

Ultimately, procurement aims to procure services which are fit for purpose and the characteristics that give this may be determined by the specification.

Once the service requirements have been established/specified, it is important to summarise the details with the user or customer to ensure that what is being sourced is to the specification they require. Additionally, lines of communication will need to be established to ensure there are minimum delays should problems occur, and areas of responsibility should be highlighted and agreed.

Sourcing

The important aspects here are that:

* The number and location of suppliers will influence the prices in the marketplace.
* There are often other buyers looking to obtain the same services and this will likely mean a review by the supplier of just how "attractive" the buyer could be as a customer.
* The power of each party also has a part to play, for example:

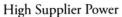

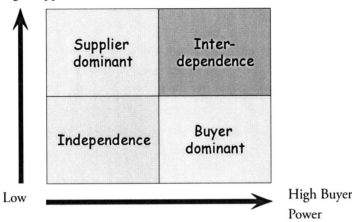

This "power view" on sourcing is am important one and also relates to our earlier discussion on Kraljic. (This and other aspects are covered fully in *Excellence in Procurement*).

Enquiry & Evaluation

As explained in *Excellence in Procurement*, this may take the form of pre-qualifying suppliers and is used to invite suppliers to apply for potential business. It ensures that suppliers conform to certain required criteria, before further detailed information is provided to them.

In making and dealing with enquiries to suppliers, approaches need to be seen as ethical and a "level playing field" must be maintained for all proposals.

A set procedure should be laid down to deal with the response proposals based on size and spend. Analysis of the proposals can include commodity value, delivery, quality, technical merit, after-sales service, security of supply, health and safety and environmental polices.

Some organisations, for example, those in the Public Sector, however, make enquiries by tendering; again this is more fully explained in *Excellence in Procurement* and involves using a formal process with the following steps:

* identification and selection of suppliers from whom to seek bids.
* issue of Invitation To Tender (ITT) documentation to the selected suppliers.

- receipt and assessment of tenders.
- selection of a preferred tender.

Tendering may not always give the intended open competition and fairness. Indeed tendering may be merely "going through the motions" as the processes can be influenced by those who have some power and influence over the eventual selection process.

Tenders may also be selectively issued and suppliers' responses are then being influenced. In this regard, a procurement manager once said to us, "We are always able to pre-cook the tender board."

The private sector will usually disregard tendering completely and move straight to negotiating, as they see the following disadvantages of the tendering process:

- Sometimes it is necessary to clarify technical points.
- The supplier may wish to give better alternatives that can only be found when negotiating.
- Tendering is slow and expensive to administrate and is also expensive for suppliers.
- Tendering is of no use in a "monopoly".
- Tendering conflicts with "newer" collaboration approaches and working more closely together with suppliers.
- Tendering prevents post-tender negotiations.

The supplier appraisal will be governed by the strategic significance of the product or material being sourced. The results will be based on criteria established by the purchaser in liaison with the user or customer and the purchasers' knowledge. Again *Excellence in Procurement* has a full discussion on the options available here, for example a detailed assessment of supplier's:

- Ability.
- Attitude.
- Organisation.
- Financial Data.
- Organisational Structure.
- Product Data.
- Supplier Production Process.

Negotiating

The private sector will generally move straight to negotiating with suppliers and not be involved in tendering. However as discussed in *Excellence in Procurement* the Public Sector may also undertake direct negotiations and we have covered there the conditions where this may occur. This book also covers more fully all the "mechanics" of conducting negotiations.

Who is responsible for the pre-order stage?

As has been seen this stage covers Need/Requirements – Specify – Sourcing – Enquiry – Evaluation – Negotiation/Selecting that all work towards the implementing of a contract and order placing,

The level of a procurement department's involvement in managing contracts and order fulfilment must be established; for example, who has responsibility for:

- Support and advice; for example the decision on which source to use may be with the budget holder/end user or, if the product has not been sourced before, then there may be an opportunity to develop a supplier.
- Contract negotiation; here it could be the direct responsibility of the buyer to negotiate terms and conditions on behalf of the user or internal customer.
- Contract management; who should have the responsibility to manage the total procurement process from identifying the need, agreeing specifications, identifying potential suppliers, supplier appraisal, contract negotiations and contract implementation, including the performance measurement.
- Collaborative partnerships; these would need to be based on trust and cooperation, shared information and shared goals, and without these, then the partnership merely becomes a long-term contract.

It is important that organisations determine who owns the relationship with suppliers and whilst we have explored this topic more fully in our book *Excellence in Supplier Management*, the standard answer, if there is such a thing, and one that is often given by people during our training courses/consultancy assignments, is that as the need is determined by the user, the user, or their delegated person, has such responsibility.

In textbook terms, theoretically, this seems entirely logical. However, in organisations where the responsibility is ill-defined, or where schoolyard politics have a part to play, it can happen that most users will choose to believe that it is actually the procurement department that has the responsibility for the relationship with suppliers. They also often believe this to be true without making any formal delegation; therefore they have a viewpoint that "we passed it on to you, so get on with it."

Whilst one can fully appreciate that the procurement department is involved in-sourcing and finalising the deal, it should not be the case that procurement is systematically left to do this in a vacuum and in total isolation from the rest of the organisation. Unfortunately, however, the authors know of too many examples where this actually happens.

Contract Management

As noted in *Excellence in Procurement* it is essential that all parties involved are aware of their roles and responsibilities and the contractual arrangements must be structured to match the particular requirement. Requirements can, of course, vary, and examples of different types of arrangements are found as follows:

- Spot orders are placed as and when required.
- Framework agreements for a fixed term for a specified supply, but with no initial commitment to buy, and when eventually buying, the use of call-offs. There is then an agreement to buy.
- Contracts with varied rates, dependent on certain criteria, for example, on volume quantity order, on payment terms etc.

Procurement departments are usually responsible for ensuring that the best fit commercial conditions are applied to the particular purchase and must also take account of any relevant legislative requirements. All contracts will involve the legal aspects as follows:

- Offer.
- Acceptance.
- Consideration.
- Legality.
- Capacity.

It is usually the responsibility of procurement department to ensure that:

- the appropriate terms and conditions are specified.

- there is a definition of when offer and acceptance takes place.
- there is an approved digital signature or equivalent.
- all legal principles have been followed.

In this regard, *Excellence in Procurement* covers the main legal aspects involved, so that all parties involved are aware of their roles and responsibilities. For example, it was noted there that The Supply of Goods and Services Act 1982 (SOGAS 1982) extends the provisions of the Sale of Goods Act to contracts which are not just purely for goods.

The key points for SOGAS 1982 are as follows:

- The Supply of Goods and Services Act 1982 requires a supplier of a service acting in the course of business in England, Wales and Northern Ireland to carry out that service with reasonable care and skill and, unless agreed to the contrary, within a reasonable time and make no more than a reasonable charge.
- These terms apply unless they have been excluded and there are strict limits on the circumstances in which an exclusion or variation will be effective.
- Common law in Scotland has similar effect to the 1982 Act. Suppliers of services or their customers should obtain legal advice about the common law in Scotland if necessary.
- If a supplier of a service breaches the conditions of a contract (for example by failing to carry out the work ordered) the user/consumer has a choice either to continue the contract (treat it as still in existence) and claim compensation from the trader for his failure to carry out what was agreed or rescind (cancel) the contract.
- If the supplier does not carry out the work with reasonable care and skill the law treats the matter as a breach of contract and the user/consumer can seek redress. Often reasonable compensation in these circumstances will be repair or replacement.
- If no agreement has been made with the supplier about completion of the work, or about the charge to be made, then if it is not completed within a reasonable time or the price is unreasonable, this is also treated as breach of contract and the consumer may be entitled to compensation.
- Any goods supplied in the course of the service must be as described, of satisfactory quality and fit for their purpose. If they are not the user/consumer is entitled to a repair, replacement or compensation.

- A supplier of a service who has broken a contract may also be liable for any consequential loss which is suffered by the consumer. Ultimately it would be for the courts to decide whether or not a breach of contract has occurred and the redress, in the form of damages (compensation), to which a consumer might be entitled.
- A claim can be pursued though the courts for up to six years providing it can be shown that the problem was due to the work not being carried out properly or the goods or materials used not being of satisfactory quality.

Source: Department for Business Enterprise and Regulatory Reform (www.berr.gsi.gov.uk)

Contract types

However beyond the above "mandatory" legal aspects, there is a range and continuum of variations and choices to be made. What follows therefore is an ideal-typical view to indicate this range and under each contract type, is the key determining aspect from Kraljic, which was covered earlier.

Whilst for some, this idealised view will be entirely practical and realistic; for others, the following division will not be fixed and definite. There can be a mixing across this continuum and it is not therefore a "tablets of stone" view, but is designed to show the key aspects that have to be considered before the buyer makes a choice; a choice of course that should usually be undertaken in conjunction with other internal departments in the organisation.

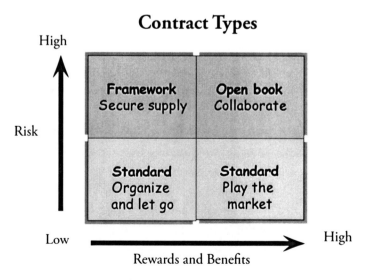

Contract Types

The buyer's views of risks are: any thing that may stop the operations of the business or prevent it from achieving its objectives. For example, poor health and safety, unreliable supplier lead times, low product quality with high levels of defects, using new untried technology, working in political environments with constant changes to regulations, supplier closure, exchange rate variations. We have already discussed risks more fully above using the Kraljic portfolio.

The buyer's view of rewards and benefits are: reduces costs, improves service, quality, time to market, innovations etc.

The key aspects that are involved in the different contract formats are as follows:

Aspects	Standard Contract	Framework Agreement	Open book Contracts
Other names used	Closed Fixed price	Call-offs	Cost plus
Typical Kraljic items	Leverage and routine	Leverage, routine and bottleneck	Bottleneck and critical
Contract description	Standard fixed terms and conditions, covering Quality, Quantity Time, Price and Delivery, plus many others, for example: -Assignment & Sub-Contracting -Arbitration -Bankruptcy -Equipment -Terms of Payment -Damages/ injury -Designs / drawings -Liability -Passing of property —Inspection / testing -Information -Copyright / Patent Rights -Statutory Regulations -Termination	There is no initial commitment to buy as the agreement just anticipates doing business. It "prepares the groundwork" and details the standard contract terms and conditions. When orders are placed by issuing a PO (known as a call off in a framework agreement), upon the order acceptance by the supplier, (without the supplier varying the terms), then there is a contract.	All costs are visible to the buyer, as the "books are open." All costs are therefore reimbursable to the supplier or maybe are paid direct by buyers. This is the "cost" aspect and the "plus" aspect can be: -a fixed management fee, or -a percentage of costs, or -agreed fees that maybe dependent on order volumes. As well as having fixed terms and conditions, there may also be some "moral" expectations/ agreements covering the preferred relational aspects.
Risk for buyer	Usually risks are well known and are often passed to the supplier. (Although of course, any subsequent supplier failure will likely impact the buyer).	Maybe shared or maybe with the supplier.	Maybe not fully known in advance and maybe accepted by the buyer.

Rewards/benefits for the buyer	Perceived as being "fully protected". Penalties for supplier non-conformity. Likely to be able to easily withdraw.	As for standard contract but with no initial commitment to buy. "Ready to go" immediately when wish to place orders.	Full visibility of costs and therefore all of the processes involved. Collaborative working.
Disadvantages for buyer	Hides supplier's profit. Supplier may include too much "contingency" cost in the price and may cut corners to improve profits. Suppliers may only do what the contract says and do not innovate or suggest improvements.	Supplier may become "disappointed", for example, they have to wait for orders, which can then fall below what they had expected.	Buyer needs cost knowledge. High administration. Could be little incentive for the supplier to reduce costs and improve service; however, the supplier may also do whatever is needed to make improvements, as mutual gains and goals "rule."
Rewards/benefits and disadvantages for the supplier	Supplier from the buyer: "you have the business, for now;" the supplier is therefore uncertain of the future. Supplier does not have to suggest any improvements.	As for standard contract but on bottleneck items, some form of incentives can be available as the buyer needs to secure supply.	Supplier incentives/ performance bonus. Incentives can follow from: -Cost reductions -Performance improvements -Delivery on time
Term	Short	Medium	Long
Performance expected	Standard	Satisfactory	Successful and can go beyond expectations
Trust	Low and is boundary trust that is determined by the contract.	Some trust beyond what the contract covers, and should become established by the reliable performances of both parties.	High and is goodwill trust. This has been built up during the working together experiences.
Relationships	Transactional, adversarial, contractual.	Cooperative	Collaborative, strategic alliance, mutuality, commitment.
Contract price	Known /fixed by price agreements	Fixed by the PO/contract, but may not have been initially fixed in the agreement.	Cost plus. The total cost price may be estimated in advance and therefore may become a variable if the estimating was wrong.
Buyer controls after orders have been placed	Low efforts needed as measures by non compliance and can easily change suppliers if needed.	Low to medium effort needed	High effort needed and both parties may measure and jointly agree remedial actions
Control of costs	With supplier	With supplier	With buyer

Meanwhile a good contractual legal agreement should provide:

- the overall groundwork and framework for the future supply.
- a perceived feeling that we have minimised risk and have a "safety umbrella".
- a formal "place of last resort" to resolve any ensuing problems.

However, legal agreements will not automatically in themselves prevent problems, nor will they provide automatic protection on a daily working basis. Legal agreements will only provide a formal structured framework for handling problems that have already occurred. Any problem handling may, of course, be handled without recourse to any formal legal involvement/judgements, as legal costs can be high/prohibitive and involve long timescales/delays.

Small wonder, therefore, that some may question why the initial time and cost in agreeing legal agreements is entered into in the first place. It is also not unusual to find one party will quickly agree to the tabled terms to prevent these expenses. Additionally, they may also agree because one party has the power to force through their terms. However, as explained in *Excellence in Procurement* the use of industry standard contracts and terms and conditions will mitigate the set up expenses.

Indeed, we have suggested before, that with complex purchases, most of the value obtained from the supplier is actually going to be driven by the post-contract management, rather than from the upfront negotiated contractual terms.

It will also have been seen that the different types of contracts have connections to Kraljic and therefore to procurement strategy and the relationships aspects. Suffice to note that a successful relationship is mainly made not on legal contracts, but on aspects like trust, fairness, respect, promises and mutual benefits that will occur daily between all of the players involved. It is how these are handled that will determine success; success is often unlikely to be because of the rigour of the legal contract.

The 3Cs of Contract Management

Contract management activities will always cover three areas:

1. Contract administration; this handles the formal governance of the contract and changes to the contract documentation.

2.   Commercial and service delivery management; this ensures that the service is being delivered as agreed, to the required level of performance and quality.

3.   Collaboration and relationship management; this keeps the relationship between the two parties open and constructive; it aims to resolve or ease tensions and identify problems early.

(Office of Government Commerce 2002 Contract Management Guidelines - principles for service contracts)

All of these above activities have to be managed, with the third one especially being not well handled by many organisations. This is important to appreciate as managing suppliers and contracts it is more than mere governance and ensuring "they" do what the contract says.

The "added extra" comes from being proactive in the relationship area. This is especially so in long term contracts, where interdependency between customer and provider is inevitable, therefore it is in the interests of all parties to make the relationship work.

Factors for success in relationships have been extensively covered in *Excellence in Supplier Management.* Briefly, these factors are trust/respect, communication and recognition of mutual aims. All of these factors being well understood by Toyota as shown in the following 3PL case study:

Case Study: Toyota USA & Freight Provider Selection

Toyota-NAPO (North American Parts Operation) is responsible for receiving and shipping $2 billion worth of service parts and accessories globally.

The Toyota Way can be called a mindset and an attitude. Toyota says, "It is the way we approach our work and our relationships with others". The Toyota Way is based upon two pillars:
*   Continuous Improvement.
*   Respect for People.

Each pillar has five (5) major principals:
-    Challenge
-    Kaizen

- Genchi Genbutsu (Go look, go see)
- Teamwork
- Respect

NAPO Mission Statement

"To provide our customers with the right parts at the right time in the right place at the lowest cost".

Toyota felt compelled to translate this message into one that would be applicable to their carriers. The translation would allow them to effectively convey the right message to their carrier partners, thereby connecting all of the parties, at least, philosophically. "At NAPO, we wanted our mission statement to convey the following: the Toyota philosophy; the objectives that NAPO strives to achieve; and to lay the foundation for the expectations that will be placed on the carriers."

Carrier Relationships with Toyota

Relationships are based on three (3) principals:

- Mutual Trust
- Respect
- Work together to reduce waste

Toyota only seeks new carriers when:

- A new facility or new geographical responsibility is required.
- A new program such as returnable program is required.
- The existing Carrier is closing down.
- The business objectives change and a carrier is unable to accommodate new requirements.
- Carrier is no longer able to do an effective job and countermeasures have not been successful.

When looking for replacements, the NAPO bid process is initially issued only to those carriers who are current partners, or, if the transportation requires a niche or specialized carrier, then they may bid the business to new carriers.

How Does NAPO Select New Carriers

By incorporating all of the principals addressed above, Toyota's selection criteria are presented in a manner that tests the viability of their philosophy and principals:

- Can the partners build a successful relationship?
- Will the Toyota Way be realized?
- Will the partnership withstand the long term, 5, 10, or 15 years?
- What are the business drivers?
- What is the legislative environment?
- What issues or challenges may be on the horizon?

What does it mean to be a Toyota NAPO Carrier?

Toyota has established a set of guidelines that will help the partnership prosper. Through this process the parties re ordered their principles by employing the following techniques:

- Continuously seek improvement:
  - Can we move this part better?
  - Faster?
  - Cheaper?
  - Most importantly: All three constraints are balanced equally.
- Toyota will not compromise:
  - We will not give up quality to save a buck
  - Do not carry more inventory if it does not make financial sense
- Genchi Genbutsu:
  - Who better to tell how we can improve than those actually doing the work! Ask your partners, what can we do to be a better shipper?
    And listen!
- Teamwork:
  - We took for "partners" to achieve Respect, not "vendors & carriers".

Toyota-NAPO has established and maintains a process that defines the organisation and its philosophy in ways that foster the development of strong logistics partnerships.

Source: www.transportgistics.com

Clearly here, the relationship aspects are given a high level of importance and represent the main key aspects of the "deal" for 3PL service suppliers.

We also will look at 3PL services in more detail in part 5 of this book.

Best Practice Contract Management

In our book *Excellence in Supplier Management* we identified the following aspects of good contract management and this can be summarised as follows:

1. Good preparation. An accurate assessment of needs/requirements helps to create a clear technical and/or performance based specification. Effective evaluation procedures and selection, against the specification of requirements, will then ensure that the order/contract is awarded to the right supplier/contractor.

2. The right contract. The contract is the legal foundation for the relationship. It should include aspects such as allocation of risk, the quality of service required, and Value for Money mechanisms, as well as procedures for communication and dispute resolution and the contractual obligations of the customer/contracting organisation.

3. Empathy and understanding. Each party needs to understand the objectives and business of the other. The customer must have clear business objectives, coupled with a clear understanding of what the contract will contribute to them; the supplier/contractor must also be able to achieve their objectives, including making a reasonable profit.

4. Service delivery management and contract administration. Effective governance will ensure that the customer gets what is agreed, to the level of quality required. The supplier's performance under the contract must be monitored to ensure that the customer continues to get what they expect.

5. Collaboration and relationship management. The eventual success of a contract depends on mutual trust and understanding, openness, and excellent communications. These being just as important (and may be more so), then the fulfilment of the legal terms and conditions.

6. Continuous improvement. Improvements in price, quality or service should be sought and, where possible, built into the contract terms and the benefits shared.

7. People, skills and continuity. There must be people with the right interpersonal and management skills to manage these relationships at all the multiple levels in the organisation. Clear roles and responsibilities should be defined, and continuity of key staff should be ensured as far as possible. A supplier/contract manager (or supplier/contract management team) should be designated early on in the procurement process.

8.   Knowledge. Those involved in managing the contract must understand the business fully and know the contract documentation inside out. This is essential if they are to understand the implications of problems or opportunities over the life of the contract.

9.   Flexibility. Management of contracts requires some flexibility on both sides and a willingness to adapt the terms of the contract to reflect a rapidly changing world. Problems are bound to arise that could not be foreseen when the contract was awarded.

10.   Change management. Contracts should be capable of change (to terms, requirements and perhaps scope) and the relationship should be strong and flexible enough to facilitate it.

11.   Proactivity. Good contract management is not reactive, but aims to anticipate and respond to business needs of the future.

A report by the Aberdeen Group (*The Contract Management Benchmark Report-Procurement Contracts, March 2006*) also indicates just what organisations need to consider and a summary of the report follows:

- Define and communicate procedures for the administration of contracts.
- Ensure executive and stakeholder support.
- Increase collaboration amongst internal stakeholders.
- Define information and reporting requirements comprehensively.
- Invest in management process capabilities.

This report also indicates what happens when there is poor contract management: a summary follows with our views on what is needed:

Problem Issue	Impacts	Needs
Fragmented procedures	Users start maverick buying. Increased finance and supply risk. Under leveraged spending.	Internal liaison. Kraljic segmentation.
Labour intensive and bureaucratic processes	Long supply lead times.	Internal and external liaison.
Poor visibility into contracts and terms	Poor compliance. Inconsistent terms. Poor spend analysis.	Influence suppliers. Internal liaison.
Ineffective compliance monitoring	High price variance. Overpayments. Performance risks.	Agreed KPIs. Work with suppliers.
Inadequate performance analysis	Policy and regulation violations.	Agreed KPIs.

Part 1: Summary

- Procurement is one part of an integrated supply chain that connects suppliers and customers.
- Procurement can be handled differently and structurally by organisations.
- Kraljic provides a valid view of such differences in the procurement process by examining risk and spend. Accordingly "one size does not fit all".
- The procurement cycle shows procurement is a process that goes across and through organisational departments. We specifically looked at in part one, the pre-order stage.
- The 5 Rights of procurement (quality, quantity, time, place and price) clearly show the connections between suppliers and customers and also provide the key performance indicators for both parties to use.
- 11 points for best practice contract management were discussed; Good preparation, The right contract, Empathy and understanding, Service delivery management and contract administration, Collaboration and relationship management, Continuous improvement, People, Skills and continuity, Knowledge, Flexibility, Change management, Pro-activity.

2: Services and Service Quality

Introduction

Services procurement encompasses the strategic management and procuring of complex category services such as the professional services of accountants, lawyers, advertising agencies, market researchers, facilities management, and consultants to name but a few.

Given the essential nature of professional services, it is surprising that so little work has been done looking specifically at how these services are assessed, selected and used by businesses.

As mentioned earlier, much of the existing knowledge in the field of Procurement and Supply Chain Management has mostly been aimed at buying goods and now, as a result of a growth in outsourcing, an increasing part of organisations' purchasing expenditures is being spent on services.

Services spend represents an enormous expense and while organisations try to control the costs, for many organisations, few have the same visibility on their services expenditure as they have for goods and materials. As a significant amount of corporate procurement spending is for services; for even the most proficient enterprise, services spending can still represent an abyss of lost savings opportunities due to direct buying by internal users that bypasses the dedicated procurement department.

Consequently, leading organisations are looking at methods for tracking this spend with the significant savings which a correctly centralised services procurement strategy can deliver.

The business of procurement is about defining what the purchaser wants and then finding a supplier who can supply it at the right price, on time and to the required quality standards. This is challenging enough with simple commodities such as furniture and stationary, but when it comes to the complex procurement of services, then the important aspects of a professional purchasing approach involving specification, sourcing, evaluation, contract and supplier performance management can be more difficult and risky.

Research shows that spending on services (such as marketing, consultancy, contract labour, facilities management, travel, print and other categories that involve people doing things), is difficult to control, yet represents one of the largest potential opportunities for savings. In fact, many purchasing directors simply don't know how much their organisations spend on services.

It is the case that, in a large number of organisations, purchasing directors often hugely underestimate how much their organisations are actually spending in these service areas. As a key element of corporate expenditure, services are much more significant than many professional purchasers seem to realise. Nevertheless, recent studies in Europe suggest that purchasing directors increasingly understand the importance of services as a spend category.

Having tackled the simpler 'hard' or direct goods, the big challenge for many organisations now is to bring services procurement under the professional purchasing banner.

With several large multinationals known to the authors, procurement has visibility of only around 50 percent of spend on hard goods, such as capital and office equipment, office supplies and IT equipment. However, with spending on services such as consultancy, facilities management, travel and print, they had visibility of around 40 percent of spending.

There seems to be general confusion about how much is spent in service categories and whilst some research has shown that organisations typically devote about 50-60 percent of spend to services, according to other sources, services spend represented on average only 15 percent to 20 percent of the total.

This disparity, suggests that a huge part of the service category expenditure is simply "not on procurement's radar at all" and that we really do not know.

Case Study: Abbey Financial

At Abbey financial services, the key issue is to identify who is spending money in the organisation. *"The key to success is to work out what your governance model is in each category"* and *"you have to understand who is making the sourcing decisions and how much they're allowed to do. You have to be able to control them, to make them not do what they're doing or at least do it in a way that's acceptable to your sourcing strategy."*

Another challenge is quality control. *"With direct purchases like truck parts, you're buying the same thing year after year in huge volumes to a specification that barely changes. But when you're buying the services of individuals, what you get will vary hugely. You can have a very clear specification for cleaning, for example, but the delivery is often difficult to regulate. Likewise, in consultancy the performance of individuals is very variable. Each category requires a totally different procurement approach".*

The approach at Abbey appears to be paying off. A target of saving 9 percent of spending over three years, that is £71 million on a total of about £81 0 million, has been met. Savings in individual categories have typically been between 15 percent and 30 percent. Organisations increasingly accept that they must bring services spending under control and, though they face huge challenges in doing so, there are steps they can take. Even more than for simple goods, it is essential for procurement professionals to gain credibility with their internal customers and to develop good working relationships. This is especially true of: for example, marketing, where the nature of the services being sourced is in many ways difficult to analyse precisely.

Case Study: Motorola

Motorola, who controls a budget of $150 million to $200 million a year, believes it is essential for procurement to sell itself to the marketing department, because this is an area where there has traditionally been little involvement.

"The biggest challenge has been persuading the internal clients that procurement has something to offer. You have to convince them that there is genuine expertise in the procurement function, and that it's materially worthwhile getting procurement involved. Marketers want to know what you know about what they do."

Marketing is to a large extent subjective, *"One of the buzz words you hear from marketers is 'chemistry'. It's all about finding people who understand your brand and your business objectives. It's an area where the relationship between the supplier and the client is often very close. People talk to each other on a daily basis and develop good personal working relationships. They're working around*

> *perceptions and ideas rather than something tangible. This is one of the last areas where procurement has been able to secure a foothold."*

Services are different purchases

This is true for several reasons, for example:

•   Many professional service purchasers are "distress" purchases. We either have no choice (e.g. auditors) or else make the purchase at a time of crisis or problem.

•   Service quality is difficult to assess (as a result of the intangible nature of the service).

For example, with consultants, organisations may employ them for a variety of reasons:

•   Insecurity about a strategic decision.
•   Ignorance of rules, methods or techniques in a particular area.
•   Lack of time to develop a particular strategy, policy or function.
•   Desire for substantiation of a decision or strategic choice.
•   Specialised input.
•   Developing knowledge and understanding of an issue, technology or technique.
•   Need for independence in looking at an issue.

Services have the following characteristics:

Intangibility: Services are often something one cannot touch or feel. Services may be associated with something physical, such as an airplane, a table and chairs, a legal brief, or a hospital bed. What people are actually buying, however involves something intangible. It is not the airplane that is valued as much as the travel. It is the resolution of the problem, not the legal brief. It is good health and not the hospital bed itself that is valued. When a service is excellent, it is typically because of the intangible nature of what has been provided, not the associated physical things. An empty seat on a plane today, is lost forever.

Inability to inventory: the consumption of a service is often nearly simultaneous with its production. One typically cannot inventory a service. Because one cannot inventory services, capacity choice becomes critical. The size, the layout, and the exact location of a service operation are tremendously important.

Service production/consumption often physically together: Often services are created and delivered on the spot. That is, the intangibility of the service results from a service process accomplished precisely where the customer is located: the trip to the doctor's office, the night out at a restaurant, the airplane flight. There may also be a lot of customer interaction with service providers in the course of this production and consumption. The service process itself is often more on display in service operations than in manufacturing. Quality control thus becomes more critical. One cannot be saved by a quality control check at the end of the line as one can in manufacturing. One has to create a quality service straightaway. Training of employees and good employee relations are especially important to service quality.

Easy entry: A high proportion of service operations, although by no means all, require very little in the way of capital investment, multiple locations, or proprietary technology. For many services, therefore, barriers to entry are low. Low barriers to entry in turn imply that service operations must be very sensitive to potential as well as actual competitive actions and reactions.

Spectrum of services

The following diagram shows the typical spectrum of services, categorised by degree of interaction and customisation of the service provision.

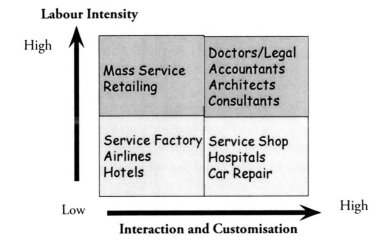

Service Procurement in Manufacturing Organisations

As highlighted above, one characterising feature of services is that they are produced and consumed as interactive processes between buyers and sellers. Services marketing/ services management professionals have strongly emphasised the importance of these ongoing interactions: the interactions between the customer and the service provider in specific service encounters, in which the service is simultaneously produced and consumer, rather than the mere transaction (exchange), should become the main focus point.

It is in these encounters that buyer and suppliers co-create value.

In one classification of business services, a distinction is made between instrumental and consumption services:

- Consumption services are used up within the buying organisation (e.g. office cleaning at an airline).
- Instrumental services are used to modify the way the buying organisation carries out its primary processes (e.g. management consultancy at an airline).

This implies that to be successful at services buying, manufacturing organisations should assess how services are used and differentiate their interactions with their service providers accordingly. Understanding and being able to manage the interaction with a supplier is therefore just as important as being able to specify and contract the desired services.

Service procurement is moving from being a rather reactive and unstructured activity, where a lot of purchases were randomly made only when the organisational needs occurred, to one that is more structured and forward looking that acts in line with the overall organisational goal.

Objective setting of services, in terms of developing carefully crafted specifications and contracts, for instance, has been seen as a central ingredient of this change. It is therefore argued that this facilitates a comparison between different providers, and transforms the services into commodities that can be exchanged in a competitive market.

On the other hand, complex services of strategic importance to the organisation business may require a different procurement approach, for example those critical items in Kraljic in the first section of the book. Here, there is a need for a close and relatively open ended buyer-supplier interaction. Like products then, it is important that "services" are not treated as one category, and that the procurement approach is adjusted to the specific service being bought.

In general, on one hand, efforts are made to standardise services at certain stages of the procurement process, while the focus is on customising services in close buyer-supplier interaction at other stages.

There is also a move towards buying more solutions, or entire functions, rather than individual specific service parts. This movement is primarily driven by an aim to decrease the number of suppliers and become more cost efficient; additionally, internal clients often want to outsource an entire function out of convenience.

Solutions are difficult to buy: it is very resource demanding to buy solutions and to handle supplier relationships for such services. Solutions are also difficult and tedious to specify and, even when they are seemingly well developed, unforeseen issues remain to be negotiated; for example:

"You think you have agreed, but when you look at the details you realise that a lot of things remain to be specified. Who's responsible for what when things fail? It is very costly to solve all the problems of responsibilities when things fail."

The various procurement approaches are often adjusted to different service categories; some services were bought as broad functions or solutions to specific needs, whereas the majority was still bought on the basis of detailed specifications.

As with all procurement; the process starts with an identification of organisational need defined by the internal client. This is then followed by the development of a detailed specification of the service to be bought. Thereafter, suppliers are selected guided by the formal procurement processes, implementation of the contract, with efforts into evaluating and following up on the implementation.

Service Specification

Surveys reveal that buyers put much effort into the initial stage of the procurement process, as that is where the need is identified. Many define their service needs by organising them in specific categories according to their usage and according to their specific features (e.g. in line with the Kraljic portfolio model). By organising needs into different categories and assigning category teams responsible for ensuring the needs are fully met, this facilitates the structuring and planning of current, as well as future, need of various services.

Once the need has been identified and a sourcing decision has been made, carefully developed specifications are the key.

In this process, the service need is assigned certain, often calculable, characteristics. The specification then serves as the basis on which suppliers develop their offerings. The purpose of clearly defined specifications also enables comparable offerings to be exposed to competitive tendering and evaluation.

Specifying complex services might be very time consuming as whilst there is a requirement to cover every eventuality, there is also a need to remain flexible so that suppliers have room for creativity and to make improvements.

In particular, it is very difficult to specify the results of a creative service, such as the ones provided by architects or PR organisations; after all, they are being used to provide creativity!

Supplier selection

The supplier selection process is above all guided by the aim of taking advantage of market competition.

Accordingly, competitive tendering, in which several potential suppliers are considered and evaluated before a decision is made, is a standard procedure in most procurement situations.

Evaluation criteria are often customised for each service as the basis for the supplier selection.

"Whether we emphasise cost or value depends completely on the type of service. A service that is of strategic importance and associated with high supply risk is evaluated based on value, whereas standardised services, such as a helpdesk, are purchased at the spot market with the focus on price".

For many purchases of services then, cost may still the most central evaluation criteria; this reflecting the use of Kraljic.

Some kinds of services however, have certain characteristics that would make a focus on value more relevant than a focus on cost. The value focus is more relevant when complex services were bought than for commodity type services. When advertising services are bought, for example, one senior buyer pointed out:

"We use rating systems for soft measures developed together with the internal client. We note on a scale from one to five the supplier's creativity and presentation skills, etc and combine these scores with cost measures".

It seems for many buyers that whilst they viewed soft measures as important evaluation criteria for certain kind of services, they were struggling with problems related to measuring and calculating them.

Conversely and perhaps paradoxically, buyers commonly argue that softer criteria are particularly important at the post purchase stage when the service contract is to be implemented. For instance, criteria such as creativity, flexibility, and ability to cooperate are often seen as pivotal for the successful implementation of advertising and consulting services.

Contract implementation

With more complex services that are close to the core competence of the organisation the preference is for long term relation orientated procurement approaches, such as Framework Agreements/contracts. These covering the future need of routine services over a longer time period.

Many procurement managers like working with Framework agreements as they see these simplify and reduce transaction costs, as well facilitating collaborative working and solutions improvements. Framework agreements being seen here as a method in which a more transactional approach was applied at the initial supplier selection stage, and a more relational approach followed once the suppliers were tied to an agreement.

Procurement managers will often note that service sourcing has long been characterised by informal and personal procurement behaviour and that to some extent, it still is. Some will also say that they struggle with internal clients, who prefer to maintain habitual supplier relationships, without the normal rigour of professional sourcing and supplier selection.

What often seems to be of great concern to procurement managers are the lack of post purchase evaluations and the follow ups on services bought. In particular, the evaluation of more complex services, of which the outcome may not be described beforehand, seems to be often problematic. In general, perceived satisfaction is a function of expectations; and if these are unknown or not clearly stated, then they are by default, going to be difficult to measure.

Specifically, the respondents emphasised difficulties of data collection, i.e. "to catch the right numbers" as one buyer expressed it. Even if the outcome was measured and recorded, procurement managers noted that it might be hard to interpret the results, as one senior buyer in the telecom industry explained to us:

"We put a lot of effort into following up but it is difficult for certain kind of services, for example advertising services, as it is generally considered hard to measure results of marketing. It is a lot easier to measure, for example, business travel."

More successful examples reported are where procurement managers systematically measured their internal client's level of supplier satisfaction.

"We have in the contract agreements that the supplier must ask for the internal customer's level of satisfaction."

Another senior buyer pointed to the fact that:

"One can only measure against the specification, what has been agreed upon, and that is why the specification needs to be carefully developed."

Indeed, several procurement managers do see that finding better methods for measuring results, is one of their major challenges in the service procurement process.

Total Cost of Ownerships (TCO), covered earlier in part 1 of this book, has been seen as one possible method to apply, but many procurement managers we know say they do not work with TCOs.

Objective setting for services in the procurement process is, however, not always automatically a simple task over all kinds of services. While some procurement managers of the organisations are introducing alternative and more value based procurement methods for complex services, others procurement managers emphasise the need for a different approach, because specifying and assessing complex services can be both difficult and tedious.

Certain services, such as professional services may, because of their complexity and intangibility, require a procurement approach where the need is specified jointly, the specifications are co-created, and where relationships between buyers and sellers of the services are to be closer and operate over the longer term.

All services, no matter how complex they are, will usually have objectives determined at some point during the procurement process, as even an integrated and customised solution is specified and described in an agreement in order for it to be tradable. To amplify this; after a decision has been made on buying or outsourcing the service, the need is transformed into a clearly specified assignment. If the specification requires involvement of the supplier, the method of buyer-supplier interaction may, at this stage, be rather relational. Once the specification is developed, it serves as a basis for the development of clearer objective offerings and for the final contract to be determined during the supplier selection stage; therefore the service has now been transformed into something tradable.

Buyers are now realising that they must put a lot of effort into making objectives very clear for their service purchases.

Clarity in Service Specifications

The aim must be to have clear objectives for services, which means reducing them to the status of simple objects. This approach aims at introducing product and production/manufacturing principles to services, by materialising, standardising, specifying or packaging services to make them more tangible and therefore objective in order they appear to be exchangeable.

In other words, the properties of services are temporarily agreed upon and specified during the procurement process. Otherwise they cannot be traded. This means that, for instance, very detailed requirement specifications are included in the request for quotation sent to the suppliers.

On the basis of the specifications, the product or service, or the quotation from the supplier, may then be measured and evaluated.

Buyers of services may benefit from standardisation of services and processes because they obtain greater predictability of what they receive from the supplier. For instance, they may receive products or services in a predetermined quantity in line with the precise specifications made by the supplier.

This standardisation also facilitates comparisons between alternative suppliers and makes it possible to apply competitive tendering.

The most important service characteristic that generates all of the others is the intangibility of services. Intangibility means *"they cannot be seen felt, tasted, or touched in the same manner in which goods can be sensed"*.

However, by looking at the degrees of intangibility of services, then for example, business services can be classified into property, people and process services.

The argument here is that such complex services are made up of intangible assets, such as services focusing on processes (e.g. professional services) or people (e.g. training), and that these are relatively difficult to specify and evaluate beforehand, because, they are composed of dimensions that are not readily visible, especially before they have been delivered. In addition, complex services are often said to have a high degree of separation between production and consumption; the outcome of a service being produced in the interaction between users and supplier/producers.

The outputs of services are not therefore separate entitles that exist independently from the relationship between producers and users.

Therefore, the alleged peculiarities of services make them relatively difficult to standardise, to count and to value, which in turn implies that they entail greater performance ambiguity.

This has led many researchers and practitioners to the conclusion that services are preferably exchanged in close buyer-supplier relationships where the role of trust between the buyer and seller is going to be central.

Because of the characteristics of services, they cannot be always specified in detail as they are co-created by buyers and suppliers in the procurement process. As products and services are not homogenous categories, there is more of a continuum ranging from intangible dominant services, to, tangible dominant goods. Only by defining and having clear objectives, will the properties of services become fit for the legal attachment and transfer of property rights. A service must therefore be turned into a "thing" before it can be exchanged.

Service Quality

Quality is the ability of a product or service to consistently meet or exceed customer expectations. The dimensions of service quality are as follows;

- Access.
- Communication.
- Competence.
- Courtesy.
- Credibility.
- Reliability.
- Responsiveness.
- Security.
- Tangibles.
- Understanding/Knowing the Customer.

These dimensions of service quality are eventually going to be perceived by the user after their initial expectations, which are based upon:

- Word of mouth, e.g. what others say about the supplier/provider.
- Meeting of the users personal needs.
- Past experiences of the supplier/provider.

These initial expectations work towards giving an expected service level and then, when the service has been provided, the above dimensions of service are determined from what was actually delivered and will be matched to the expectations.

This may result in a service quality gap between what was expected and what was actually delivered; the result being the perceived service quality. The following two diagrams expand on this:

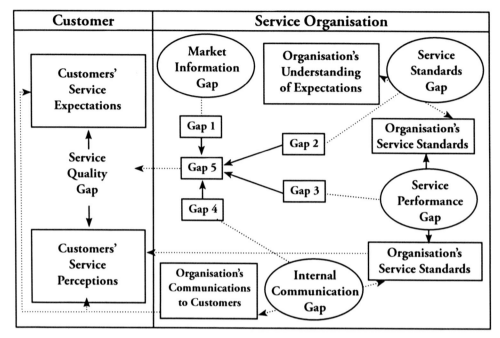

Gap	Problem	Cause/s
1. Consumer expectation/ Management perception	The service features offered don't meet customer needs	Lack of marketing research, inadequate up communication, too many levels between contact personnel and management
2. Management perception/service quality specification	The service specifications defined do not meet management's perceptions of customer expectations	Resource constraints, management indifference, poor service design
3. Service quality specification/service delivery	Specifications for service meet customer needs but service delivery is not consistent with those specifications	Employee performance is not standardised, customer perceptions are not uniform
4. Service delivery/external communication	The service does not meet customer expectations which have been influenced by external communication	Marketing message is not consistent with actual service offering, promising more than can be delivered
5. Expected service/ perceived service	Customer judgements of high/low quality based on expectations vs. actual service	A function of the magnitude and direction, the gap between expected service and perceived service

Managing Perceptions and satisfaction

Procurement managers must become fully attuned to their internal customers and understand how perceptions of a service develop during the service process.

The diagram below combines the levels of expectations and zone of tolerance, and the outcome of a service, level of satisfaction and dissatisfaction. It looks at how expectations give way to perception of satisfaction using the service process (Johnston 1995). The diagram shows the zone of tolerance extending from expectations, through the process to the outcome of satisfaction.

It is vital that procurement departments communicate with their internal customers regularly in order to ensure that they fully understand what is, and what is not, acceptable in terms of service delivery.

Managing perceptions and satisfaction during the process

Satisfaction Continuum

Expectation	Process	Outcome
More than Acceptable		+5 Delighted
Acceptable	Zone of Tolerance	0 Satisfied
Unacceptable		-5 Dissatisfied

The diagram is similar to a control chart that procurement managers can use to identify customer's expectations, see what is acceptable, less than acceptable and is more than acceptable. Then they can assess during the service the impact of each stage or transaction in a single service transaction or encounter, or a series of service encounters. This helps procurement managers to understand how they can jointly design their service to have the appropriate interventions at appropriate times to achieve the desired outcomes.

A number of suggestions have been made about the use of this model (Johnston 1995). We shall take, for example, a service of maintenance and apply this model. We might consider there to be several transactions here:

- Response time (e.g. one hour).
- Arrival at the client.
- Diagnosis.
- Actual time taken to fix on first attempt.
- Discussion of findings.
- Departure; total elapsed time for the service.
- Need for recall to fix again as was a unsuccessful first attempt.

Expectations may have been managed by Procurement through its Contract and Service Level Agreement (SLA), for example, this informs customers that they should have to wait no longer than one hour for a response to the breakdown/maintenance problem, that they will be treated with care and consideration and that all facts explained to them in a meaningful way. (See the following diagram).

Managing Satisfaction - Maintenance

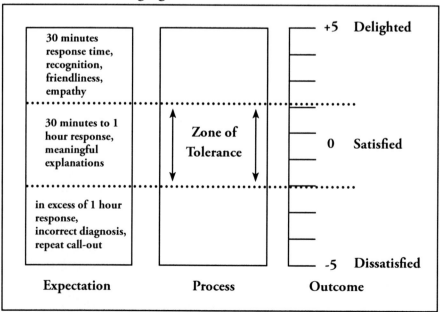

Performance within the zone of tolerance results in satisfaction. Providing the customer's perceptions of the transactions are not greater or less than acceptable, the outcome will be a "satisfied" customer with a "score" somewhere within their outcome zone of tolerance, as shown below.

Adequate Performance Satisfies the Customer

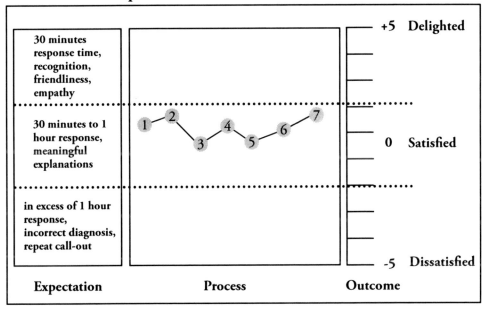

It has been suggested that the quality of a performance within the customer's zone of tolerance may not always be consciously noticed. Therefore, for a procurement organisation wishing to make an impact, they will need to design in positive interventions, such as self-assessment of the level of service provided, and then feed this back to customers to show how performance is improving and is being maintained.

Sufficient incursions above the zone of tolerance threshold will result in a highly satisfying outcome (customer delight).

By including one or more enhancing factors the service provider may be able to delight the user. For example, the maintenance service provider greets the user by name and illustrates their competence by immediately explaining the likely problems, the time needed to fix the problem and the options available. This might be quite unexpected (at least on the first occasion) and will therefore delight the customer, as shown in the following diagram.

Using Enhances to Delight the Customer

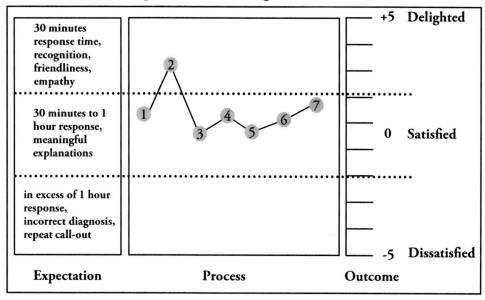

The outcome "score" may not be a mean score but delighting (and indeed dissatisfying) incidents may have the effect of skewing the resulting level of satisfaction.

Sufficient incursions below the zone of tolerance threshold will result in a dissatisfying outcome. A delay of 10 minutes may be forgiven, but this coupled with a brusque treatment and a cursory examination may well lead to dissatisfaction, as shown below.

A Dissatisfying Outcome

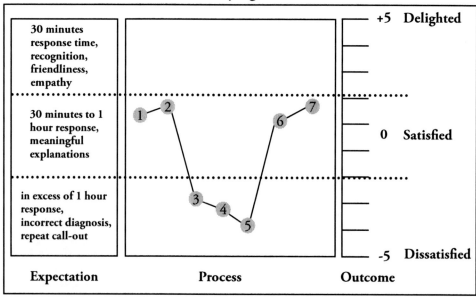

Some dissatisfying and satisfying transactions may be compensatory; for example, a lack of a timely response resulting in a customer waiting around, with the uncertainty of when the maintenance service provider is arriving, will count as a dissatisfying transaction, but a profuse apology from the maintenance provider with an explanation, coupled with particularly caring service delivery, may compensate for the initial problems. The following diagram shows this change:

Enhancers Compensate for Failure

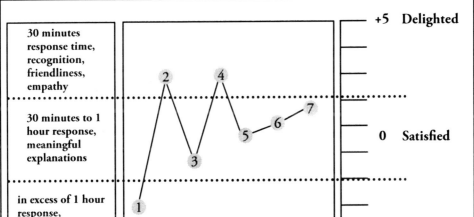

Several satisfying transactions will be needed to compensate for a single dissatisfying transaction (as above).

A failure in one transaction may raise the dissatisfaction threshold.

A dissatisfying experience may also have the effect of shifting the zone of tolerance upwards and/or maybe reducing its width. For example, if the customer has had to wait for a much longer time than specified, their dissatisfaction with this transaction may be such as to negatively dispose them towards the rest of the service. This could mean that future transactions that might previously have been within their zone of tolerance are now felt to be dissatisfying. This shifting of the zone increases the likelihood of the outcome being a feeling of dissatisfaction.

Dissatisfaction Shifts the Zone of Tolerance

Conversely, an enhancing transaction may lower the zone of tolerance (and/or widen it) so that further transactions that might before have been within the acceptable range are now felt to be delighting.

This has also been referred to as the "halo effect" (Wirtz and Bateson 1995) whereby, say, prompt completion by the service provider, a feeling of being important and welcome by the customer, all the forms ready to be signed, and an overall swift, efficient and effective response service may not only delight but positively dispose the customer to the rest of the service and increasing the likelihood of a delighting outcome; the following diagram illustrates this.

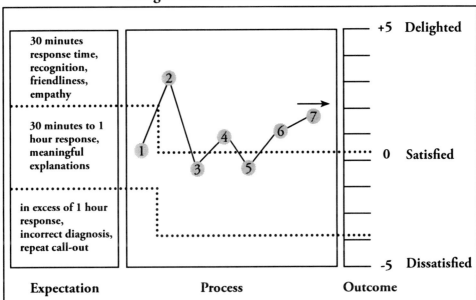

Delight Shifts the Zone of Tolerance

Category Management and Services Quality

As we have mentioned earlier, with the lower complexity and potential higher savings categories, they will have their procurement processes automated and controlled, and the procurement team will now have to shift its focus to the more difficult categories.

Most early savings will came from procurement of goods and materials which are more easily controlled and processed by enterprise resource planning (ERP) or e-procurement systems. Today, in the more advanced organisations, these categories are well managed using electronic catalogues tied to automated purchase order systems that link to preferred suppliers. Through this means, spend becomes fully visible and controlled and transaction costs are minimised.

We would therefore suggest that these organisations must now turn towards services procurement to achieve further price/cost reductions. Services procurement may be as much as 75% of non-manufacturing organisation total spend, but these will not, in most organisations, have been similarly automated or controlled. They therefore represent a huge opportunity for procurement.

However, to successfully manage services spend, procurement needs tools and processes that are more sophisticated than the catalogue and purchase order systems used in regulating leverage and routine goods and materials. Services usually do involve a broader range of customer stakeholders and suppliers. Most of this spend is likely to lie outside of the sourcing agreements managed by the procurement staff, thus making it more susceptible to higher prices, lost savings opportunities and higher risk. Benefit will also be "hard" and "soft" making their quantification and tracking more challenging.

Changes in procurement objectives

Procurement's early objective of consolidating product spend and reducing purchasing prices, is now giving way to more complex process initiatives of automating basic transactions, reducing processing costs and identifying. The challenge is now to identify the right solutions, manage migration of suppliers and users and manage/measure the change, progress and impact of future price reduction opportunities by improving market intelligence.

Procurement is continually being asked to prove value to the organisation by improving quality and the business impact of procured services in a significant way that will directly improve the organisation's performance. Building an effective, hard-hitting business case for the upfront investment in technology and people procurement needs is the first step towards performance-centred procurement that will focus on best product/service management and integrate relationships, processes and outcomes.

Building the business case

This begins with an opportunity assessment. The objective is to assess the potential for savings or value additions using a rigorous, consistent analytical process and state of the art tools; it determines if there is a credible, fact driven case to initiate a project to achieve the benefits.

The opportunity assessment provides all the information needed to develop and convincingly communicate a business case to stakeholders and management. When done properly, it establishes a solid foundation to launch a strategic procurement project by building clear understanding of the spend category, people involved and the processes and organisational impacts. It establishes credibility with stakeholders and management by clearly presenting facts in a disciplined, analytic format and helps to decide where and when to commit resources to bring the best probably return based on the facts of each case. Finally, it sets initial baseline to evaluate on going progress and the ultimate success of the project.

The opportunity assessment has four key parts:

1. Define the category
2. Identify the opportunity
3. Define the business impact
4. Integrate results

As will be demonstrated below, each key part has several operational steps.

Part 1: Define the category

Defining the category is a five step process consisting of:

1. Determining facts we need to know
2. Identifying potential sources of data
3. Performing the analysis
4. Summarising findings
5. Developing, documenting and testing hypotheses

The objective here is for the project team and stakeholders to understand the spend information.

Step 1: Determining the facts

As a minimum, explore the following questions which apply to services procurement. Category facts we need to know are as follows:

- How much do we spend? (current and future spend, lifecycle costs)
- Who buys it?
- How does the organisation buy it?
- What processes or technologies are used?
- Is there a contract? If not, what are the risks of not having a contract?
- How do we use/maintain written contract?
- Who are the main users?
- Who sells it to us?
- Who are the top suppliers?
- How many suppliers account for the top 80%, bottom 20% of the volume and total spend?
- How do we pay for it, especially SLAs, complex billing arrangements?

- What are the various deliverables from this service category?
- Geographical dispersion of services ordering /delivery?

Step 2: Determine sources of data (to answer questions in Step 1). Typical sources of data are as follows:

- Accounts payable.
- Financial database.
- Suppliers' reports and interviews.
- Business users and buyers.
- Industry websites, industry sources and contacts, market research.

Step 3: Analyse the spending

A thorough analysis will consolidate, organise and manipulate data to create a profile of the category spending by digging into the questions in Step 1. The project team's greatest challenge will be determining accurate measures that will be broadly accepted by all players.

Despite information technology advancements, information availability is the greatest barrier to accurately measuring cost and savings potential. Even if data is available, it is often inaccurate or incomplete; the second most common barrier. Specialised "spend analysis" systems and consulting organisations are now available to assist in collecting, cleansing, and analysing spending by category.

In evaluating different systems options it may be relevant to construct a Total Cost of Ownership (TCO) model where all costs associated with acquisition, installation, on going operations and disposal are considered. For example, several large multinationals with which the authors have had contact with over many years, readily recognised that it is this stage of the project which is often the most difficult as a result of varied approaches to categorisation of spend. One country's business unit may describe and allocate a service spend differently to another, and therefore detailed analysis is complex.

Step 4: Summarise Findings

Summarise findings with supporting facts for each finding. The following is an example of how this could be done using housekeeping services data from a major retailer:

Category: Cleaning			
Supplier	**Total Expenditure**	**Spend %**	**Cum. %**
		27.8%	27.8%
		24.2%	52.0%
		20.2%	72.2%
		5.6%	77.8%
		5.5%	83.3%
		4.8%	88.1%
		3.9%	92.0%
		2.6%	94.5%
		1.6%	96.1%
80 Others		3.9%	100.00%
Average Spend £			
Analysis: **For example:** • Did business with over X Cleaning suppliers • Top 3 suppliers account for 72% of spend volume • 80% of volume is spent with top 5 suppliers • Two of the top 5 in spend do not have a signed contract			

Step 5: Develop and Test Hypotheses

Develop and test hypotheses with further investigation into the data:

- What are the hard savings?
- What are the soft savings?
- How do we score the benefits and costs?
- Can we achieve 20% cost savings by strategic sourcing contingent staffing?
- Can we further reduce cycle time and reduce the Total Cost of Ownership (TCO) such that the Return on Investment (ROI) is competitive with other high profile projects?

Part 2: Identify the Opportunities

The objective of Part 2 is to look for opportunities to reduce service costs and process costs.

1) Service Cost Savings

Service cost savings are achieved through negotiating better pricing using a more strategic sourcing. Signs to look for are as follows:

- Many suppliers in different locations for a nationally consistent service.
- Single, non-competitive source in a competitive market.
- Cosy relationships with supplier.
- Unclear or non-existent corporate policy on procurement of a major service spend.
- Many buyers for the same service.
- Is spend being leveraged?
- Are these different specifications for the same service causing duplication of contracts?
- No written contracts or existing ones are old and automatically renewed.
- New contract each time service is bought.
- Multiple contracts with same supplier or its subsidiaries.
- Paper intensive ordering/approval process or no process at all.
- Price for similar service are varied or are out of line with market benchmarks.

2) Process Cost Opportunities

In addition to better prices, look at ways that additional costs can be taken out by simplifying the process or replacing costly, replacing time consuming error prone steps with automation and better internal controls. Potential process flow savings questions to analyse are:

- What are the obvious control points? Are they commercial? Technical? Procedural?
- Does any supplier have a dominating position?
- What are the potential value changes, upstream and downstream?
- Why and where might we want to change the relationship between links in the chain? What leverage do we have to do so?
- Are there any other linkages to exploit?
- What is the best possible solution that offers lowest upfront investment, low or no ongoing operating costs and quickest installation and implementation?
- What options offer flexibility and ease of systems updating when innovations and improvement upgrades become available?

Part 3: Define the Business Impact

The objective is to identify points of resistance or support for the project and build this knowledge into the sourcing strategy and tactics. It begins with listing and profiling key stakeholders (people who have a substantial interest in the success of failure) of the project. They are then grouped by the real or perceived impact of the project on them. Finally, different management strategies are prepared to deal with anticipated resistance from each group. The following is an example of a stakeholders mapping followed by possible strategies to deal with each.

Part 4: Integrate the Results.

The objective is to pull together all the results identified so far into an overall assessment and establish the initial project direction.

Service Quality Improvement

Below are some examples from BP of processes in place to ensure continuous improvement in the quality of their services received from external contractors:

Case study: BP Egypt

BP has a scorecard for Well-Testing Services:

- Traditionally, once a contractor has passed the minimum requirements at the technical stage, they were then chosen on the lowest price criterion at the commercial stage.
- One of the consequences of this was that over time, it was noticed that there were gaps between the standards expected by BP from the contractor's staff, and the actual performances provided.
- An analysis of the situation found that there were gaps between expected skills and competency levels and the actual levels of the staff being supplied on the contracts.
- Following a benchmarking exercise with BP Trinidad, BP Egypt devised a Skills Assessment Model.
- This sets down the levels to be provided by the contractors and measures actual skill levels against these standards to identify gaps.
- Clearly it was necessary to agree the standards, as well as for both sides to agree the existing levels of skills for the staff on the contracts.

- Contractors were asked to measure the skills themselves and BP would then measure and agree a mutually acceptable level.

The following areas were measured:

- Experience 45% weighing.
- Interpersonal 20%.
- HSE 15%.
- Technical 20%.

Each of the above area was broken down into skill definitions and both sides assessed each one according to the levels below:

0 = no experience in the assessed area
1 = basic
2 = competent
3 = highly competent

Once gaps in skills had been identified, a joint action plan was agreed to develop the skills to the required level.
As a result, skill levels improved and performance overall as a consequence ensuring:

- Lower total costs.
- Less downtime.
- Higher efficiency and effectiveness.

Obviously such a Skills Assessment Model has to be continually applied to ensure continuous improvement.

Following the successful introduction into the Well Testing Services function it is intended to roll–out the model to other services and will be embedded into any future supplier appraisal and selection process.

Source: Shaer, S.E (2008)

Case Study: BP KPI Scorecard

Below is an example of a KPI scorecard for Drilling Services.

Key Area	Weight %	KPI weight in section	Key performance Indicator (KPI)	Target	Actual Score	Score % Within Section	Total Score
HSE	40	15	Safety Observations	100	90	13.50	94.00
		15	% of offshore employees trained	95	90	14.20	94.00
		20	Recordable Accidents per month	0	0	20.00	94.00
		15	Non-recordable Accidents per month	0	1	11.30	94.00
		25	Lost Time Incidents per month	0	0	25.00	94.00
		10	Environmental Incidents per month	0	0	10.00	94.00
Cost	10	50	Actual v planned (% Difference)	0%	0%	50.00	90.00
		50	Actual planned (% Difference)	0%	12%	40.00	90.00
Efficiency	25	50	Average % Rig NPT per month	5	3	50.00	100.00
		50	Actual versus planned job time (%)	10	9	50.00	100.00
Quality	25	20	Incorrect equipment occurrences	0	0	20.00	100.00
		20	late equipment/In excess of 3 days	0	0	20.00	100.00
		15	Test unsuccessfully 1st attempt	0	0	15.00	100.00
		20	# of failed removals/landings	0	0	20.00	100.00
		10	# of failed landings on 1st attempt	0	0	10.00	100.00
		15	# of failed tree test on 1st attempt	0	0	15.00	100

Score **96.58**

Source: BP Egypt (2008)

These KPIs are measurable and therefore are objective criteria. They highlight areas for further improvement. Subjective criteria may also be involved based on the buyer's perception, for example to commitment, attitudes and mannerisms including:

- Motivation toward individual contract commitments, future business etc.
- Response to constructive criticism, problem solving.
- Input into problem solving, innovation.

Recent studies have shown that if buyers communicate as openly as possible with their suppliers about what they expect, they will be given more information on such areas as stock levels, lead times and quality problems.

Part 2: Summary

Services procurement encompasses the strategic management and procuring of complex category services such as the professional services of accountants, lawyers, advertising agencies, market researchers,facilities management, and consultants to name but a few.

Research shows that spending on services (such as marketing, consultancy, contract labour, facilities management, travel, print and other categories that involve people doing things), is difficult to control, yet represents one of the largest potential opportunities for savings.

Service quality is difficult to assess (as a result of the intangible nature.)

In one classification of business services, a distinction is made between instrumental and consumption services where Consumption services are used up within the buying organisation (e.g. office cleaning at an airline) and Instrumental services are used to modify the way the buying organisation carries out its primary processes (e.g. management consultancy at an airline).

Quality is the ability of a product or service to consistently meet or exceed customer expectations. The dimensions of service quality are as follows:

- Access.
- Communication.
- Competence.
- Courtesy.
- Credibility.
- Reliability.
- Responsiveness.
- Security.

- Tangibles.
- Understanding/Knowing the Customer.

Procurement managers must become fully attuned to their internal customers and understand how perceptions of a service develop during the service process.

To control the Procurement of Services effectively, and to ensure Service Quality Improvement, it is advisable to adopt a Category Management approach as follows:

- Define the category.
- Defining the category is a five step process consisting of:
  - Determining facts we need to know.
  - Identifying potential sources of data.
  - Performing the analysis.
  - Summarising findings.
  - Developing, documenting and testing hypotheses.

3: Outsourcing

Introduction

Outsourcing often raises emotional concerns in people over job security and arguments that contractors and providers are making profits. Whilst such concerns may be understandable to some degree, outsourcing is growing only because it makes good business sense and presents new opportunities for the organisation that "contracts out" what it has determined to be non-core activity and has therefore chosen to leave this to the an appropriate expert.

As has been noted:
"Organisations should outsource all possible support services, excluding the very few that represent the source of core business of an organisation."
Source: Tom Peters

"Outsourcing may indeed be the only way to obtain productivity in clerical, maintenance and support work."
Source: Peter Drucker

Outsourcing can have a profound impact on an organisation's financial performance; there are therefore a number of issues to be considered before making the decision. The first is whether the service is a core competency. If the service is critical to an organisation, like, for example, warehousing is for Amazon, then it may be seen as central to the organisation's strategy and the best decision is to maintain all, or part, of the current in-house operations.

The second main reason is financial and whilst service providers may argue that they can lower costs, this may not apply where organisations are already running an efficient operation. Other financial reasons relate to the fact that, as the service suppliers may operate in a low margin business, your own people and resources can be better employed on more profitable work, or the limited available capital is now invested in an area that delivers a better return; e.g. those retailers who use limited capital to open more shops/outlets.

Without a mandate from top management, outsourcing will fail. Additionally, the organisation must have people with the skills to manage an outsourced relationship.

Those skills are very different from the managing of current physical service operations, for example, good warehouse managers are not necessarily going to be good at managing 3PLs.

The final question an organisation should ask is whether it is outsourcing for the right reasons. Too often, organisations outsource to get rid of a problem, but this will rarely work, because the problem is usually being caused by an unidentified source within the organisation's underlying business processes and is therefore destined to re-surface regardless.

The following checklist covers the important aspects of outsourcing in summary form:

Checklist: 10 rules of outsourcing

1. Develop a strategy for outsourcing. Outsourcing should always be measured against in-house solutions. This will help identify relative strengths and weaknesses for each alternative.

2. Establish a rigorous provider selection process. Check industry sources, existing clients, and financial health. Carefully analyze management depth, strategic direction, information technology capability, labour relations, and personal chemistry and compatibility.

3. Clearly define your expectations. Outsourcing relationships most often fail because of unrealistic expectations by organisations that lack accurate or detailed knowledge about the volume, size and frequency of their shipments. Such inaccuracies result in arrangements that don't reflect reality.

4. Develop a good contract. Provide incentives to improve operations and productivity with both parties sharing the benefits. Clearly spell out obligations, expectations and remedies.

5. Establish sound policies and procedures. In the ideal world, an operating manual will be developed jointly with the provider and contain all policies, procedures and other information necessary for the efficient operation of the outsourcing arrangement.

6. Identify and avoid potential friction points. Both parties are usually aware

of friction points that may arise. Develop a procedure for dealing with them in advance.

7. Communicate effectively with your service partner. Poor communication is second only to poor planning as a cause of outsourcing relationship failure.

8. Measure performance, communicate results. When setting up a relationship, clearly identify, agree upon and communicate standards of performance. Then measure performance regularly.

9. Motivate and reward providers. Don't take good performance for granted. Compliments, recognition, awards, trophies and dinners are all proven motivators. Do whatever works for your particular circumstances, but do something.

10. Be a good partner. Good partnerships are mutually beneficial. Your service provider's ability to serve you and your customers often can hinge on your own performance or lack thereof.

Source: Bob Trebilcock, Modern Materials Handling, 3/1/2004

Definition and History of outsourcing

The authors' definition of outsourcing is:

"The practice of handing over the planning, management and operation of certain functions formerly carried on inside the organisation, to an independent third party."

There are many examples of outsourcing, for example:

- ICT.
- Cleaning.
- Security.
- Transactional accounting.
- Engineering design.
- Construction management.
- Legal services.

- Catering.
- Market research.
- Travel.
- Procurement.

The history, development and future of outsourcing can be seen below:

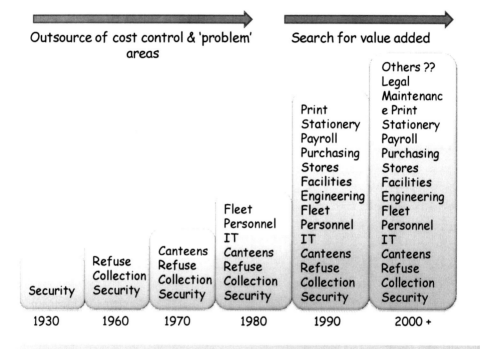

					Others ??
					Legal
					Maintenanc
				Print	e Print
				Stationery	Stationery
				Payroll	Payroll
				Purchasing	Purchasing
				Stores	Stores
				Facilities	Facilities
				Engineering	Engineering
			Fleet	Fleet	Fleet
			Personnel	Personnel	Personnel
			IT	IT	IT
		Canteens	Canteens	Canteens	Canteens
	Refuse	Refuse	Refuse	Refuse	Refuse
	Collection	Collection	Collection	Collection	Collection
Security	Security	Security	Security	Security	Security
1930	1960	1970	1980	1990	2000 +

Outsource of cost control & 'problem' areas — **Search for value added**

Checklist: Some Reported benefits of Outsourcing

- Total cost reduction.
- Focus on core activities.
- Contracted service levels; continuous improvement.
- Reduce capital investment.
- Investment saved is available to be spent on core activity.
- Continual efficiency/technical improvements.
- Improved support service.
- Fixed costs are converted to variable costs.
- Increased flexibility.
- Obtain specialist knowledge/management capability.
- Improved control.

Checklist: Concerns when Outsourcing

- Avoid losing control.
- Lack of effective reporting.
- Manage use of confidential data.
- Avoid hidden costs not in contract.
- How to capture benefits.
- Resource availability.
- Manage impact on internal morale.
- Lack of contract management and relationship skills.
- Lack of flexibility.

Outsourcing Process – A Model

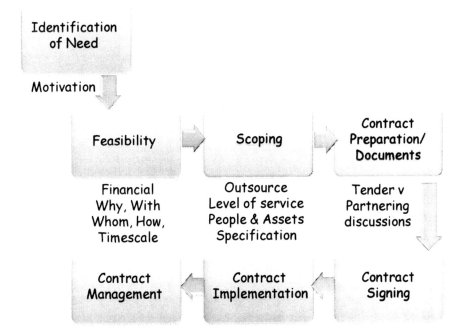

Important aspects for buyers

These include the following:

- The availability of bespoke management information, realistic KPIs.
- An open and honest relationship with their chosen partner.

- A reduction of risk.
- An understanding of the Transfer of Undertaking (Protection of Employment) Regulations of 1981 or TUPE and 2006. (This topic is covered more fully later in this section.)
- Effective Supplier Relationship Management (SRM). (This is also covered later in the book.)

Three important issues to avoid operational difficulties are as follows.

- Do not underestimate the resource requirements involved in contract management.
- Both parties must understand and agree the communication process/protocol.
- Do agree responsibilities and the reporting process (both ways). (Regular reviews, frequency, agenda, KPIs).

The authors have found that, while organisations recognise that they must focus their own resources on the things that give competitive or strategic advantage and/or on the things that they do better than anyone else, few of them have developed their thinking much beyond this point. Unfortunately, there is rarely a clear organisational focus for determining which activities are "core competencies", or for determining any strategic impact.

The following will therefore assist in deciding what should be outsourced:

1. Why should we outsource?
2. Who should we select?
3. What are the risks?
4. How should we develop and maintain 3rd party relationships?

To realise the benefits of outsourcing an organisation has to decide what to outsource. The approach to this is frequently quite haphazard based on a loose identification of what is "core" to the business and what is "non-core".

A possible model for helping to decide what might be suitable for outsourcing i.e. what is non-core, is to place all the activities which an organisation undertakes within a traditional four box matrix, the axes of which consist of importance to the organisation (vertical axis) and extent to which the organisation is competent in that activity (horizontal axis).

Outsourcing Matrix

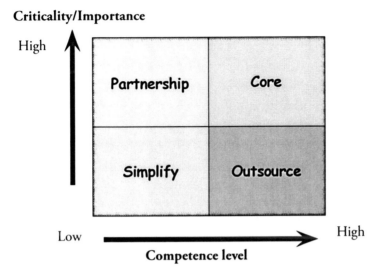

Nowadays effective relationships are based on the sharing of risk and reward, as shown below:

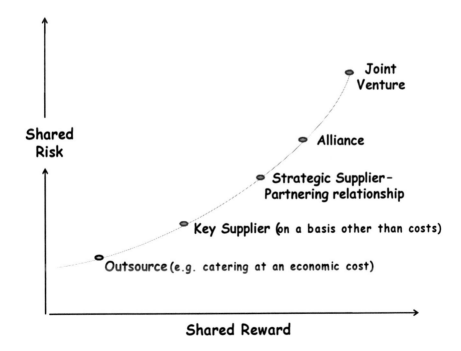

The types of relationships are also described in the above diagram.

Sourcing and Selection of Suppliers

Outsourcing partners require careful selection and development. The two organisations need to have close communication ties, technology transfer, address supply chain costs, early supplier involvement, and how the relationship is going to develop and be maintained.

The organisation may wish to expand their market abroad and must decide whether to use the same outsourcing organisation (who use their existing networks or by encouraging them to expand also) or whether to use a new regional organisation for their outsourcing activities.

A third important fact for consideration is whether the outsourcing organisation is a suitable partner. Successful partnerships often have similar technical competencies, bargaining power, cultures, strategies and visions.

Checklist: Key partner selection factors are:

- Careful analysis of the outsourcing organisation and suppliers to align competencies, strategies and transportation processes.
- Consideration of the extent to which long term competitiveness will be affected by outsourcing, obviously only applied to outsourced activities which affect competitiveness.
- Recognition of the mutual dependency and how this will affect the outsourcing organisation.
- Possible loss of flexibility.
- Recognition of the existence and scope of mutual bargaining positions.
- Consideration of the extent to which suppliers will fit with other suppliers, the outsourcing organisation's other partnering organisations.
- Establishing whether the outsourcing organisation has the competencies to manage outsourcing.

IMD Lausanne, Switzerland has suggested that competencies can be divided into five distinct groups. Consideration of this model might also be of assistance in deciding what to outsource.

Distinctive	**Future technologies, use of scarce resources, risk of failure in new product development**
	The competencies associated with these should not be outsourced.
Essential	**Have no/few suppliers, essential for quality, throughput time.** Competencies which affect these latter two aspects should probably not be outsourced. Obviously if there are no suppliers of an activity associated with the competency, then outsourcing is not possible.
Spillover	**Scale Economies, raw materials costs, high entry barriers**. These can confer a market advantage which can facilitate the outsourcing of an activity. An example is Benetton which buys conservable volume of the world's wool and gives it to suppliers. This facilitates low cost supply and could diminish the necessity to take manufacturing in-house.
Protective	**Confidentiality, exclusivity, supplier power;** as mentioned previously these impinge on outsourcing decisions
Parasitic	**Supplier's cost advantage, no capacity in an emerging technology, specialist organisational skills greater than the outsourcing organisations, new business involving unknown risks** These activities all lend themselves to outsourcing

Organisations considering outsourcing need to consider whether a supplier exists which can undertake the activity better than the organisation itself. If not, can an existing supplier be developed and, if so, how? (For more on Supplier Development, this is fully covered in *Excellence in Supplier Management* by Emmett and Crocker 2009). It is also important to consider whether the supplier might either have or can obtain economies of scale as a result of the new outsourcing deal.

Whilst the outsourcing of ICT and other activities is directly concerned with swiftly changing technology, it is particularly important to consider whether the outsourced relationship will confer an ability to cope with any changed and new technology shifts. In some cases, the effect of outsourcing on new product development should be considered, with for example, the outsourcing of design engineering.

If the outsourced activity requires confidentiality (for example as with engineering services or legal services), then the need for having exclusivity in the relationship should be considered. It could be that an organisation of solicitors should not deal with competitors or possibly suppliers.

Other aspects to be considered are the risk of supplier failure and the extent to which outsourcing is perhaps more suitable for one part of a product life cycle than another.

Checklist: Managing outsourced contracts

- Ensure that the activity is well defined with a clear specification.
- Roles and responsibilities of all parties must be made clear and communicated to all stakeholders.
- Effective supplier selection is undertaken to ensure the high quality of suppliers.
- Do not outsource if the market in that geographical area is not mature enough.
- Effective client management/monitoring/Supplier Relationship Management(SRM).

It is no surprise that clear specifications should come first in the above checklist; without them, there is little basis for a working relationship in a service context.

An important part of managing outsourcing is the consideration of potential exit strategies. Many people take the view that the decision to outsource is effectively irreversible, particularly where human and physical resources are transferred to the incoming supplier. However, there are many instances where outsourced services have been taken back in-house; clear evidence that even if you outsource, you can still retain long term control.

There are related changes to be seen in the recent styles of contractual relationships. These changes indicate a modest decrease in the number of contracts whose main characteristic is to penalise poor performance and a greater increase in those which reward good performance. Also of interest, are that more contracts are being based on the sharing of risk and reward.

Taken together, these trends are indications of a significant shift in client perception, away from the contractor as a potential adversary towards the contractor as potential partner. However, the ability of many organisations to deliver effectively within this new style of relationship can be questioned. For example, most of those who are looking to make increased use of open book mechanisms or performance-based contracts currently have very little experience of doing so and therefore could be "at risk"; experience with monitoring mechanisms is another requirement.

As outsourcing becomes extensive and relationships with suppliers more complicated, the level of skill and sophistication necessary for effective monitoring may increase beyond the current capability and competences found in many organisations.

Relationship management

It is important to manage the relationship between the customer and the supplier as it is to manage the contract. In pursuit of this, strategic sourcing is more willing to share risk and reward and less likely to rely on penalising poor performance. This is in line with a greater use of partnership type contracts, where incentives and the sharing of risk and reward are more common features.

Outsourcing Strategy

Many organisations tacitly admit they have little enough control over their in-house support departments and that a legally enforceable contract with an external supplier is a way of keeping the lid on costs and improving the quality of the service they get. Some questions that should be asked here are as follows:

- What are the proposed savings measured against?
- Does the outsourcer have economies of scale not available to you?
- Is the guaranteed price a good deal?
- Can the outsourcer buy equipment and hardware more cheaply?

However, in-house support operations should only be outsourced if they are cost effective as well as low risk in terms of service delivery non-compliance.

As mentioned earlier, if the customer succeeds in transferring responsibility for, say, its logistics to an outsourced supplier, the customer will be able to focus on its core business and look for advantages from the supplier such as strategic development advice, economies of scale, transformation activities (where business change needs to be managed) and benefiting from lower cost provision.

Case Study: Thomas Cook
Reasons for outsourcing and the business case

The main reason for Thomas Cook to outsource was to enable the IT department to respond to the constantly changing requirements from the business who are operating in a competitive and customer driven marketplace.

To maximise the potential of the IT department, the strategic and business management interface was retained, with the operational elements being transferred to a leading technology and service organisation, thus creating a virtual IT organisation.

Thinking strategically about outsourcing

There are four broad issues which need to be considered prior to making the decision and signing the contract:

- Think strategically about outsourcing.
- Think on the limits to the organisation's knowledge and competence.
- Think about the changes in the balances of power during the contract period.
- Consider the effects of supplier failure.

The most serious strategic risks of outsourcing are that it can lead to the organisation outsourcing its core activities.

Outsourcing of problematic functions often leads to disappointing results (as the organisation is unable to communicate its requirements adequately to the supplier). It may be that the troublesome activity is of some value to the organisation or, perhaps more significantly, it may acquire greater importance in the future. Just because it is problematic does not mean it will never be an activity that is critical to competitive advantage.

When a service has been provided in-house, certain aspects are taken for granted, and consequently it is often not identified explicitly. These can be aspects of the service provided in goodwill, or possibly by employees in other parts of the business. This can lead to them being omitted from the contractual agreement, and can mean that such extra charges are not built into the original cost comparisons.

Another crucial issue which an organisation needs to consider when it outsources is the way in which the balance of power in the relationship between buyer and supplier can change during the course of the contract.

Suppliers may fail to achieve the high standards required by the organisation, or, more significantly, go out of business altogether.

The lean business model is also pushing organisations towards concentrating on what they do best and adopting more "virtual" forms of enterprise with a small core, here the organisation manages many outsourced services and processes and is able to operate more efficiently with a smaller workforce.

However, if wrong decisions have been made, or circumstances change from those originally determining outsourcing, then maybe the outsourced service can be returned in-house, giving rise to what is called in-sourcing or backsourcing.

Case Study: RMC and In-sourcing

RMC UK cement division, part of one of the world's largest building materials and concrete suppliers, has moved its multi-million pound logistics operation back in-house.

Reasons:
Going back in-house will enable them to:

- Achieve better control.
- React more quickly and effectively in the marketplace.
- Make cost savings.

The contract includes managing customer processing, vehicle route planning, and collection and delivery of about 80 percent of RMC UK's raw materials. RMC's decision to bring its logistics back in-house bucks the industry trend and is because RMC wants more direct control of operations. The main reason for doing so is to have more direct control to reduce overall costs.

Outsourcing implementation guidelines

While outsourcing can often help control costs, simplify operations, and keep an organisation focused on its core competencies, it won't work unless it is properly implemented. Here are some guidelines on implementation.

- Determine what business you are in.
- Evaluate costs: try to determine just how much is being spent on a function and whether or not it can be done more cheaply by an outside organisation.
- Set objectives: Realistically decide what an outsource partner can do for the

organisation. Whether it is to cut costs, improve focus, or free up resources, make certain the goals are attainable.

- Monitor: if you decide to outsource, set up regular performance reviews or similar criteria to measure the provider's performance
- Be flexible: even after deciding to outsource, look at ways it can be improved. Don't be afraid to make changes in the ways a process is being handled.
- Don't jump on the bandwagon: just because outsourcing is a growing trend does not mean it should be automatically embraced.

Choices should be made only after these questions have been answered.

- What will the net gain or loss in efficiency and cost effectiveness be of using outsourcing?
- What will the net gain or loss in performance quality be of using outsourcing?
- What will the net effect be on the strength, versatility and resourcefulness of the department?
- What dependence on a third party will be created by outsourcing, and how vulnerable would the organisation be if that third party somehow became unable to perform as expected?

Procurement management needs to pay attention to six key areas in particular, these are highlighted in the following checklist.

Checklist: 6 Key Areas for Procurement when outsourcing

1) Service quality

The supply of services needs to be defined carefully and broken down into separate sub-services, each of which should be measurable.

Comprehensive performance reporting will enable both parties to ensure that services are delivered as part and as agreed.

This part of the contract is often referred to as a service level agreement (SLA). In this, the customer's objectives must be clear, and the parties need to agree performance levels for the services relating to availability, liability, serviceability and response, as well as either or both of productivity and quality.

The parties also need to agree service credits, which will be payable to the customer if the supplier fails to meet the SLA.

2) Intellectual property rights

At the start of the contract, the customer's intellectual property right (IPR such as copyright, patent and design rights, for example) in its processes, drawings, written material and software need to be made available to the supplier.

But over the course of the contract, new rights will arise as new material and processes are created, mainly by the supplier, so it must settle which side owns these rights.

For the main, they should be owned by the customer. However, where the supplier uses its own expertise to bring benefit to the customer, it will want to own the relevant rights.

3) Legal liabilities

The customer needs to make sure that the supplier can offer compensation if the worst comes to the worst.

4) Supplier openness and transparency

The customer will be committing important aspects of its business into the hands of the supplier. In return, the supplier must provide assurances on three particular issues: Data security, business continuity and the right of the customer to audit the processes of the outsourcer to ensure everything is being run efficiently and cost effectively.

This includes the need for the customer to audit the work of the supplier and its subcontractors for effectiveness of the services and costs and savings

5) Termination

The parties should always be aware that however well the contract relationship goes, at some point it will end. It is important for the customer to define all the triggers for terminating a contract, but it is also vital for the consequences of termination to be agreed and planned in advance. The customer needs, for its own performance, to secure a smooth handover, either back to itself or to another supplier, whenever termination occurs. In terms of the triggers for termination, they must include material default by the supplier, the insolvency of the supplier and the change of control of the supplier to an organisation that might harm the customer's trading operations.

A smooth handover is best achieved by creating and updating an exit plan, which details all the activities of both parties that must be undertaken when a handover starts. In that way, there will be no surprises for the customer at what will be a critical time.

6) Contract management/Supplier relationship management (SRM)

A continuing, successful working relationship is vital if the outsourcing of supply chain tasks is to work. The contract should therefore set up structures for regular meetings, the escalation of difficult issues and the resolution of disputes. (We give more details about contract management below, and SRM is also covered later in this book.)

Following on from point 6, contracts, the following will assist:

Checklist: Outsourcing - Contractual Issues

Key Requirement	Contract Clauses	Contract Schedules
The external and the internal business customers' requirements	A description of the services	Detailed service level agreements (SLAs)
Culture and commercial requirements	Reporting, meetings, quality, change control and escalation procedures	Contract management procedures
ICT requirements	Service provision, Data records and security, warranties and breaches	Service management and a statement of work
HR requirements	Staff and T & Cs, TUPE and pensions	Staff transferring
Finance requirements	Pricing mechanisms, penalties	Detailed pricing and controls
Legal requirements	Entry (set up) and exit and other essential legal clauses.	Transition plan and exit plan

Contract Management

The worst way to 'manage' a contract is simply to leave it take its course; it will then more than likely go wrong and leave an incomplete audit trail. Let's be very clear here, control cannot be outsourced and management control must remain a core activity. Effective contract management involves the 3Cs of contract management; the Contractual, Commercial and Collaboration aspects:

1) Contractual: Performance to a required standard and compliance with the contract conditions, for example, costs and services supplied, are in accordance with the requirements of the contract and its terms and conditions. Contract control involves actively keeping the contractor's performance to the required standard. If this is to be successful, participation by both parties is needed so that any problems can be quickly identified and resolved. It is therefore important that a sound working relationship is established.

If monitoring indicates that a contractor's performance has deteriorated, action will need to be taken. The nature of the action will depend upon the level of the under-performance or from any complaints. If regular monitoring is effectively carried out, then problems will be spotted early and the degree of any disruption from corrective action will be minimised. In most cases a discussion of the problem will be all that is required to secure agreement on remedial action.

2) Commercial: Clear and documented records are vital, with evidence where necessary to invoke any non-compliance procedures, for example, recording complaints received from customers of the service and recording customer satisfaction with the service. It is important for contract managers to have clear and documented evidence if contracts do not run smoothly. Records of all meeting and telephone conversations should be held on file. The contractor should be notified in writing of all instances of non-compliance, and a written timetable for rectification should be drawn up. It is likely that the contractor will also be keeping records of the problems incurred with the contract.

If the contractor continually fails to perform, this may constitute a breach of contract. The severity of the failure and the cost to the organisation will need to be assessed. Legal advice may be required before any further action is considered. Below are examples of where default in a contract may arise from a failure to:

- Perform any part of the services.
- Provide financial or management information.

- Employ appropriately qualified, experienced, skilled or trained staff.
- Comply with legislation.
- Make payment to the supplier on time (clearly both parties must fulfil their contractual obligations).

3) Collaboration and relationships between the parties, the way they regard each other and the way in which their relationship operates, is vital to making a success of the arrangement.

Although it is sometimes difficult to predict accurately where problems may arise, good contract management with regular dialogue between the contractor and customer will help to identify potential problems earlier. This will enable problems to be dealt with swiftly and effectively and so prevent major disputes.

Active contract management therefore requires efficient two-way communications between both parties which will anticipate problems, so that these are dealt with quickly and corrective action is taken to prevent similar problems from arising in future. This requires established lines of communication and an overall approach that will jointly and seamlessly manage and control change, for example, in making collaborative improvements.

As identified by the OGC (2002), good contract management goes much further than ensuring that the agreed terms of the contract are being met – whilst this is a vital step, it is only the first of many. Whilst a successful relationship must involve the delivery of services that meet requirements and the commercial arrangement must be acceptable to both parties (such as offering Value for Money for the customer and adequate profit for the provider), the collaboration between the parties, the way they regard each other and the way in which their relationship operates, is what is really critical in making a success of the arrangement.

No matter what ever is the scope or the terms of the contract, there will always be some tensions between the different perspectives and perceptions of the customer/buyer and the supplier/contractor. Contract management is about resolving such tensions and to do this, there must be an effective collaboration with the supplier/contractor that is based on mutual gains, understanding, trust and open communication.

Control of change

Contract requirements are often subject to change throughout the life of the contract.

We live in a fast changing world with a future of "stable turbulence" and it is not therefore always possible to predict such changes and variations in advance, or, at the specification stage.

It may therefore be decided during the course of the contract, that a slight change to the requirements are needed.

Such changes to the requirements will often affect the cost and so will need to be recorded. Changes to the contracts may also affect the following:

* The initial specification (it can be now out of date).
* The cost and service, for example, changed delivery times, locations.
* The nature of the services being provided.

It will normally be the role of the contract manager to ensure that any need for any contract variation is recorded and the contract is changed to be line with the newly agreed procurement procedures. The variations being clearly tied in with the main contract so that a clear audit trail is possible. Audit trails being especially important for those organisations in the public sector who find it essential to keep records of dealings with suppliers whether written or verbal as such records are required for:

* Information if problems arise.
* Reviewing meetings and re-negotiations.
* Audit purposes.
* Planning for any subsequent re-tendering processes.

End of Contract/Completion Reports

It is good practice at the completion of any contract to review and place on record what went well and what lessons can be learned for any future contracts, for example, using a Contractor Evaluation Report. The information on this report will be used to evaluate and monitor the effectiveness of the organisation's contractors. This essentially covers the outcome and extent to which the expected benefits (deliverables) were achieved.

What can go wrong with outsourcing?

Unfortunately many outsourcing contracts, with which the authors are familiar, have floundered as a result of having a prime focus on savings, rather than on improved service and bringing in a new competitive advantage. The research findings below highlight contributory factors that shows most respondents actually placed contracts more on the price/saving money aspects, instead of on other performance/service aspects:

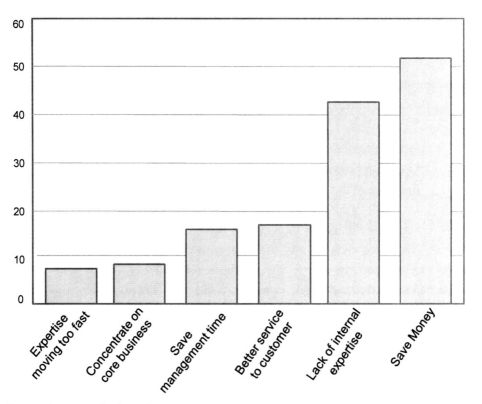

Source: Arminas, D (2003)

Case study: IBM

Services which have been outsourced range from customer call management and marketing support to education and training, warehousing and property management. From the diversity and scale of these operations the organisation has gained a broad based, practical expertise in outsourcing strategy.

At the heart of IBM's approach has been the drive to define the absolute minimum resources and critical "value add" skills which are the very core of its business. These are IBM's definition of the core competencies, which fall into the following four categories:

- They provide management and direction.
- They maintain competence and control.
- They differentiate IBM from its competitors.
- They sustain IBM's uniqueness.

Case Study: Digital

When considering the definition of outsourcing Digital suggests that it is necessary to question both the motives of the outsource seeker and the potential supplier, and to evaluate the various options available. It defines outsourcing as the *"contracting out of one or more business or information systems functions"*. Outsourcing is further defined by them as:

- Long term; two to five years.
- A relationship.
- A merger of cultures.
- Joint working.
- Risk sharing.
- Strategic motivation.
- For mutual benefit.
- Only by sharing risks can both parties truly share in the potentiality of the partnership.

Pitfalls versus benefits

- Lock-in, no easy escapes.
- Price rises dependent on supplier.
- Loss of control.
- Non-performance of the service provider.

As well as the above pitfalls, there are also **inhibitors** which may be due to fears, however real, which may stop the outsource seeker from looking further. These are:

- Fear of losing control.
- Outsourcing being tantamount to admitting failure.
- Not want to be on the 'bleeding edge' (in this case outsourcing).

- Seeking outsourcing as a one way street.
- Technology developments which may be difficult to include such as new work being carried out by key insiders.
- Contract term with may be too long.

While some may be real, these can be weighed against the **potential benefits**, which are:

- Cost savings.
- Better cost control.
- Improving balance sheet by removal of fixed assets.
- Ensuring flexible matching of resources to business.
- Staying in tune with fast evolving technology.
- Securing access to scarce skills.
- Enhanced employees' careers.
- Achieving guaranteed service levels.

Case Study: Boots

Boots the Chemist admits that while it could "squeeze another half a percent" out of its indirect budget itself, a third party will save significantly more.

Checklist: Outsourcing Pitfalls

- Organisations often fail to achieve their objectives when outsourcing because of poor planning and lack of communication.
- One critical success factor is having a carefully drafted contract from the outset. Benefits often fail to materialise because the written document does not set down common objectives and marry key performance indicators with the service level agreements. They also fail to include the right mix of incentives and penalties for the provider.
- The contract largely determines whether an arrangement works.
- The contract has to include a mechanism with incentives and penalties.
- If this is not right, the various parties in the contract will drive in different directions. The provider has to be incentivised; you cannot want large savings and not put incentives in the contract.

- It is essential that outsourcing arrangements track changes to the business. The word here is "flex". Businesses can go through a whole series of changes over time, which can cause the service provider and client to diverge in terms of the service that is being delivered.
- The negative effect that "outsourcing" may have on employee morale. The effect can be minimised, through a high level of consultation and communication of intentions, however, the fact remains that most employees perceive the practice as a negative development.
- Motivation of contractors. Many organisations report that contract employees are rarely as prepared as in-house colleagues to go beyond their immediate remit and take the time to work out ideas which may be of benefit to the organisation as a whole.

Outsourcing of the Procurement function

While years ago outsourcing might have been seen as an option for only certain areas, such as cleaning and catering, now practically every function is viewed as a candidate for it, including payroll, IT support, fleet management, and even procurement. If you can achieve cost savings and improve service levels outsourcing IT support, for example, why not place procurement with a third party?

Checklist: Procurement Outsourcing Best Practice

- Concentrate on what the organisation does well and allow specialists in other areas to handle your noncore services.
- Adapt to new ideas and developments; what was an acceptable practice in the past may not be so in the future.
- Choose a third party service provider that can understand all your needs.
- Benchmark current costs, this is crucial.
- Ensure that the outsourcing delivers the planned benefits and meets the agreed service, cost and time targets.
- Acknowledge that information equals power in areas such as spend and service level requirements.
- Have a strategic partnership with your providers that are based on mutual trust.
- Opt for an initial, phased, controlled service, with monitored service levels at all stages.

- Develop the right corporate culture.
- Monitor the outsourced function and measure its performance regularly.

A survey by Accenture of more than 200 procurement directors from a variety of industries in the European Union and the US found that nearly half of them were considering outsourcing at least part of their procurement within three years. Deutsche Bank announced plans to outsource it to consultancy Accenture, as has Goodyear, in a £30 million deal with IBM. NHS selected DHL in 2006 to carry out non-critical purchases totalling £22 billion per year, with expected saving of £1 billion per year for 10 years. However outsourcing, as already mentioned, is not without potential pitfalls.

Outsourcing and "Service Level Specifications"

Determining appropriate service level specifications is a crucial foundation for a successful outsourcing relationship.

In outsourcing, an organisation turns over the ownership of a non-core business process to a service provider in order to leverage the provider's expertise, economies of scale and access to resources.

Service level specifications play two vital roles in an outsourcing agreement.

- They ensure accountability on the part of the provider.
- They determine the price of the service.

The only way to ensure a comfort level for the buyer is to set required service level specifications, and to then regularly measure the provider's performance to determine whether they have achieved those levels.

A service level specification should be established for every important component of a process, and then buyers will know it is getting what it is paying for. Each component will then focus on one of the buyer's desired results (such as accuracy, timeliness, customer satisfaction, ensuring regulatory compliance etc.).

If, for example, with the services of a call centre, the buyer wants a very high service level to minimise the amount of waiting time before calls are answered, then the price will be higher because of the need for more resources, both people and technology.

The buyer's desired results (that will be specified in the service level specifications) do determine the price; therefore, it is crucial to define service level specifications clearly. By avoiding ambiguities and ensuring service levels are directly linked to desired results, the service level specification can actually drive down the price.

Definition of a Service Level Agreement (SLA)

A Service Level Agreement (SLA) is a legal document within (or attached to) an overall master contract for an outsourcing agreement. It is an agreement between the provider of an outsourced service and its principal or customer which quantifies the minimum acceptable service to the latter. An SLA contains a description of the services to be provided pertaining to the buyer's outsourced business process.

The SLA also states the service level specifications, which clearly describe the level of performance and therefore the results the buyer expects to receive from the service provider. The service provider must meet or exceed these performance standards and disenchantment will arise from unspecified expectations which are not met by supplier performance.

Checklist: Examples of service parameters

- Availability.
- Turnaround of delivery vehicles.
- Delivery times.
- Response times.
- Security.
- Quality levels.
- Rates/fees.
- Organisational objectives.

Checklist: Examples of elements in the SLA

- Mission statement.
- Business targets.
- Corporate plan.
- Specification.
- Service level specification.
- Capacity plan.

Some examples of Service Level Specification Types

Before the buyer determines service level specifications, it must first define the results it effectively is buying. An organisation might want to outsource, say, one or more of its human resource (HR) functions and for example, it may want to achieve the following results:

- To gain flexibility and economies of scale necessitated by mergers, acquisitions.
- To consolidate and standardise data and the disparate services currently provided to employees.
- To implement web-based, self-service formats for delivery of benefits services
- To reduce operational costs.

What should be measured, and thus stated in the service level specifications, will vary greatly for each of these results. Furthermore, the buyer, before they can measure results objectively, must clearly determine the scope and boundaries of the outsourced process. To outsource the HR process, for example, the buyer will need to determine whether to include in the scope:

- Health and welfare benefits.
- Pension.
- Savings.
- Recruitment.
- Training.
- Retention.
- Payroll.

Each of these decisions will be reflected in the drafting of the service level specification, and each will be a cost factor in the provider's service.

Service Level Specification Styles

Utility

This style of service level specification is similar to what we expect from an electric organisation or a telephone organisation. If the service is on, all is well. If the service is off, we want a credit applied to our invoice for the amount of downtime. Basically, there are two levels of service: acceptable and unacceptable. A penalty (a credit to the buyer's account, for example) is associated with the unacceptable level.

The role of value creation

The next two of the three styles are tied to creation and capture of additional value that can be achieved by outsourcing. The objectives in this type of outsourcing are to contribute value beyond the reduction in costs that are associated with a particular function or transaction.

As an example, the objective for a "utility style" service level specification in a hospital's outsourced food service process might be to centralise the operation, and thus reduce operational costs. But if the objective for outsourcing the food service process is to improve patient nutrition and satisfaction, the impact of the outsourcing will create a far greater value in addition to the cost reduction.

Where the objectives in outsourcing are to add value with a strategic impact on the organisation, the service level specification style to use will be either the "process improvement" or the "value added" style.

Process improvement style

This style or service level specification is used when the buyer's business objective is process improvement after the service provider takes responsibility for the process. The service level specification for a process improvement objective will measure success of changes introduced to the process, rather than the end result.

It is not uncommon for organisations to write utility service level specifications when what they really want and expect from the service provider is process improvement. In such an instance, the wrong things will be measured.

Value added style

This style of service level specification must describe the actual value, the quality of the desired result. Using an HR recruiting example, the service level should measure the right fit of talent in a position or duration of employment, not just how many people are recruited. A well constructed value added service level specification will therefore measure the effectiveness of results in creating value for the buyer's organisation. This is also applicable when the buyer and service provider both share the risk and reward.

Steps to determine a service level specification

No process is too complex to measure, if the buyer simply follows the steps outlined overleaf:

1) Select the service to be measured.

This will be one of the following:

- Achieving the objective(s).
- The process itself.

It is this step that determines which style of service level specification to use (for example, utility, process improvement or value added).

2) Choose the attributes to measure

These attributes are the things the buyer determines to be the most critical components of service and the relationships (e.g. time, cost, quality, quantity). Together, the attributes paint a clear picture of what success looks like.

3) Determine the current in-house service level

Determining the current in-house service level and the cost for that service level eventually enables comparison. By comparing the figures to industry standards and benchmarking, as well as best of breed service level specifications, you can then determine how much improvement is desired.

The process to determine the current in-house costs is full of pitfalls, as most organisations are not aware of all the hidden cost factors affecting the total cost. If this procedure is not performed adequately, the parameters the buyer uses to determine its desired level of spending will not be accurate and may give rise later to perceived dissatisfaction with the outsourcing decision.

4) Components of service level specifications

Each service level specification must have:

- A definition of the metric and what is being measured.
- A description of the method and process for capturing the data.
- A statement of the timing interval for measurement.

Note: Metrics are the value that defines the data points that will be measured and reported; value is a description of the level of performance to measure against; typical values will be:

- Service level; an acceptable level of service; however, a service provider is usually expected to perform above this level.
- Impact level; where performance is unacceptable and adversely impacts the buyer's business.

Below is an example of the process improvement type.

Outsourced process: Call Centre

Style: Process Improvement

Step 1: Determine the service to be measured:
- First call resolution rate
- Cost per call
- Customer satisfaction

Metric for First Call Resolution Rate

Values	Metrics
Service Level	90% answered with 50 seconds
Impact Level	90% answered within 60 seconds

Outsourcing: risk elimination

The most important focus for buyers when writing an outsourcing contractual agreement is to eliminate risks. This is best accomplished through clear, effective descriptions of the process to be outsourced (including scope and boundaries), along with clear, effective, objective service level specifications.

To achieve a win-win relationship, both parties must be able to rely on the service level specifications to determine where the provider's focus should be, as this is based on the buyer's critical needs. It identifies both the buyer's goals and the service provider's guarantees and also lays out the path toward continual improvement in the outsourced process. This simplicity however, does not seem to borne out by most organisational practice, as shown in the following case study:

Case Study: Research

Not every organisation has had a good experience taking functions out of house.

According to research by Brunel University, 18 percent of organisations in the UK that had outsourced a function experienced higher costs, a third cancelled the contract within five years and half found themselves in dispute with the third party.

Of these disputes, more than a third concerned failure to meet service level agreement, while 23 percent were to do with unclear contractual issues, 21 percent changed requirements and 18 percent unforeseen charges.

Most organisations decide to outsource a function because:

- It is under performing.
- There is a genuine business case for outsourcing the activity.
- They are facing a major challenge, such as the need to develop quickly or enhance a competence to stay competitive.

These factors are often linked to other motivations, such as:

- Pressure from suppliers and customers.
- Poor results in benchmarking studies.
- Limited staff and space.
- The expansion or discontinuation of products or services.

There is generally a mixed bag of reasons behind a decision to outsource, a good number of which actually seem to set up problems that will inevitably lead to eventual disaster. Therefore the challenge for procurement staff is to have an impact on the decision from the start.

This means influencing stakeholders who have the power, and developing robust risk assessment and management tool for the whole business; unfortunately, the initial contract often fails to adequately cover the four key areas.

- Service Level Agreements.
- Penalty clauses.
- Changing circumstances clauses.
- Early termination provisions.

The Brunel research mentioned previously found that only 26 percent of the organisations that had outsourced felt that they had covered all four areas sufficiently.

Some of the problems encountered are actually as a result of outsourcing something that should have actually been left in-house.

As we mentioned earlier, being influenced too much by price when making an outsourcing choice is one of the most common pitfalls; service factors are nearly always the absolute key. Those procurement people that have a mindless search for the lowest price, will ultimately get the service they pay for. (This is discussed more in our section on government services procurement and the Value for Money principle).

Outsourcing as a Paradigm Change

Through the outsourcing decision, an organisation often moves from a focus on protecting the "how" of business to managing the "what" of its business. This means changing the organisational structure from a focus of internal corporate competencies in the higher risk/strategically important zone to the external sourcing of lower risk/non-strategically important competencies.

This requires a paradigm shift in the organisation's management from being process/operationally minded managers towards now being contract managers. The key attitudinal changes required as follows:

Respect the Contractor. Often, two different business cultures come together in an outsourced service relationship, for example, a 3PL is contracted because they are "the experts" and the organisation's staff must now present themselves professionally and acknowledge the 3PL's ability to do the work.

Develop Rapport. An outsourced service arrangement is an opportunity to move away from adversarial/transactional relationship to a collaborative/partnering supplier relationship. This requires the development of rapport between all of the key players.

Focus on Project Milestones. Regular meetings are required to report on transition, optimization and process improvements. The service provider must be regularly accountable but must also receive regular and clear guidance.

Clear Statements of Deliverables. There should be no doubt about the deliverables of the service provider. They should be stated in the agreement but also clearly understood by the key players and regularly reviewed by them at an appropriate forum.

Staff Interaction. Interaction is vital at both the management level and the working level. Contract management should always be on the lookout to facilitate interaction to head off potential problems and to encourage innovation and synergies.

Any eventual gap between planned and actual benefits of outsourcing and the non-achievement of the expected performance will not only be caused by the external service provider; but also by internal barriers, such as resistance and failure to change attitudes. Consequently here, the required support to the new ways of working together may be stifled and prevented.

Transfer of Undertaking Protection of Employment (TUPE)

No discussion of outsourcing would be complete without reference to the Transfer of Undertaking Protection of Employment (TUPE) regulation which is considered by many to have created problems for the government in the implementation of its public sector CCT (Compulsory Competitive Tendering) and market testing policies.

These regulations, which implemented the 1977 European Acquired Rights Directive, provide that where there has been a transfer of an undertaking, either in its entirety or in part, the new employer takes over the contracts of employment of all employees. The intention is that employees should not suffer from unemployment or loss of earnings as a result of an organisation deciding to outsource any of its operations.

The Transfer of Undertakings (Protection of Employment) Regulations 1981, otherwise known as TUPE, usually apply where an employer transfers all or part of its business to another employer.

However, the question of whether and when TUPE applies has become notoriously complex in situations where what is being proposed does not fit neatly into the definition of "transfer".

The updated 2006 regulations made it clear that TUPE would apply to most outsourcing situations, for example, where services are initially outsourced or taken back in-house, or when a replacement service provider is appointed.

This meant that it would no longer be possible for an incoming employer to claim that TUPE does not apply on the grounds that it will be performing the services in a substantially different way to the outgoing employer.

Another big change was a new obligation on the outgoing service provider to give the incoming provider details of all transferring employees, their terms and conditions of employment and any other employment related liabilities. This has proved very useful in labour intensive service sectors, such as cleaning, where incoming providers are often faced with little or no knowledge of the number of employees they may become responsible for and also, with having to agree to the existing wage agreements and costs.

The new Regulations introduced joint liability on both outgoing and incoming service providers/employers for any failure to inform and consult with affected employees. This way, outgoing and incoming employers are incentivised to co-operate in their information and consultation obligations.

One area of uncertainty had been, whether, incoming employers can lawfully change the transferring employees' terms and conditions. The new Regulations therefore clarified when and how employers can lawfully dismiss or change terms and conditions of employment in connection with a transfer.

Private Finance Initiative (PFI) and Compulsory Competitive Tendering (CCT)

As is fully discussed in the next part of this book (public sector procurement of services), one of the major driving forces for the increase in outsourcing is the take up of the Private Finance Initiative (PFI) deals and Compulsory Competitive Tendering (CCT) by the public sector. This in turn has led to a large expansion in the Facilities Management (FM) industry.

The PFI has resulted in long term 25-30 year deals for service provision of roads, hospitals, prisons and government offices. The FM organisations themselves are also expanding and merging. For example, ServiceMaster, a large FM organisation in the

USA, teamed up two years ago with UK's Tarmac in order to compete for big PFI contracts.

As businesses contract out more of their non-core activities they are being forced to confront the question of what exactly they exist to do in terms of the process and not the function.

Case Study: RAC

The business changes at the RAC saw a refocus on motoring and mobility, as a result of this strategy, there was a need to reduce the number of offices and divest part of the non-core business.

They were lead to consider outsourcing with an assessment that the systems for some processes had a finite life, such as RAC Insurance Services, the relocation of IT from the insurance office and the non-core nature of the administration processes.

They key objectives of the business case reflected the need for IT to keep aligned with the business to provide excellent support, through key skills and knowledge retention, Value for Money and flexible services and to ensure that there was not business disruption.

These objectives were all factored into the final outsourcing solution and formed the basis of the supplier selection process.

Case Study: Morgan Stanley Bank

Outsourcing is usually understood to mean that an organisation is getting out of some part of its business.

Morgan Stanley handed over responsibility for about a third of its $1bn of annual technology spending, and 900 staff, to a grouping of computer service and telecoms organisations. Over the life of the contract, it expects to save 15 percent of the money it would have spent on this technology.

The bank will benefited from its suppliers' depth of expertise, freeing its own people to focus on the areas most important to creating competitive advantages.

Case Study: Boots

Boots have signed a multi-million pound deal with IBM to outsource all of the administration of its indirect procurement operation.

It covers £52 million of non-strategic categories such as stationery, couriers and lab supplies.

It also covers the transactional procurement and accounts payable processing for all goods not for resale activities worth around £650 million annually.

No purely strategic sourcing staff would be transferred to IBM because Boots has a shortage of this type of staff and wants to concentrate efforts in new spending areas including goods for resale procurement. To cut operating costs, they have already centralised people and reduced numbers, re-engineered processes and introduced purchasing cards.

The next level – automating additional processes, which would have meant an outlay on technology or moving jobs off shore, but Boots does not have the time or resources to get into that sort of thing.

Case Study: BBC

The BBC has outsourced its IT services arm as part of a £2 billion outsourcing project. The corporation expects to save £20-30 million a year by outsourcing BBC technology.

The division supplies 26,000 personal computers and IT services for the BBC and handles contracts for other media groups such as British Sky Broadcasting.

The 10 year contract offer followed an internal review of the BBC's technology requirements, which found outsourcing technology services would lead to savings.

Outsourcing: Summary and Conclusion

Outsourcing may still be the latest fashion, but it needs more careful handling as there have been many unsuccessful ventures.

For example, an estimated half of all ICT outsourcing deals in Europe fail to meet expectations as organisations focused excessively on the process of selecting a service provider and negotiating the deal, at the expense of working out how to make it work for the business.

The following is a summary of reasons why outsourcing fails:

Checklist: Reasons for failure when outsourcing

- Failure of the outsourced organisation to invest in Research and Development.
- Failure of the outsourced organisation to keep abreast of competitors.
- Disorganised setting up of the partnership leading to greater costs incurred than the in-house function.
- Trade union opposition.
- TUPE regulations in terms of the restrictions placed on the outsourcing organisation's choice of staff and in terms of the lack of consistent TUPE rules (i.e. TUPE is developing in case law).
- Lack of trust on the part of the organisation leading to intrusive and costly, checking systems into the outsourced organisation.
- The organisation's inability to manage the supply chain organisation and supplier development.
- The outsourcing organisation, if large and holding several organisations' contracts, using the same approach for all and not differentiating between the different requirements of their customers.
- Poor contract drafting, for example, confidentiality and data ownership.
- Failure to account for the indirect costs of outsourcing.

Outsourcing involves at least two organisations working together, therefore a relationship exists. Any relationship is dependant on trust, as without trust, there is effectively no relationship. This is a large topic, covered fully in *The Relationship Driven Supply Chain*. Meanwhile the key ingredients for creating high performance relationships are:

- The right mix of internal skills.
- Formal relationship management processes.
- Active trust between the customer and service provider.

Supplier relationship management skills (covered in part 6 of this book) will grow in importance as organisations became reliant on external and increasingly global deals.

Organisational agility and the ability to create value require flexibility and creatively that go further than process excellence.

These factors are often negotiated out of outsourcing deals owing to traditional approaches based on control, but we have seen that relationships with higher trust levels do really deliver more value, less waste and resolve problems more effectively.

Checklist: Pitfalls when outsourcing

- Leaving contract negotiations until very late in the process.
- Poor specifications, which fail to define services and service levels in detail.
- Inflexible contracts.
- No attention to building relationships.
- Lack of effective reporting of KPIs.

Checklist: Benefits of outsourcing

- Economies of scale.
- Specialist suppliers expertise.
- Possibly improved quality.
- Freeing management time to concentrate on the core business.
- Increased strategic flexibility.
- Fixed costs become variable costs.
- Investment saved can be spent on core area of business.
- Lower total costs.

A report from E-E International concerning the outsourcing of distribution logistics services identified the main benefits of outsourcing as:

- Increased flexibility.
- Improved service.
- Reduced costs.
- Investment avoidance.
- Increased flexibility.

Poor contractor management and insufficient controls were the principal problems encountered along with the perceived following drawbacks:

- The risk of being locked into commercial contracts which later lose relevance.
- Supplier and buyer become complacent.
- The difficulty of reverting to in-house services.
- Loss of responsiveness to the customer vase.
- The tendency for suppliers to put profits before user business benefits.

The following factors for success included the following:
- The driving forces behind outsourcing can be combinations of financial problems, a need for a clear focus on core competencies, and cost efficiency.
- The outcome of outsourcing is more successful if based on strategic decisions including core competence and cost efficiency considerations.

Case Study: HMSO

HMSO identified the following areas to be considered when outsourcing:
- Retain in-house control over the strategic direction of the service.
- Retain the responsibility for setting the standards to which the supplier must conform.
- Make the supplier responsible for the delivery of the service.
- Be prescriptive about the service requirements rather than the methods.
- Always be aware of the business reasons for outsourcing.
- Avoid being locked into a single supplier.
- Expect Value for Money, but don't lose sight of the fact that the supplier is looking for financial gain.
- Understand the wider perspective of the outsourcing contract.
- Be clear about what is expected of the supplier.
- Spend time choosing a person to manage the contract.
- Regularly review the contract and the relationship with the supplier.

- Re-tender contracts at defined intervals.
- Keep an eye on the outsourcing market in order to keep up with the changes and good practice.
- Monitor the supplier's resources and business knowledge.
- The contract should be flexible enough to allow for change.
- Aim for continuous improvement.

Part 3: Summary

Definition of outsourcing

The authors suggest that outsourcing is *"the practice of handing over the planning, management and operation of certain functions, formerly carried on inside the organisation, to an independent third party."*

Reported benefits of outsourcing

- Total Cost reduction.
- Focus on core activities.
- Contracted service levels-continuous improvement.
- Reduce capital investment.
- Investment saved is available to be spent on core activity.
- Continual efficiency/technical improvements.
- Improved support service.
- Fixed costs are converted to variable costs.
- Increased flexibility.
- Obtain specialist knowledge/management capability.
- Improved control.

Key partner selection factors are:

- Careful analysis of the outsourcing organisation and suppliers to align competencies, strategies and transportation processes.
- Consideration of the extent to which long term competitiveness will be affected by outsourcing, obviously only applied to outsourced activities which affect competitiveness.
- Recognition of the mutual dependency and how this will affect the outsourcing organisation.

- Possible loss of flexibility.
- Recognition of the existence and scope of mutual bargaining positions.
- Consideration of the extent to which suppliers will fit with other suppliers, the outsourcing organisation's other partnering organisations.
- Establishing whether the outsourcing organisation has the competencies to manage outsourcing.

Managing outsourced contracts
- Ensure that the activity is well defined with a clear specification.
- Roles and responsibilities of all parties must be made clear and communicated to all stakeholders.
- Effective supplier selection is undertaken to ensure the high quality of suppliers.
- Do not outsource if the market in that geographical area is not mature enough.
- Effective client management/monitoring/Supplier Relationship Management(SRM).

4: Public Sector Service Procurement

Background

The UK public sector procurement environment has undergone considerable change over the past forty years. The 1970s was a period of considerable socio-economic and political upheaval with the late 1970s seeing a change of government and, in the early 1980s, an increasing emphasis upon competition. This meant that quite a number of commercial organisations ultimately went out of business; there was also the introduction of the emphasis upon the concept of Value for Money (VFM) and a recognition that reducing costs could impact upon the bottom line for organisations as well as by increasing of sales (especially when gaining additional sales was difficult anyway!)

The then new Margaret Thatcher highlighted a variety of things in public sector spending in an introduction to a report on public sector procurement (for the then new Central Unit on Purchasing that is now evolved into the OGC, the Office of Government Commerce). Comments were made on the spending on "paperclips, desks, fuel and other essentials; let alone what is spent on warships and the like". It was perhaps a time when the recognition that the effect of improving purchasing performance could impact the overall profitability of commercial organisations, then in due course a similar view was taken that such approaches could apply in the public sector. Such approaches would not increase profitability in the public sector but in a similar manner to the increase of profitability in the private sector, this could then allow for more goods or services to be obtained for the same amount of money.

As the 1980s progressed and the 1990s were entered, the public sector, just as the private sector had been for many years, was now under pressure for increased efficiency. Arguably, although this also included 'effectiveness' and 'economy', it was seen by many as cost cutting. Managerial approaches that had been successful in the private sector were now being considered and applied in the public sector environment as efficiencies.

During these two decades, organisations that were part of the public sector were taken into the private sector. Examples included the public utilities such as:

* Gas and electricity.
* Transport such as trains and road freight.
* Communications such as British Telecom (originally part of the Post Office).

The remaining parts of the public sector were now placed under increasing pressure to act in more commercial or entrepreneurial ways. In effect, trying to emulate best practice in the private sector became generally the driving force for the public sector. Much of this being centred upon what could be outsourced to third party organisations; frequently many of these were for contracts covering the provision of services.

Context and Scope

It is also useful to consider the scope and complexity of the public sector as a whole. In generalising the term 'public sector,' what is meant here are the assets which come under control of the state, as opposed to the private sector, where the assets and wealth belong to the private individual or to a group of people.

It is important that a distinction is made between the public and private sector for there are differences which impact upon the way in which services are procured, as will be discussed throughout this part of the book.

Whilst many of the processes for the procurement cycle and the obtaining of quotations are based upon those that you will have read about in earlier parts of the book, and apply to the private sector and can apply in the public sector, there are however, considerable differences in the underlying approaches that are applied in practice. This is because ultimately, as it is public funds that are being spent (i.e. the taxpayers money), there has to be seen a visible adherence to legal and ethical codes and practice.

For the sake of simplicity, the discussions within this section of this book will largely pertain to the public sector as a whole. However, it is important to bear in mind that the public sector consists of organisations which are neither unified nor uniform, but rather the term 'public sector' is used as a means to group the assets and wealth which come under control of the state. To give an idea of the scale of the UK public sector, Central Government public sector spending in the period 2007/2008 was recorded as £586.35 billion. This amount reflecting the procurement spending by a vast array of departments which come under central government control, and which also operate in a variety of contexts. Therefore there are different working practices and requirements between them in all of their functions, including the procurement of services.

The varieties of departments which fall under the public sector include:
- Central departmental organisations such as:
    - Ministry of Justice.

- Ministry of Defence.
- Foreign and Commonwealth Office.
- Department for International Development.
- Department of Health.
- Department for Children, Schools and Families.
- Department for Business, Enterprise and Regulatory Reform.
- Department for Transport.
- Department for Culture, Media and Sport.
- Department for Work and Pensions.
- HM Revenue and Customs.
- Devolved spending
  - Devolved Spending in Wales.
  - Devolved Spending in Scotland.
  - Devolved Spending in Northern Ireland.
- Communities and Local Governments
  - Regional Governments.
  - Local Governments.

To add to the complexity of the public sector, devolved governments and governing bodies at regional, county, district and parish level all receive funding from the central government. This may be spent on areas related to or even allocated by central department organisations. Therefore, as well as those responsible for procurement functions having to operate within different contextual environments, which invariably alter the nature of their procurement practices, so too is there a need for an understanding of the requirements that come with different contextual practices with the devolved and subdivisions of government.

As an example, although the NHS may be responsible for providing health care throughout England, local governments may be responsible for providing it within their localities.

Case Study: NHS Structure for Delivering Public Sector Health Services:

As a way of managing the complex system for the delivery of health services the NHS is divided into two sections, these are:

- Primary Care – the front line services which act as the first point of contact for the general public and is often delivered by a wide range of independent contractors.

- Secondary Care – also known as acute health care and can be elective or emergency. This is usually the specialist care which follows on from referral from the front line health professionals.

Dividing the service delivery structure into two distinct (albeit interconnected) areas allows the NHS to better deal with the complexity of service delivery that results from the subdivisions of the public sector, and thus accountability noted earlier.

The primary care is administered by Primary Care Trusts (PCTs) and have the major role of providing community care services. As such they control 80% of the NHS's budget. The PCTs are administered at a local level, and thus are local organisations. It is viewed that this means that such organisations are in a better position to understand the needs of their communities and so can better organise and streamline them to ensure that the provision of health and social care services is done so to best affect for the area. The PCTs oversee 29,000 GPs and 18,000 NHS dentists.

Secondary care is delivered through several areas which are administered at different levels according to the requirements for England. These include:
- 175 acute NHS trusts and 60 mental health NHS trusts which oversee 1,600 NHS hospitals and specialist care centres.
- Foundation trusts are a new type of NHS hospital of which there are currently 115 available across England.
- Emergency vehicles are provided by the NHS ambulance services trusts. There are 11 ambulance trusts in England. The Scottish, Welsh and Northern Ireland ambulance services provide cover for those countries.
- NHS care trusts provide care in both health and social fields. There are few care trusts and they are based mainly in England. There are none in Scotland and the Scottish NHS has no plans to introduce them.
- NHS mental health services trusts provide mental health care in England and are overseen by the PCT.

- There are also agencies under the umbrella of the NHS. These include the National Institute for Health and Clinical Excellence (NICE).

The complex nature of the system requires effective structures for communications so as to be able to effectively deliver health and care services. This also requires clear accountability and understanding of responsibility, particularly where as mentioned above primary care is increasingly being delivered by a range of independent contractors such as GPs, dentists, pharmacists, and optometrists (as mentioned above).

The way in which the Government deals with the issue of complexity caused by the many contexts and with the procurement functions, is by the use of a central framework and policy, designed to provide guidance for these operating procurement functions and for those undertaking procurement activity within the public sector. There are both benefits and challenges found in the use of a centralised framework, such as ensuring legal compliance and ensuring that all procurement activity is in line with the central policies of the state.

Central guidance can be valuable and understood in the provisioning of 'general' requirements (such as the desks and paperclips highlighted by Thatcher in the earlier quotation!)

It is more difficult however, to ascertain the value of specific guidance when it comes to more complex contexts; such as specific procurement of services. Therefore, the individual entities within the public sector are allowed to develop their own procurement policies which are more contexts specific to their own functions and activities.

There are services which will be required generally across the public sector, a good example being cleaning services for public sector offices; whereas other services will be more context specific, for example private sector health staff being used by the NHS, or the supply and maintenance of a naval vessel such as with the Offshore Patrol Vessel (OPV) Private Finance Initiative (PFI) and Contractor Logistic Support (CLS) agreements.

Case Study: Contractor Logistic Support (CLS) Agreement

The provision of several Offshore Patrol Vessels (OPV) was contracted out to VT Shipbuilding Group through the use of a private finance initiative (PFI) where the vessels were constructed and delivered at the expense of the contractor and leased out to the Royal Navy over a period of several years. As part of this agreement VT took on full responsibility for the contractor logistic support (CLS), ensuring that the ship remains at sea for a designated number of days a year, operating at over 6,000 miles away from the home base. VT retains ownership of the ships and charters them for a period of five years; added to this is a daily charge for full Contractor Logistics Support.

The fundamental element of the charter and CLS service is that VT Naval Support gets paid by results. Only when the ships are available for MoD tasking is the MoD liable for costs, working to a minimum requirement that VT must make each ship available for 320 days a year and this demands a comprehensive, capable and effective CLS organisation which has a demonstrable track record.

For the Batch One River Class OPVs, VT Naval Support guarantees availability of 960 days per annum across the fleet to the RN. In the first year, the River Class ships achieved 97.5% availability of the required number of operational days, compared to an average of 82% availability for the ships that they replaced. Besides availability, the quality of accommodation on board and operational effectiveness have both underlined the value of the design and the package that VT has put together to provide such an innovative solution.

VT Naval Support is required to make the OPV available for sea for at least 282 days a year through a round-the-clock, global maintenance commitment including repairs and spares. The Minor Warships Auxiliaries and Boats (MWAB), Integrated Project Team /IPT) says the River Class programme is providing valuable experience for the latest project, with VT and MWAB (now part of Boats and Sea Survival (BASS) Integrated Project Team) co-operating closely in areas of performance monitoring, joint risk management, and close communication and liaison between the contractor, the MOD and the ships' crews.

In all VT Naval Support's CLS work, partnering is an essential principle and delivering a successful River Class project has involved close collaboration between the contractor (VT), customer (IPT, ship, MOD) and other interfaces. VT works to an agreed set of stringent Key Performance Indicators that incentivised the company to deliver the support service against the contract specification in terms of vessel availability to ensure that it earns its daily fee. For its part, VT has carefully assessed the risks and developed a support solution that minimises its exposure.

VT utilises modern automated equipment and commercial maintenance practices. Major elements of the CLS process include maintenance management systems, interactive technical publications, configuration control and obsolescence management, supported by a dedicated organisation of VT personnel in the South Atlantic and the UK.

All of these are important factors which VT is much more likely to address given the incentive to provide a good service given that the contract is for a fixed period and does contain the option for discontinued use. By outsourcing the support service the Royal Navy is free to concentrate purely on its operational requirements rather than day to day maintenance and support issues, whilst ensuring standards of equipment through a vested contractor interest in the vessels success.

This unique agreement places the onus on the contractor to support his product through-life. However, the challenge of providing a CLS system for a the OPV(H), operating more that 6,000 miles away provides a additional test of VT's logistics capabilities. VT already had a strong presence in the Falklands Island before the awarding of the contract through a team that maintains power generating facilities and strategic communications. The staff on land; the personnel on board the ship and other regional resources all play a key role in keeping the ship at the maximum levels of availability.

Taking on such a challenge has already attracted interest from overseas. The River Class design and this latest development are regarded as ideal ships to fulfil the Economic Exclusion Zone (EEZ) patrol duties to which all maritime nations must now adhere.

To ensure that we retain a practical application in this book, we shall therefore avoid delving into the specifics of individual departmental considerations and we will address the general and important issues of the public sector as a whole. We will, however, use some more specific contextualised examples to substantiate the points raised on some of the issues and challenges that are faced in the procurement of services in the public sector.

The guidance that the government provides with regard to procurement generally, and to the purchasing of services specifically, is, of course, subject to fluctuation and change. This reflecting the current operating environment in which services are procured.

The environment for the procurement of services

The environment for the procurement of services can be generally characterised by several tenets:

It is not static: procurement practitioners, specifically in services, have to operate in a profession which is characterised by change and transformation as a result of the vast variety of influential variables.

It is not uniform in context: practitioners operate in a variety of contexts which impose the need for different context specific considerations e.g. defence acquisition and notions of deterrence; care of the elderly and notions of home care; and the use of social services.

It consists of practitioners who are not unified in a single acquisition profession: procurement practitioners come from various cultural and functional backgrounds which impact upon their decision making, the tools they choose and the way in which they choose to implement them. *(Source: J P Davies, UK Defence Academy)*

Such variables require consideration whatever the procurement area of focus, and are acknowledged in the change requirements which force changes to be made in public procurement policy. To illuminate this, it is worth looking at how the guidance related to the procurement of services has developed in line with the changing of practices used within the public sector.

A Timeline

As mentioned above, the UK public sector procurement environment in general has been the subject of considerable change over the last 40 years. The vast majority of people would agree that this has come as a result of the adoption of private sector commercial and managerial practices (neo-liberalist principles) resulting in the increasing emphasis on competition and the increasing privatisation of public sector services. Specific examples here include utilities such as gas (The Gas Act, 1986) and electric, transport such as trains (British Rail, 1992), and communications such as British Telecom (1984).

It is interesting to note that the Thatcher quote used earlier does not reflect the increasing amount the public sector is spending on the procurement of services, particularly the vast amounts spent on consultancy. For example, it was reported by the OCG that the Government spent £1.8 billion on consultants in FY2006/06 *(Source: www.nao.org. uk/publications/0607/government_use_of_consultants.aspx).*

Additionally, the opposition Conservative party recently stated that up to £4 billion will be spent on consultancy services over the next four years. *(www.telegraph.co.uk/news/newstopics/politics/5215852/Government-spending-4bn- on-consultants-say-Tories.html, 25 April 2009).*

This reflects that the purchasing of services and the adoption of commercial practices did not occur in an instant, but that the greater application of such practices takes place over time, as shown in legislation and guidance outlined below.

We can see that it is the adoption of private sector commercial practices (also known as New Public Management), and particularly that of the role of competition, that has now come to define the UK public sector's approach to the procurement of services. What follows, therefore, is a brief timeline reflecting the adoption, or rather adaptation, of private sector (commercial) practices to the public sector procurement of services, over the last 40 years:

1970s

The 1970s was a period of considerable socio-economic and political upheaval with the early 1970s seeing a three day working week and the issuing of petrol rationing coupons (although not actually utilised). The latter part of the decade was characterised by the 'winter of discontent' with public sector strikes resulting, for example, in refuse not being collected from peoples' homes.

The culmination of such acts can be argued as the catalyst for a transformation in public sector approach to procurement as a whole, beginning with the election of Margaret Thatcher in 1979. What followed was an increased application of private sector commercial practices in the way by which the public sector operated. Emphasis was placed upon competition with the introduction of Compulsory Competitive Tendering (CCT) as a local government public procurement policy with regards to construction, maintenance and highway work (Planning and Land Act, 1980).

1980s

What followed in the 1980s, as a result of the perception that the application of such practices was producing effective results, was the application of the CCT policy to other areas of public sector procurement. Health Authorities were instructed to introduce CCT for their support services such as catering, cleaning, portering and estates management; blue collar services such as ground maintenance and refuse collection; white collar services such as public libraries and arts centre management; and sports and leisure management services.

1990s

The trend of greater preference for commercial policies and practices, plus competition continued into the 1990s as the public sector continued to feel the pressure for increased efficiency with the introduction of the Private Finance Initiative (PFI) in the Autumn Statement 1992. This was a means to fund and operate public sector construction and services such as schools, hospitals and prisons.

What PFI did was create the policy where the public sector would look to the private sector to meets its future service requirements as opposed to offloading its existing service requirements and capabilities. The introduction of PFI demonstrates further recognition that savings could be made and efficiency attained by keeping assets off the account books, a concept which drove the wave of privatisation during the 1980s and 1990s.

As part of the privatisation of services, in 1994, guidance was issued on the Transfer of Undertakings (Protection of Employment) regulations (otherwise known as TUPE, already considered in this book). The application of this law protected the terms and conditions of employment for workers who are transferred to the private sector under CCT, with the effect of slowing down the rate of outsourcing.

Such guidance was deemed a necessity due to the scale of outsourcing in comparison with the past. Further professional 'white collar' services came under CCT legislation in 1996, namely those provided by councils such as legal, construction and property, and personal.

2000s

Although CCT had demonstrated an ability to deliver significant cost savings, at least in the short term, the 1990s brought the increasing realisation that CCT, which essentially was aimed to use competition to get the best price, may not necessarily have been delivering the best service.

Given the notion of 'social responsibility' which exists with regards to delivery of services by the public sector, this was an issue which was to be addressed in 1997 with the Labour government. When winning the general election, the new Labour government replaced CCT with another concept taken from the private sector, that of ensuring best practice through attaining best Value for Money (VFM).

The previously, arguably, vague notion of Value for Money began to take precedent in the public sector and became a driving force. Rather than be solely concerned about achieving the lowest possible price, VFM is actually instead about achieving the optimum combination of 'whole life' cost and quality; as we have discussed in the first part of this book.

VFM still required that the public sector continue to look at outsourcing its service requirements but also considering factors other than cost alone. This is because the cheapest option may not always guarantee a sufficient quality of service, a fact the government continued to struggle with.

This has recently been highlighted by the reverse e-auctions for services to provide care to the elderly. Reverse auctions place a greater focus on cost as opposed to quality of service, which 2009 media attention has highlighted to be insufficient. (See for example www.timesonline.co.uk/tol/life_and_style/health/article6401002.ece, and www.timesonline.co.uk/tol/life_and_style/health/article6401122.ece).

The Labour Party also embraced and expanded upon the Private Finance Initiative, with the then Prime Minister Tony Blair being against public sector monopolisation. He stated: "what matters is what works".

This was demonstrated in 2000 when Labour signed a 'concordat' with the private health industry under which it agreed to send thousands of NHS patients to be treated in independent hospitals.

On the back of such perceived successes with regards to the application of commercial practices, Labour was re-elected with a party manifesto which explicitly stated that private or voluntary sector providers should be brought in where public providers are failing to improve, or where there is the potential for them to add value to the public service.

For more on Hospital PFI see:
- www.nao.org.uk/publications/0405/darent_valley_hospital.aspx.

For the Labour Party manifestos see:
- www.labour-party.org.uk/manifestos/2001/2001-labour-manifesto.shtml (2001).
- http://news.bbc.co.uk/1/shared/bsp/hi/pdfs/13_04_05_labour_manifesto.pdf (2005).

Whilst there is of course an ongoing debate on the degree to which increased outsourcing of required services and the use of PFIs, has actually been successful in delivering VFM; the application of commercial practices and the buying of services from the private sector has continued in the 2000s; with

- Private health companies invited in 2002 to compete for multi-million pound contracts to run fast track surgeries specialising in routine NHS surgery.
- Ministers announcing that they will consider drafting in private management teams to run NHS trusts that perform consistently badly.
- In 2003, Labour agreed to statutory code guaranteeing wages 'no less favourable' than in the public sector for new staff hired by public services contractors, as well as those transferred under TUPE. Although the Unions hailed this as an 'end to the two tier workforce', private contractors stated that they were losing faith in government's commitment to partnership with the private sector.

Generally, there has been little change to the emphasis placed on the application of commercial practices and the outsourcing and procurement of services through competition. These still take precedence in public sector procurement policies.

Case Study: Darnet Valley Hospital PFI Success

In 1997 Dartford & Gravesham NHS Trust awarded the first NHS PFI contract to The Hospital Company (Dartford) Limited to provide the facility of Darnet Valley Hospital, as well as select services.

A national audit office review into the success of the PFI agreement found that THC Dartford both:

- Delivered the new hospital to the Trust two months early and for the price agreed in the contract.
- Maintained hospital availability and the provision of catering, cleaning and portering services with only occasional lapses.

However, such initial successes were not attained without complications. As the first NHS PFI hospital, it was found that even with the greater risk transfer involved with the PFI contracts, that managing both the contract and clinical activities requires a large amount of senior management engagement.

Likewise, it was found that there were significant lessons to be learnt from the refinancing which took place in 2003, where in return for its share of the financial gains the Trust has accepted additional risks. The Trust benefited from a lower annual contract price, but in return extended the contract an extra seven years. The decision to do this did reflect the overall satisfaction in the service provided.

Where the service lapses noted above did occur were in important areas such as waste collection, cleaning and food production but the problems were overcome and service performance returned to a satisfactory level within an acceptable timeframe. This is also reflected in the low level of payment deductions (0.1 percent of THC Dartford's charges up until 2005). This shows the importance of the decisions made, when contracting for a service, is essential to take into account issues such as performance measurement

Though not without issues as mentioned, it was found that THC Dartford's stakeholders benefited significantly from the PFI arrangement, thus both parties on the whole have deemed the agreement a success thus far, but not without lessons to be learnt.

Policy surrounding the procurement of services has generally remained relatively unchanged since the adoption of VFM as procurement policy. The term 'generally' is used here because although new procedures have been introduced to improve procurement in the public sector, the policy goals are still underpinned by VFM.

The current policy for VFM has remained relatively unchanged since 1997. However, as has been highlighted in this section, change in the future will to occur to some degree. For example, the financial crisis of 2008 did impact upon public sector spending and policy as shown later in the outsourcing slow down of the part privatisation of the Post Office' and the part nationalisations of east coast rail services; at least for the short term. On the other hand, the crisis has also seen the increase of the money spent on some services such as consultancy and military logistics.

We have looked so far at the purchasing of services from the private sector; this being because of the weight of policy and the focus that is generally placed on these approaches. What must also be noted, however, is the internal purchasing of services, which is all too often not given enough consideration as a means to attaining better working practices.

As compulsory competitive tendering and outsourcing have increased within the public sector, much of what was originally provided by internal groups or departments has ceased. However, efforts should be made to consider the 'in-sourcing' of services as there have been occasions when public sector organisations have outsourced activities only to find that they had not managed the planning, the processes and decision making as well as they might have.

Hence, most recently there have been examples, to obtain best Value for Money, of either in-sourcing or through adopting the so-called, and arguably lean processes, that the provision of services has been possible. This should be borne in mind when undertaking procurement of services for the public sector as it is an important aspect for public procurement professionals and their stakeholders.

UK Government policy

Now that the scope and context of buying services for the public sector has been addressed, this section will provide a more practical element for the procurement of services.

In discussing the buying of services in the public sector there are two areas which always need to be considered.

The first is the actual buying or contracting for the service; whilst the second concerns the effective management of the service contract through the life of the service requirement.

The procurement of services for the public sector, as with any other form of public sector procurement, is subject to a set of rules, regulations and frameworks which instruct and guide the individuals in the public sector in their procurement activities. Some examples of these have been mentioned in the timeline above.

Each public sector organisation is ultimately responsible for determining the methods, tools and techniques it uses in developing its context relevant framework, practices and policies used in its acquisition activity. For example, the Ministry of Defence (MOD) has developed its own Acquisition Operating Framework (AOF).

It is important that this is done, so as to ensure that purchasing services considerations are made within the relative contexts in which they operate. It could be, for example, that for the defence acquisition practitioner this might be determined by the cost of maintaining the state's own logistic support, versus the operational risk of outsourcing the logistic support to a contractor. For a practitioner in the NHS, it might be determined by the through-life cost of procuring a new prescription drug versus the potential life extension of an individual. Some others might emphasise time saved, whilst others the cost.

Just as there is a need for contextualisation, there is also a need for an overall framework and guidance to ensure that the procurement is in line with the central government's policies and is therefore seen to be in the interest of the state for which the areas of the public sector account.

Central government communicates its policy via the guidance, frameworks and information delivered by the Office of Government Commerce (OGC), defined simply as *"an office of HM Treasury, responsible for improving VFM by driving up standards and capability in procurement"*. The OGC ensures a uniformed working practice and that a set of standards is maintained within the public sector.

There are two main reasons why it is necessary for public sector procurement practitioners to adhere to the guidance provided by the OGC and Central Government when looking to contract for a service.

1.) Firstly it is to ensure that the contracting of services is done so in a manner that achieves the policy of Central Government; that of attaining Value for Money (VFM) in a socially responsible manner.

2.) The second is to ensure that, when buying a service, that it adheres to the EU legal framework to which the UK, as a member of the EU, is subject.

Both of these reasons will be addressed in turn below, highlighting what the guidance states, why it states it, and how the government ensures adherence.

1) Delivering the policy of Value for Money (VFM)

Due to the scale of the public sector and the numerous stakeholders involved (as has been noted above and which will also be addressed further in this book in the following section called Some Issues), the OGC makes its procurement policy and standards framework as widely available as possible via its website. It is here that all the key principles and processes governing public sector commercial activity can be found. As such this section will provide a précis of the processes which determine how a public service contract is made, followed by an analysis of the issues involved.

By producing an overarching framework for the procurement of services what the OGC is doing is ensuring that its current policies are being considered (if not always adhered to in practice) by all of the organisations operating within the public sector, see www. ogc.gov.uk/procurement_-_the_bigger_picture_policy_and_standards_framework.asp This is necessary because as all of the organisations are spending public money distributed to them through the Treasury, and as such, the government needs ensure that its key policy principles are being met, and that such policies and principles are visible and provide for informed public accountability.

Anyone involved in the procurement of services in the public sector must remember that they are spending the taxpayers' money. The key policy principles that should be considered when buying services can be summarised as follows:

- Delivering VFM; 'buying the product or service with the lowest whole life costs that is 'fit for purpose' and meets specification. Where an item is chosen that does not have the lowest whole life costs, then the additional 'value added' benefit must be clear and justifiable.'
 (Source: www.ogc.gov.uk/documents/VFM(1).pdf)
- Ensuring that government projects deliver on time and on cost performance.
- Getting the best out of the governments civil estate.

- Delivering other policy goals through procurement concerning:
  - Environmental sustainability.
  - Addressing of social issues.
  - Innovation.
  - The creation of opportunities for Small and Medium Enterprises (SMEs) and third party organisations.

As mentioned above, VFM has been central to policy since the Labour government came to power in 1999. The current definition for Value for Money can be found in HM Treasury Managing Public Money – Annex A 4.4 and is as follows:

'Value for Money is a key concept running through Managing Public Money (see paragraph 4.2.3). It means securing the best mix of quality and effectiveness for the least outlay over the period of use of the goods or services bought. It is not about minimising upfront prices. Whether in conventional procurement, market-testing, private finance or some other form of public private partnership, Value for Money will involve an appropriate allocation of risk.'

The driver here is to attain a mix of quality and effectiveness in the procurement of services for the perceived through life cost. Generally this is perceived as best attained through competition.

The weight to which one should consider quality and effectiveness against cost is left open to interpretation, as it will differ depending on the individual requirements and the risks involved. How quality and effectiveness is defined differs with the individual service procurements or projects.

When considering suitable procurement options, VFM should always be assessed over the whole life of the contract. This should also include the disposal (either sale proceeds or decommissioning costs) and take into account all costs and benefits to society as a whole. These include the environmental and social benefits and costs, and not just simply those directly relevant to the purchaser.

Additional guidelines are as follows:

- **Assessment of supplier bids** should only be conducted in relation to a published set of evaluation criteria, which must be relevant to the subject of the contract. Any 'added value' that justifies a higher price must flow from these defined criteria and is assessed from the perspective of the contracting authority.

- **Affordability should be considered**; clearly, goods or services that are unaffordable cannot be bought. This should be addressed as soon as possible within the process, ideally at the organisation case stage before procurement commences. In order to address this issue, a change in procurement approach, specification or organisation strategy may be required.

- **VFM should normally be established through the competitive process**. A strong competition from a vibrant market will generally deliver a VFM outcome. But where competition is limited, or even absent, other routes may have to be used to establish VFM.

Earlier in the book, how the 'Kraljic' portfolio was used in consideration of the differing procurement approaches within a commercial organisational context was discussed.

That approach can also be adopted for Public Sector procurement of services. The point here is not on which the right procurement strategy is, but rather which is most appropriate in the contextual setting. (This may of course be different for the procurement of medical consultancy for a regional health authority, as against the procurement of civil engineering services in the construction of a restaurant/rest rooms in a national park, or the services to provide maintenance services for an IT system for air traffic control).

As in the earlier examination of differentiation, there are some areas where a procurement professional might wish to spend more time. With the procurement of services, the emphasis should be upon those that have a strategic impact upon the organisation; these tend to be the ones that will fall into the high risk yet high VFM impact (i.e. the Critical box in Kraljic). Meanwhile the other three Kraljic boxes show the approaches that can be generally adopted; bearing in mind the public sector legal aspects and directives

Nevertheless, unlike the commercial sector consideration of differentiated strategies, all of the other boxes have to be carefully considered and given due process and procedure. These can offer potential to optimise performance, not just for an individual organisation within the public sector but for many, as there may be a greater potential purchasing power, especially in services, when a number of public sector organisations work together in collaboration or through shared services.

It can be seen that although most of the approaches in each Kraljic box have much in common with commercial organisations, there are some elements that are different. An example is that in the Critical box (high risk yet high potential for enhanced Value for Money) where there will be a need to develop a Stakeholder Engagement Plan as the influence and the impact on public sector stakeholders, can be considerable and is also open to much scrutiny and potentially, controversy. The following diagram summarises these aspects:

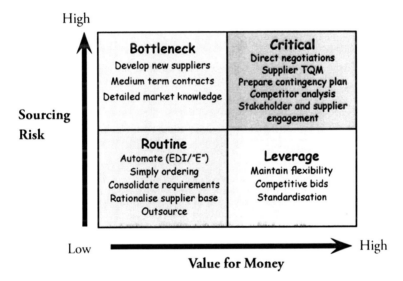

2) Ensuring concordance with the European Union Treaty and Procurement Directives

Although flexibility exists as to how to interpret VFM and how best to attain it, the policy as outlined by the OGC clearly states that VFM must be in compliance with EU procurement law.

This directive is repeated in the majority of OGC documentation and is part of the central policy framework. This ensures that the purchasing of services is undertaken in compliance with not just UK, but EU Law, which oversees the public sector procurement activities of those countries who have signed The EU Treaty.

The UK ascended to the European Union on 1 January 1973, and as a member is subject to EU laws requiring free trade and open markets. One such legal framework is the EU Procurement Directives. *(Source: OGC, EU Procurement Guidance, March 2008.)*

The EU Procurement Directives set out the legal framework for public procurement which the EU Member States must follow. The purposes of the directives is to ensure that there continues to exist the free movement of supplies, services and works within the EU.

It is also worth noting that the EU procurement policy rules also apply to states outside the UK through the Government Procurement Agreement (GPA). Negotiated by the World Trade Organisation, the GPA ensures that GPA signatories' suppliers etc. have the same rights as those within the EU. Therefore, compliance with EU procurement law ensures compliance with the GPA. The current signatories include: Aruba; Canada; Hong Kong, China; Iceland; Israel; Japan; Republic of Korea; Liechtenstein; Norway; Singapore; Switzerland and USA.

There are several ways EU procurement law affects the procurement of services for the UK public sector, for example:

- Defines three stages which make up the procurement process, with criteria outlined at each state.
- Defines four procedures by which contracts can be awarded.
- Determines the means by which procurements must be advertised should they reach predetermined procurement thresholds.
- Enforces the EU procurement regulations to ensure accountability should they be breached.

We shall examine these in detail shortly.

Because of the requirements to abide by EU law, taking particular note of the last point, the EU regulations have been translated into UK procurement law. This is communicated in two documents:

- Public authorities (the State, regional and local authorities and other public bodies), The Public Contracts Regulations 2006 (SI 2006 No.5): www.opsi.gov.uk/si/si2006/uksi_20060005_en.pdf

- Utilities (i.e. certain operators in the water, energy, transport sectors), The Utilities Contracts Regulations 2006 (SI 2006 No.6) www.opsi.gov.uk/si/si2006/uksi_20060006_en.pdf

Because of this it is possible to show the current UK requirements for the procurement of services, as determined by EU law, through discussing the four points highlighted above.

This has a direct impact on the buying of services in that, if in the planning stage, it is deemed that a contract will be over a certain value (or threshold) then it needs to be advertised to all of the countries within the European Union.

Although the specific enforcement of the EU (supra-national level) regulations is determined by whether the value of a contract is perceived to be above a certain threshold (that is to re-affirm, it is required to be advertised through an OJEU notice in the European journal), the principles by which the EU treaty stands, that of *"non-discrimination, equal treatment, transparency, mutual recognition and proportionality" (www.ogc.gov.uk/documents/Introduction_to_the_EU_rules.pdf)*, do continue to apply and are directly translated to UK policy and guidelines.

Though based on the relatively fixed rules Treaty of Rome, the directives themselves are not fixed and continue to transform and adapt. An example would be the consolidation of public sector regulations on services supplies and works contracts into a single regulation.

EU regulations and laws impact upon the UK in other ways, such as driving the need to procure services. An example of this is the 'Managing the Waste PFI Programme', where the EU introduced, through the EU Directive in 1999, the requirement for all member states to reduce the amount of biodegradable municipal waste (BMW) sent to landfill; as this requirement could not be met with the current infrastructure, local authorities with the help of government sought to solve the problem through means of a PFI.

The UK Public Sector Procurement Process

1) The three stages of the procurement process.
EU procurement legislation clearly defines the procurement process as composing of three stages. It makes this clear definition so as to make the procurement process more manageable by associating specific criteria that has to be met at each stage.

The three stages to the procurement process are as follows:

Stage 1: Pre-procurement: the planning stage where the specifications and requirements are identified, and the project appraised.

Stage 2: The Tender Process: where the best solution to the service requirement is identified.

Stage 3: Contractor and Supplier Management: where the contract itself is managed.

You will recall that earlier in the book we discussed the procurement process for the procurement of services and although we showed this in more detail in respect of commercial organisations, for the public sector this is, in a simplified manner, how such a process can be interpreted. However, it must be borne in mind that this will be an oversimplification of Value for Money, and the legal adherence to UK and EU legislation is fundamental.

What is clear from looking at the OGC guidance is that, due to the complexity and range of considerations that have to be made in the buying of services, there is a need for flexibility with regards as to how a particular service is procured.

This flexibility is reflected in the range of options available within a framework which encourages the use of competition, as the way in which the service is bought may be reliant on other contingencies.

A good example would be whether or not a plan exists to invest in relative infrastructure at the same time. If there is a requirement for infrastructure but the buying authority does not wish to directly invest in it then the procurement of the asset then the service can come in the form of Public Private Partnership (or PFI) where both the service and the asset is provided. The alternative is where the government wishes to build and directly own (or already has) the asset where by the service is brought in separately, e.g. I.T. support or financial consultancy.

Although a range of options for tendering exist in order to provide flexibility, there still remain restrictions in the forms of EU law and the emphasis on meeting the competitive tendering requirement, regardless of whether the buying of the service is a simple, complex or collaborative procurement.

This preference is made clear in the "Public Contracts Regulations SI 2006", which outlines the four methods by which the tendering process can take place, with the stated preference being for competitive procedures; particularly when it comes to complex procurements (which will often be the case with procurement of services).

Framework agreements can be an effective means used to escape from an ongoing requirement for CCT; although they do have their drawbacks in that they can only provide the specific services that are outlined.

This obviously depends on how narrowly the agreement is specified and the supplier with which it is agreed upon (an example would be the South West One framework agreement for shared services). The competition requirement is still met, as the initial framework agreement would have been competed for.

As a general rule, it is stated that VFM can best be attained through the use of competition, though the there is no definitive placed on the use of certain practices in certain instances. Rather this is left for the procurement processional involved in the acquisition of the service to determine which method to use.

2) Four Procedures by which Contracts can be Awarded

So as to ensure fair and even competition, the procedures which can be used in the second stage, i.e. the tendering process, are clearly defined within the EU procurement directives. These are directly translated into the UK framework where the OGC states methods/approaches by which to go about public sector procurement activities.

Currently these are:

The Open Procedure: any party is invited to tender and all who respond to the OJEU notice receive full contract documentation; notice is given by placing the information in the Official Journal of the European Journal (OJEU). There is no pre-qualification process, no ability to shortlist candidates and contract negotiations are not allowed. All tenders are received, evaluated and the contract is awarded.

The Restricted Procedure: contracting authorities undertake a pre-qualification process and invite short-listed candidates to tender. Contract negotiations are again prohibited.

The Competitive Dialogue Procedure: contracting authorities undertake a prequalification process first before inviting short listed candidates into a process of dialogue. During this dialogue any aspects of the project may be discussed and solutions developed. The authority continues the dialogue process until it identifies one or more solutions which satisfy its requirement. It will then close the dialogue in order to invite final tenders.

The Competitive Negotiated Procedure: similar to the Competitive Dialogue Procedure in that a pre-qualification process takes place and then an invitation to negotiate is issued. Unlike the Competitive Dialogue Process there is no formal end to the negotiation phase before the contract signature.

The word 'currently' is used when noting the procedures for the Competitive Dialogue Procedure has only recently been added. It is important to note this for this reflects that although the EU Treaty and its policies are for the most part very much fixed, the procurement directives are subject to change. This is also reflected in the thresholds (which will be discussed later).

Currently, as VFM is determined as best attained through competition there is a preference placed on the Competitive Dialogue Procedure. However, that there are more options available than just this one reflects that different service requirements may call for different procurement solutions.

There are positives and negatives to each approach, just as there are when seeking an external service solution as opposed to an internal solution. It will be the requirements which will likely dictate the preference, for example, there are different minimum timescales associated with each process which must be adhered to if it is chosen. This is also dictated by point 3) below, on how procurements must be advertised.

3) Procurement thresholds and the means by which contract opportunities are to be advertised.

The requirements placed on the scale of advertising are determined by the perceived value of the potential contract. Should the procurement include more than one contract, then the advertising requirement is determined by the total value of all contracts associated with the specific service procurement. As with the EU procurement directives, the thresholds are subject to change and as such must be checked regularly. Because of this they are readily available on the OGC website. *(Source: www.ogc.gov.uk/procurement_ policy_and_application_of_eu_rules_eu_procurement_thresholds_.asp)*

The particular value of the threshold depends on the contracting authority, as well as whether the contract falls under the a) Public Contracts Regulations or b) the Utilities contract regulations. Currently the thresholds for services are as follows on the 13 July 2009.

a) Public Contracts Regulations 2006; from 1 January 2008:

	Services
Entities Listed in Schedule 1	£90,3192 (€133,000)
Exceptions from Schedule 1	£139,893 (€206,000)
Other Public Sector Contracting Authorities	£139,893 (€206,000)
Indicative Notices	£509,317 (€750,000)
Small Lots	£54,327 (€ 80,000)

Schedule 1 is found in the Public Contracts Regulations 2006, and lists the central government bodies which are subject to the WTO GPA mentioned above. The exemptions noted above which are subject to the higher threshold are:
- Part B (residual) services.
- Research and Development Services (Category 8).
- The following Telecommunications services listed in Category 5:
  - CPC 7524 – Television and Radio Broadcast Services
  - CPC 7525 – Interconnected services
  - CPC 7526 – Integrated Telecommunication services
- Subsidised services contracts described under regulation 34.

b) Utilities Contracts Regulations 2006 – From January 2008:

	Services
All sectors	£279,785 (€412,000)
Indicative Notices	£509,317 (€750,000)
Small Lots	£54,327 (€80,000)

If the threshold value is met then the requirement is that the potential service contract must be advertised to the whole of the European Union (or the signers of the GPA) so that the requirement for the free movement of goods and services is met.

To ensure visibility of the potential contract, and thus compliance with the principles of the EU Treaty which stand for of 'non-discrimination, equal treatment, transparency, mutual recognition and proportionality', the invitations to tender must be placed on the Official Journal of the European Communities (OJEU) in the form of a Notice (often referred to as an advertisement). As to the specific content of the Notices, the OGC provides its own guidance as to what should be outlined in a Notice.
(Source: www.ogc.gov.uk/documentation_and_templates_ojeu_advertisement.asp)

The length of time each advertisement is to run is determined by the chosen process as mentioned above. This is so that ample opportunity is allowed for competition with regards to the service procurement opportunities and the following timescales are found:

- **Open Procedure Timescale;** must be advertised on OJEU at least 52 days prior to the closing date for the receipt of tenders, with 11 days allowed from the dispatch of the notice before advertising in the UK press. Under no circumstances must the advertisement in the UK press appear before the publication of the OJEU notice.
- **Restricted Procedure Timescale;** must be advertised in OJEU and at least 37 days allowed for applicants to register interest. A further 40 days is required from the date of dispatch of tenders to the closing date.

- **Negotiated Procedure Timescale;** must be advertised in OJEU and 37 days allowed for applicants to register interest.
- **Accelerated Procedure Timescale;** must be advertised in OJEU and 15 days allowed for applicants to register interest, and 10 days from the date of dispatch of tenders to the closing date.
  (Source: http://mendip06.web-labs.co.uk/CouncilService.asp?id=SX9452-A7804530&cat=134)

It is worth noting that this period can be reduced:
- If a prior information notice (PIN) has been published sufficiently in advance of the procurement.
- When authorities offer full and restricted website access to tender documents.
- When the OGC notice has been submitted in accordance with the SIMAP requirements.

4) Enforcement of EU and UK regulations

The enforcement of the EU procurement directives comes in the form of the regulations derived from the Remedies Directives. The possible actions are:

- Actions by suppliers or contractors against an individual purchaser of supplier through the High Court.
- Action by the EU Commission against a Member State in the European Court of Justice (ECJ).

The High Court can suspend a procurement contract and award damages, though this is the extent of the punitive measures available. The ECJ on the other hand also has the power to overturn a contract. As with the procurement directives, the Remedies Directives are subject to change, which can also be found in the OJEU. When such changes are made, the UK has two years to implement the changes into its procurement legislation.

In order that time is allowed for the awarding of a competition to be contested (should it be appropriate to do so), the ECJ enforces a mandatory 10 calendar day 'stand still' period between the time that the contract is awarded and the time it is signed.

By highlighting the means by which the ECJ can enforce the regulations, as well as the punitive measures which may occur as a result of failure to comply, it can be understood why the UK would wish to ensure that its public sector organisations listed earlier in the 'Context' section comply with the regulations!

Failure to do so may result in significant costs in both time and money as a result of damages awarded or a forced renegotiation of the contract. Despite these penalties, 'workarounds' do exist which are often used by governments. Though improper use of such exemptions is ill advised, an awareness of the potential to misuse is valuable.

An example relating to defence is Article 296 of the EU Combined Treaties. Because defence contracts fall under Internal Market rules, Directive 2004/18/EC discussed above applies to contracts subject to Article 296 TEC which is as follows:

"(1) The provisions of this Treaty shall not preclude the application of the following rules:

(a) No Member State shall be obliged to supply information the disclosure of which it considers contrary to the essential interests of its security;
(b) Any Member State may take such measures as it considers necessary for the protection of the essential interests of its security which are connected with the production of or trade in arms, munitions and war material; such measures shall not adversely affect the conditions of competition in the common market regarding products which are not intended for specifically military purposes.
(2) The Council may, acting unanimously on a proposal from the Commission, make changes to the list, which it drew up on April 1958, of the products to which the provisions of paragraph 1(b) apply. (Note from Policy Sponsor: see Appendix 1 to Annex C)'.

It is therefore up to the individual member states to define and protect their own security interests, and as such there have been tensions and controversy as a result of some states taking a broader definition of what constitutes their security interests than others.

This highlights that there is both pressure and scope to refine EU law and the associated directives. It is for this reason that the Directives are subject to amendment and change. Changing the provisions of a Treaty once it has been ratified is more difficult, which is why the terms of the European Constitution remain heavily debated; including the equivalent statement of Article 296 discussed above.

(Source: www.whoswholegal.com/news/features/article/15862/battle-stations-defence-companies-go-alert-new-eu-procurement-directive/).

It is important to note though, that where the Directives do not apply for the numerous reasons already mentioned above, they also will not apply for all the principles of non-discrimination, equal treatment, transparency, mutual recognition and proportionality.

Other Policy Principles with the Public Sector Procurement of Services

It will have been noted in the discussion of VFM that the list of policy principles presented contained issues other than achieving VFM and abiding by EU procurement regulations. The reason why these issues are separated in this discussion is so as to reflect that weight should not be given to such issues in relation to the two policy goals mentioned earlier. This is something stipulated throughout the guidance documents provided by the OGC.

That other policy considerations have been mentioned reflects an awareness of the potential wider impacts that the procurement of services may have on various stakeholders.

The possible benefits that may come as a result are acknowledged by the OGC when they identify areas of consideration other than, but not at the expense of, the overarching policy framework which prioritises VFM and abiding by the EU Treaty and Directives (as was noted above).

Each of the areas noted will now be discussed in relation to the specific procuring of services. These are:

- Sustainable Procurement.
- Innovation.
- SMEs.
- Social issues.
- Skills.

It is important to note that although each of these is being discussed as a separate issue, consideration of such issues may indeed be a factor in determining Value for Money.

Likewise due to the complex nature of the procurement tasks, the consideration of such issues can often not be taken in isolation, but rather as a mixed balance.

Because there is a vast array of information regarding procurement policies on the OGC website, these areas will not be covered in great detail. Rather, what follows is a brief outline as to why and how such factors should be considered.

Sustainable Procurement

The timeline in the section earlier, showed how procurement policy has largely been the utilisation of private (commercial) sector practices. In general it has been the private sector that has taken the lead in developing innovative solutions (and this will be discussed further soon under the subtitle 'innovation') and policy. However, one area where the public sector is, arguably taking the lead (for example, Marks and Spencer may disagree), is in sustainable procurement.

As is usually the case with such terms, 'sustainable procurement' has different connotations based on the source of the terms and individual understanding.

For example, sometimes the term is used to narrowly describe environmental sustainability in procurement, and in other cases is refers to a broader number of issues which are desirable to attain, such as maintaining (sustaining) support services or equipment.

The government guidance talks in terms of sustainable development, which incorporates environmental, social and economical sustainability issues. Sustainable development is typically defined as *"development which meets the needs of the present without compromising the ability of future generations to meet their own needs"*.
(Source: 'Our Common Future' (The Brutland Report); Report of the 1987 World Commission on Environment and Development.)

Because social and economic issues are addressed in their own right under the policy framework put forward by the OGC, we can take sustainable procurement to primarily refer to that of environmental sustainability. There are several reasons why it is preferential that the government acknowledge sustainability issues in its procurement practices; these include:

- Compliance with international treaties relating to the environment.

- Desire to be perceived as socially responsible in its procurement decision making.

Just as the government is subject to the EU laws, rules and regulations governing procurement practices, the UK Government is also subject to international treaties. Some of the better known examples include the Kyoto Protocols. Such environmental sustainability targets have been translated into the governments own Sustainable Operations on the Government Estate (SOGE) targets and delivered through the procurement action plan.

Case Study: IDeA Sustainable Procurement – translation of OGC policy.

The Improvement and Development Agency (IDeA) in its procurement policy can be seen to place significant emphasis on the importance of sustainable procurement. It defines sustainable procurement in line with that of the OGC, as about:

- Getting lasting Value for Money.
- Avoiding or reducing environmental damage.
- Delivering social and economic benefits locally.

Concern is not fixated just on environmental sustainability, but it does contain a weight of focus apart from social and economic sustainable issues.

The department provides much advice on the issue of sustainable procurement to levels of the public sector who partake in procurement activity. For example, for local authorities, 'to integrate sustainability into your procurement process, your council should:

- look at its procurement policy and strategy and ensure that they are compatible with the principles of sustainable development.
- look at the flexible framework in the Sustainable Procurement Task Force Report 'Procuring the Future' to find out where it is against this benchmark, and what it needs to do to improve and meet the recommended targets.
- look at the Office of Government Commerce sustainability guidance and advice on quick-win sustainability solutions for goods and services.

- identify its 'top 10' spend areas and prioritise them for action on sustainable development.
- prioritise contracts with the greatest sustainability opportunities and ease of implementation for immediate action.
- provide suppliers with its sustainable procurement policy and provide guidance.
- look at Forum for the Future's sustainable procurement toolkit that includes a method for prioritising supply areas for sustainable procurement, a demand review tool, sustainability review and tender planner, and a whole-life costing tool.
- engage staff at all levels in sustainable procurement and identify training and skills needs to enable sustainability to be integrated into the mainstream procurement process.

What is interesting is the documentation it provided to its own procurement professionals reflecting awareness, or at least an attempt to follow its own advice. For example, see *Sustainable Procurement – Making it Happen* referenced in the footnotes.

Source: www.idea.gov.uk

In order to help government departments meet the targets and the action plan set out by the government, the Centre of Expertise in Sustainable Procurement (CESP) was set up as an organisation within the OGC. This organisation deals solely with environmental issues at present. As the recognition of sustainable procurement and its importance for global wellbeing grows, then so will the influence of public sector procurement, particularly in respect of procurement of services.

This has implications for the way that procurement organisations and those within them are developed and organised. If an organisation is to have a collective conscience, then there are implications in respect of how that organisation deals with sensitive issues that arise from sustainable procurement.

For example, there are certain points of ambiguity that might arise when a health authority wishes to purchase new waste disposal services. It may well be that this will not be the lowest cost option and that the most effective 'green' (environmentally or sustainable) solution is the most expensive option. Arguably, this merely means that an individual buyer within the authority (or more likely a small procurement team) makes an organisation case/investment appraisal; based upon 'Value for Money' over the lifetime of the services and although it might not be the cheapest option it does meet the Sustainable Procurement agenda of that particular health authority.

As such it could be argued that it is becoming more necessary to measure the benefits of an environmentally responsible procurement of services (albeit possibly a more costly one), against, those more traditional measures of an organisation's efficiency such as keeping costs low.

However, deciding whether to incorporate a responsible approach is not so straightforward. There will be many stakeholders, not least the general public, who whilst thinking that the environmentally responsible, sustainable procurement approach is laudable, would rather have less expensive waste disposal services and (simplistically) have more patients medically treated and cured. Hence organisationally, and/or individually, procurement may take a sustainable approach, but the wishes of stakeholders will have to be taken into account and in turn this has an impact upon procurement organisation, policy and procedures.

Sir Neville Simms (2006), in leading the UK Sustainable Procurement Task Force, made it clear that using procurement to support wider social, economic and environmental objectives will be beneficial over the long term. The impact of the Task Force is significant, giving credence to the topic and high profile to the aspects that affect public procurement such as legal matters, moral imperatives and ethical behaviour. Were such an approach not to be taken there would be a lack of a cohesive approach to public sector procurement of services in respect of 'sustainable procurement.'

When procuring services, it is through the tender and contracting processes that public sector procurement organisations and personnel can build into procedures, policies and decision making a requirement for sustainability. In a number of ways it is an important aspect that, as the National Audit Office (2004, pp.36) states, Sustainable Procurement is not incompatible with the concept of Value for Money; indeed the implication is that Value for Money assessments must be developed so that sustainability can be incorporated. Indeed the OGC produces guidance that encourages departments to incorporate sustainability.

Sustainable procurement (SP) is therefore about the incorporation of sustainability into the 'total process,' and the whole life perspective of procurement. As public sector procurement organisations emphasise corporate social responsibility as an important supplier selection criteria, it will encourage more sustainable production/procurement on the part of potential suppliers.

It is interesting to note that whilst the public sector may be a leader in the area of sustainability generally, there is a mixed response from commercial suppliers to the whole agenda. Whilst most recognise the need for and have acceptance of sustainable procurement, the requirement to meet shareholder expectations can sometimes have greater influence than the desire to want to serve communities and meet green targets. Meanwhile proponents of sustainable and green practices remain convinced, as do a growing list of organisations, that the adaptation of green practices is also clear business sense and represents a win/win scenario; a topic very fully discussed in the book *Green Supply Chains: an action manifesto* (Emmett and Sood, 2010).

Innovation

The term innovation, though generally understood, can have a wide application. The government's policy on innovation covers three areas:

- The procurement of innovative products and services.
- Innovation in the design and delivery of procured services.
- Innovative procurement services.

The government encourages by policy that its departments, seek, encourage and embed innovation in its procurement functions, especially where it can help deliver higher quality services whilst achieving the policies of good VFM and abiding by UK regulations, EU Procurement Directives and EU Treaty obligations.

The best way seen to achieve innovative solutions is to engage with suppliers in the marketplace early by communicating the requirements for the service. This then allows those in the market to propose potentially innovative solutions.

Innovation is best implemented at the earlier stages of the procurement. This is when the procurement approaches to be taken are decided upon. If the processes of procurement are advanced it becomes more difficult to introduce innovative approaches.

In order to develop effective innovation, there are several things which must be considered but prime amongst these is the identification and statement of needs and outcomes. These have to be effectively communicated so that credible and innovative solutions may be put forward by suppliers in the marketplace. This can be attained through initial communications well in advance of the formal call for solutions to the service need.

The OGC outlines four possible approaches to the procurement of innovative solutions:

1. The Competitive Dialogue Procedure; as described previously.
2. Design Contests; an outlined process which may result in the award of prizes for innovative solutions.
3. Pre-commercial Procurement; a process which uses research and development contracts to progress solutions.
4. Forward Commitment Procurement; a piloted process which awards the contract once an innovative solution to an early communicated need is proven to be effective.

This shows that processes that encourage innovative solutions to the procurement of service needs are plausible within the frameworks outlined above, although as with all procurements they will require a serious degree of planning and support.

When seeking innovative solutions, clear support from those above, as well as effective risk planning, are an important requirement, particularly where solutions have not been proven.
Source: www.ogc.gov.uk/documents/Finding_and_Procuring_Innovative_Solutions_(3).pdf

'Whilst innovation should not be an end in itself, it can add value'.
Source: www.ogc.gov.uk/documents/capturing_innovation.pdf

This indicates that given a need for a particular service then suppliers can be encouraged to develop innovative solutions. Supplier innovation has the potential to add better Value for Money through:

- Better Quality.
- Faster Delivery.
- Reduced Whole Life Cost.

This means engaging with a wide range of suppliers so that the broadest range of innovative solutions can be explored. To do so requires knowledge and skill from the procurement professionals undertaking the procurement activity and the ability to take an entrepreneurial approach whilst remaining cognisant of the need for Value for Money and adherence to legal requirements. This is discussed further towards the end of this part of the book.

Small to Medium Enterprises (SMEs)

The government policy with regards to SMEs is that these organisations should be encouraged and supported in competing for public sector service contracts, where this is possible within the policy of attaining VFM whilst abiding by UK and EU regulations and the EU Treaty.

The encouragement and support provided to SMEs is meant to result in creating a more level playing field on which such organisations can compete for contracts, although of course preferential treatment should not be given, for this would be against the rules of competition.

As well as the social incentives to join there are potential benefits to be had for the public sector organisation undertaking the procurement of services:

- A wider supplier base will mean that potentially competitive suppliers will not be overlooked.
- A wider supplier base increases the possibility that innovative solutions may be found.
- Market stagnation that might come through a concentration of solutions in a decreasing number of large suppliers can be avoided.
- The procurement process is made easier.

It has been indicated that SMEs are the lifeblood and future of the UK economy and that there is an opportunity through public sector procurement of services for this to be maintained and enhanced.

Case Study: The Department for Constitutional Affairs

In 2004 the Department of Constitutional Affairs (DCA) commissioned a review of the Community Legal Services (CLS). The procurement process began with the standard OJEU call for expressions of interest. Several potential suppliers were subsequently invited to submit fully costed proposals and invited to a briefing session. Written questions were taken from the shortlisted bidders and written responses were provided to all bidders. Following the submission of full proposals, a short list of potential suppliers were asked to attend a presentation, following which Matrix Research & Consultancy Limited (Matrix), a mature SME, was designated as preferred provider.

After Matrix was awarded preferred provider status, the DCA wished to revise the project brief. Involving more Matrix staff and changing the number of case studies allowed this to be accommodated. Procurement from an SME in this case appears to have benefited from almost all of the characteristics that can be associated with such companies, namely more competition, better value for a given cost, innovation, responsiveness, flexibility and specialism in the civil justice field.

Source: www.ogc.gov.uk/documents/CP0083_Small_supplier_better_value.pdf - p.9

In considering how much to consider in respect of public sector procurement of services, an indication was given earlier of the nature and scope of that environment. However, no mention was made of charities and other small not for profit organisations. We should remember these whenever discussing or applying procurement of services they can on one hand be a purchaser of services, or on the other hand, be a supplier to other public sector procurement organisations.

Case Study: SMEs have 20% of NHS Contracts (NHS, 2005)

'Small to medium sized enterprises (SMEs) are a critical component of the NHS supply chain and a large proportion of their organisation is conducted with SMEs. In 2004/5, of the 5,500 or so contracts that were awarded, approximately 1,250 were to SMEs (i.e. those organisations with less than 250 employees). The value of SME contracts exceeded £1.14 billion.

Our internal contract information management system (CIMS) is now set up in such a way that all SMEs can be identified, and each year we submit data to the

Small Organisation Service (SBS) which feeds into their annual survey of SME success.

We have a number of ongoing initiatives to engage and support SMEs, and we have reported these in previous reports. In summary they include:

- a purchasing helpdesk to ensure we deal promptly with all enquiries
- provisions of specific guidance on any aspect of selling to the NHS, including
- relevant quality standards, compliance with public procurement procedures
- where relevant, market structure, pricing and customer requirements
- stakeholder consultation groups which include supplier representatives
- meet-the-buyer events
- production of a guide called "Selling to the NHS" and a dedicated website for suppliers.

In 2004/5, we participated in a NERA Economic Consulting study for the Small Organisation Service (SBS) of the DTI. The study examined the benefits of public sector procurement from SMEs. We submitted four cases to the study, all of which demonstrated a particular benefit to the public sector of procuring from SMEs. The report of the study is available on the SBS website.

Social Issues

There are certain key points to remember when addressing social issues when procuring services for the public sector. These are clearly outlined in the guidance from the OGC covering social issues in procurement as follows:

They must be relevant to the subject of the contract.
- Actions must be consistent with the EU Treaty and the EU Public Procurement Directive.
- Actions taken on sustainable development can have implications in the shorter, medium and longer term. Therefore, it is essential that sustainable procurement is approached from a whole life cost perspective.
  (Source: www.ogc.gov.uk/documents/Social_Issues_in_Purchasing.pdf)

The terms social issues can be a broad umbrella to refer to a number of issues. Some of the main social issues which should be addressed or given consideration include:

- Community Benefits.
- Core Labour Standards.
- Disability Equality.
- Employment and Training Issues.
- Fair Trade.
- Gender Equality.
- Race Equality.
- Small and Medium size Enterprises, including Social Enterprises, Black and Minority Ethnic Enterprises, women's organisations, disabled-owned organisations, and the Voluntary and Community Sector (sometimes referred to as the 'SME sector' in this guidance).
- Workforce Skills, including Adult Basic Skills.

Some of these issues are covered in other policy considerations which reflect the weight of importance/consideration that such issues should be given.

The OGC document *"Buy and make a difference: How to address Social Issues in Public Procurement"* (2008, pp.14) contains a list of what it considers important 'Dos and Don'ts' in the procurement process. They include:

Checklist: How to address Social Issues in Public Procurement

Do make sure:
- Social issues addressed in procurement are relevant to the subject of the contract.
- Actions to take account of social issues are consistent with the government's value-for-money policy, taking account of whole-life costs.
- Actions to take account of social issues comply with the law, in particular, the principles of the EU Treaty, around a level playing field for suppliers from the UK and other member states, and the UK Regulations implementing the EU Public Procurement Directive(s).
- Any social benefits sought are quantified and weighed against any additional costs and potential burdens on suppliers, which are likely to be passed onto the public sector.

- Not to impose any unnecessary burdens that would seriously deter suppliers, especially small and medium sized enterprises (SMEs), from competing for contracts, which in turn would reduce the choice available and could impact on costs and service standards. The suppliers deterred could include the very ones whose participation would help to further the government's social agenda e.g. those owned by under-represented groups.

Do not:

- Act in such a way as to distort competition or discriminate against candidate suppliers from other Member States.
- Add social elements to a contract without careful evaluation and justification of any additional costs.
- Leave consideration of social issues until too late in the process.
- Confuse obtaining Value for Money, which is required, with awarding contracts on the basis of lowest initial price, which is bad practice.
- Impose contract conditions that are not relevant to the performance of the individual contract.

An example of this can be seen in the issue of equality and its application to contracts for the procurement of services.

The *'government is committed to promoting a fair and equal society, where everyone has the chance to flourish, achieve their full potential and contribute to its success; a fair and equal society which makes best use of its talents will help the economy perform to its productive potential.'*

Source: http://www.ogc.gov.uk/documents/Equality_Brochure.pdf

Although equality issues are not necessarily allowed to be used as the primary factor for choosing one contractor over another, where it is not specified in the contract (which should be properly determined by Value for Money); should two bids be identical, then other concerns, such as equality, can be used to distinguish between bids. However, legal advice should first be sought.

There exist legal obligations concerning equality. Compliance with these equality laws should be standard in all public service contracts. These come in the form of duties, of which there are:

- The Disability Equality Duty.
- The Gender Equality Duty.
- The Race Equality Duty.

Other than the requirements to comply as stated by law, issues of equality should be given 'due regard'. By this it is meant that the weight given to the issues of equality should be proportionate to their relevance to the service procurement in question.

The Disability Equality Duty means that it is not unlawful to treat a disabled person more favourably. This is seen in the ability to contract specifically to employers of disabled people and avoid the requirements for competition. This reserving of contracts is allowed under Article 19 of the EC Public Procurement Directive and Article 28 of the Utility Directive.

This equality legislation of course, applies to both the public and private sectors.

When contracting out a service to the private sector, the public sector body should be aware that the contractor is representing the public sector, and as such it is important that the awarding body ensure that the contractor is compliant with the legislation throughout the life of the contract. The conditions for meeting equality requirements should be included in the public service contract. This can only be done effectively is the commercial strategy of the organisation reflects an awareness of such issues. However, it remains the case as with other areas that the most scope to address such issues can be found at the beginning of the procurement process when setting out the organisation case. What is important is that the stakeholders are engaged on such issues.

Checklist: Working on Government/public premises

In a hospital contract for building and equipment maintenance services and repair works where the contractor's staff will be working on the hospital premises and have contact with other hospital staff and patients, the public authority decided that the contractor's staff must abide by the hospital's equality code of practice which included attending their equality and diversity training session. This was therefore included and carried out as a contract condition.

Source: http://www.ogc.gov.uk/documents/Equality_Brochure.pdf - p.6

It is also important to bear in mind that other ethical areas exist and, although they may not be covered explicitly under specific duties as the three mentioned above, should be given the same attention and due diligence. These other equality issues include among other things:

- Age.
- Religion or belief.
- Sexual orientation.
- Gender reassignment.

Organisations do exist to help inform over equality issues and they can provide valuable information to help incorporate equality policies into the procurement process. For example:

- Equality and Human Rights Commission (EHRC).
- Trade Unions.
- Industry Representatives.

Failure of a potential contractor to account for such directives can be grounds for exclusion during the selection stage.

Case Study: More favourable treatment' under the Disability Equality Duty

A local authority is contracting out its sports and leisure services. The authority recognises that all services must be fully accessible for disabled people. Through consulting with disabled people in the planning stage, the authority recognises that some specific services solely for disabled people will also be required, to allow them to participate fully in the services being offered.

So, within the procurement process the authority builds in certain requirements including full accessibility of services, specific sessions in both the swimming pools and gyms for disabled people and positive mechanisms such as working with representative groups to recruit disabled people to the user groups for individual sports facilities.

Source: www.ogc.gov.uk/documents/Equality_Brochure.pdf - p.6

A specific approach for engaging with smaller organisations and particularly minority owned SMEs is Supply2.gov.uk (Supply to Government) which is a government backed internet site that can be used by the public sector to search for lower value contracts. These lower value contracts are defined as typically under £100,000 (in effect contracts that would not be advertised in the OJ). *(OGC, n.d. Tendering for Public Contracts: A Guide for Small Organisations, pp.3).*

All public sector organisations are encouraged by the government to publicise their contracts on the site with the aim to open up the market especially to SMEs and minority/disadvantaged groups (but to all organisations in general) and make it easier to develop a close working relationship between the public and private sectors.

Skills

Public sector procurement provides the opportunity to promote skills development, raise the skill level of service providers' employees, improve the quality of public service delivery, and ensure greater Value for Money.
(Source: http://www.dius.gov.uk/~/media/publications/P/promoting_skills_through_ public_procurement)

An example of how to accomplish this would be placing the requirement that trainees or apprentices be given a proportion of the work. It is permissible to address requirements for skills and apprenticeships in public procurement processes according to UK regulations, as long as they:

* Are relevant to the contract.
* Are proportionate.
* Do not compromise Value for Money.
* Do not unfairly discriminate against potential contractors.

Case Study: Improving transport skills

Merseytravel places contracts for the provision of bus services with transport providers throughout the Mersey area, and has insisted that drivers working on their contracts should hold an appropriate Level 2 qualification, or European equivalent. Merseytravel regularly works with a number of smaller operators who had concerns about how they would meet these requirements. Working with Go

Skills and the LSC outside the procurement process, Merseytravel/Mersey Learn responded to this challenge by co-ordinating activity with providers delivering to the transport sector, helping to ensure employer and individual skills development needs were met. Prior to making it a core requirement a pilot programme was run with a typical smaller bus contractor to test the approach, which enabled over 30 drivers to obtain their first level 2 NVQ.

Source: http://www.ogc.gov.uk/documents/Promoting_skills_through_public_procurement.pdf - p.6

Some Issues

From the discussions which have occurred within this part of the book, and the book as a whole, we can see that the purchasing of services in the public sector is a complex matter requiring consideration of numerous issues. What will now be identified are some of the main issues, as well as justification for why they are raised and considerations to be taken. These are:

- Public sector versus private sector innovation.
- How to determine Value for Money – efficiency versus effectiveness.
- Managing the contract through life.
- Visibility of legal and regulatory requirements.
- The need for probity.
- Identification of stakeholders.

Public Sector versus Private Sector Innovation:

So far the discussion of trends highlighted above have focused on the adoption of private sector practices by the public sector. What has been suggested is that this is generally one way and that innovation and advances in terms of the procurement of services and procurement generally has been found with the private sector.

However, as notions such as Sustainable Procurement and Corporate Social Responsibility are becoming more prevalent we can potentially see some reverse movement of influence from the public sector. Nevertheless, the real issue is public versus private sector innovation, and how to determine when one should lead the other in procurement practices for buying services.

Innovation, as related to the procurement of services, is *"the qualitative change in processes and organisations whereby new artefacts, methods or ideas penetrate the social system."* (Van de Ven, in Moore, 2008).

The public sector is an important and integrated part of most economies, as such, the changes it makes, can provide a source of innovation for the private sector where such innovation is seen as useful. Although it is true, as noted earlier, that the transfer of approaches has been a relatively one way process from the private sector, along with a time lag in adoption of commercial practices being implemented within the public sector, recent years have shown that this one way process in the creation and distribution of procurement innovation and knowledge is becoming less so.

Although the commercial private sector will likely continue to lead the way with regards to the economic issues, it is clearly the public sector which is at the forefront of developing and applying policies which are socially responsibly to its procurement activities.

This is because the public sector is ultimately spending public money, and as such has to be seen as responsible in doing so.

Corporate social responsibility (CSR), incorporates several issues which are of increasing visibility and prevalent to the general public. For example:
- The concerted effort to engage with SMEs; increasingly important with when any financial recession is of concern for the survival of small and medium enterprises.
- Being environmentally responsible, reducing waste and CO_2 emissions, increasingly important as impacts from global warming take preference
- Drawing upon services provided by the broad spectrum of our society, where it may be more profitable to outsource services to an international firm.
- The issue of morality as part of CSR, or social responsibility generally for which there is the Chartered Institute of Purchasing and Supply (CIPS) guidance on www.cips.org where a wide range of papers and discussion documents can be found by searching on CSR.

The discussion on innovation as a policy as earlier highlighted is that it is preferable to explore innovative practices. The problem comes with the adoption and implementation of such practices; this is because the ability to do this depends on the ability to distribute knowledge among procurement professionals both in the public and private sector.

This is not an easy thing to do, for there are often barriers between professions which serve to block the transfer of practices and knowledge that otherwise might serve to improve the purchasing of services across the public sector as a whole.

The challenge is found in identifying what these barriers are, and what to do to remove them. Arguably, for too long the public sector has placed considerable reliance upon processes that will deliver innovation; but this cannot be the optimal approach when adherence to processes and procedures brings in turn, more adherence and conformance. This is then the opposite of what is required for innovative, novel solutions to challenges presented in the procurement of services.

In this regard, whilst this part of the book commenced with an overview of the changes that have taken place over a period of thirty to forty years, it could be said that this is a very long time and that much has actually changed in such a time period.

However, for the UK public sector environment, change does not come quickly nor does it come easily. The reason for identifying a timeline is that there are many socio-economic and political aspects that come into play within the public sector. Thus, the need for probity and adherence to the legal requirements are always in the foreground.

Pressure for the public sector procurement organisations to change has continued to grow. This is because such organisations spend a considerable amount of the taxpayer's money and commercial organisations must appear able to take on latest thinking to make more efficient and effective use of funds available through the utilisation of new approaches.

In the decades in question, these include Total Quality Management, Just in Time, Organisation Process Re-engineering, Lean Manufacturing, Supply Chain Management etc; however, these have not been so easy to introduce within the public sector procurement organisation.

Often there has to be adaptation rather than adoption of concepts. However, there are examples where entrepreneurial thinking and taking an open minded perspective have had results that can bring change and performance enhancement, always bearing mind the need for probity and legal compliance. An example of this is the CRISP case from the MOD, which is about spare parts and the use of a wider perspective, which became a service based contractual arrangement providing considerable benefits; as the following shows:

Case Study: PROJECT 'CRISP' – ChallengeR Innovative Spares Provision

Background

Challenger II replaced Challenger I as the Main Battle Tank for the British Army in 1998. The full fleet deployment was around 400 Main Battle Tanks. It was anticipated that Challenger II will have an operational life of 25 years. The support to the earlier Challenger I was historically poor, involving £30million spend per annum with over 300 separate suppliers in an adversarial, 'arms reach' procurement approach. This was coupled with additional weaknesses such as excessive stocks at warehouses, poor availability of spares, costly repetitive tendering to a vendor base in excess of 300 suppliers and long lead/delivery times.

Procurement Strategy

Vickers Defence Systems (VDS), both the Design Authority and Prime Manufacturer, were selected as a partner to provide the specific spares support. The reasons for this included future design and technological changes or improvements could be more easily, and incrementally, introduced at less risk with Design Authority involvement, the risk of maintaining obsolescent stock was considerably reduced, tank production ended in 2000, although delivery of stockpiles and retrofitted tanks continued through 2002.

Some urgent spares requirements could still be met from production stockpiles. The MoD could also draw benefit from existing long term supply agreements between VDS and their subcontractors, which include supply chain quality assurance standards and production improvements, UK industrial expertise may be lost if VDS' involvement was reduced to conventional Post Design Tasks only whilst maintaining involvement in whole life support substantially improves the ability of VDS to compete for further orders and finally the position over Intellectual Property Rights was, as ever, complex, and would impair the timely letting of breakout contracts.

Innovative Thinking

Project CRISP has explored these ideas in an open, no commitment basis. A framework agreement, establishing a partnering arrangement, was accordingly signed in May 1999. As a result, the initial requirement and proposed contract provided for the supply of Challenger II specific consumable spares, a range of 2493 items.

Operation of the Contract

The requirement, in outline, sought to maintain the operational support chain and provide for a core of consumable items, all of which are peculiar to Challenger II. It further establishes a procedure to include additional items as user experience matures. The contract transfers the responsibility, and risk, from the MoD to VDS for the provision (calculation of requirement) procurement, storage and distribution of spares.

There was a requirement for the distribution of spares to locations around the world. The contract set challenging targets to reduce stocks and increase availability. Military units continued to demand in the normal method via their unit and onwards via a Secondary Depot to the Supply Chain Operations Centre; all changes have invisible to the users, accepting that they have experienced a substantially improved availability.

In recognising that they have little direct experience of spares provision and supply, of the scale necessary to support the fleet, and following MoD advice, VDS (following a competitive tendering action), chose a major third party logistic services provider, 'Multipart' as their partner in the project. *NB - The MoD was party to, and informed at every stage of, the tender process, although did not interfere with it, nor did they influence the decision.* In effect the demands for spares are collated at the Supply Chain Operations Centre and forwarded electronically to VDS' Supply Chain Partner – 'Multipart'. 'Surge' requirements to meet operational needs and sustainability targets are included in the contract. The ability to meet these 'surges' is a mandatory requirement within given lead time notice; such 'surges' are costed separately to the main contract price.

Pricing Strategy

To incentivise both the quality of service and overall cost, the contract includes a 'Target Cost Incentive Fee' pricing mechanism, with annual target costs and a target fee that will be paid in full or in part according to the level of service received. The underpinning contract is an enabling arrangement for the supply of spares. The annual target cost is the unit cost of the spares, multiplied by the estimated usage, plus an additional percentage for delivery and management. Adjustments to reflect the level of availability reached are made on a quarterly basis.

Benefit Analysis

The operational benefits were summarised as improved availability, reduced stock levels and therefore reduced obsolescence, reduced lead/delivery times, better asset tracking, leading to identification of the true fleet costs and identified surge capability for mission essential items. An 'output based' Investment Appraisal was employed to confirm the financial benefits using the Process and Performance Cost Model.

Risks

A risk analysis was undertaken. The procurement strategy was relatively high risk when compared to existing procurement methods. VDS were unproven as a spares provisioning agency; additionally the commercial viability of VDS was at some risk with an empty order book and rumours of takeover. However, sub-contractors and not VDS physically produce the vast majority of the spares.

A professional 3rd party logistic organisation (Multipart) carried out the provision, procurement, supply and distribution functions and has a proven track record in this field. VDS input concentrates on overall responsibility, product quality, design changes, technological insertions, configuration control and the provision of reliability data to the provisioning algorithms.

Summary

It was the combination of sharing risk and the partnering approach of 3 key stakeholders, the MoD, VDS and Multipart together with the key sub-contractors in the supply chain that have enabled CRISP to produce the efficiencies. The previous system produced low availability of <71%, with costly disposal issues and poor pipeline delivery. CRISP was subsequently running at >95% and was exceeding savings targets. It was also providing value added benefits such as improved 2nd and 3rd tier supplier relationship which has drastically reduced production lead times, a better understanding of the MoD position by suppliers, improved flexibility and drastically reduced pipeline times.

This case study is based on the events in the late 1990s (although the contract in amended form is still in existence), but provides an excellent opportunity to show that some enlightened individuals at that time were 'pushing the envelope' of what could be achieved by innovative thinking.

It is the ability to see opportunities, from a wider perspective than just the relatively narrow response to a requisition or statement of requirement from a department or group which the procurement professional serves.

As the use of outsourcing has grown so has the need for the ability for procurement professionals to see the wider picture and take a proactive (rather than reactive) approach to the increasing need for procurement of services. This is not in any way to advocate breaking the rules and to not follow processes and procedures, but it is part of the challenge in procuring services for the public sector, that taking on new approaches and strategies must still allow conformance with legal requirements and the need for Value for Money.

The latter aspect is relatively easy to deal with. Long gone are the days (we hope) when purchasers in the public sector arranged for three quotes and then just picked the lowest price!

Value for Money can be many things and prime amongst these must be whole life and through life considerations. It is vital to understand and recognise that there are costs incurred in the so-called 'lines of development' that are needed to provide a service; such lines of development include:

- Training, for example to update operators if during the course of a contract operators have to switch to updated systems.
- The cost of updates and enhancements for example, to equipment and facilities.
- Delivery of the service, for example, support given over the life time of the service needs to be taken into account.

Often, the contracts that are awarded for the provision of services to a public sector organisation may be for many years; as it is not unusual, with the use of PPP/PFI contract, that there is a 10 to 20 years contract term. Additionally, an innovative approach for the public sector, as another means to provide VFM, is that of collaboration (with other public sector users) or shared services (a variation on collaboration). We have written extensively on the benefits of collaboration and working with suppliers/customers in different ways in the books, *The Relationship Driven Supply Chain* (Emmett and Crocker 2006) and *Excellence in Supplier Management* (Emmett and Crocker 2009).

How to determine Value for Money – efficiency versus effectiveness

The notion of VFM, though clear as a policy requirement, is relatively vague when it comes to practical application. It was described earlier how the 'value' is determined by the costs, balanced or weighted against, whether the procurement meets its purpose.

This is where discussion of VFM takes place. VFM is the guiding principle which determines whether a service is bought, and from whom it should be purchased.

The EU directives state that competition is a preferred method of gaining VFM but it has recognised that, especially in the early planning stages of any procurement activity, there can be opportunity for dialogue (or even negotiation). It is the communication between Buyer and potential Seller that can highlight different, innovative or novel solutions to requirements; these often allowing new thinking that brings a whole life solution and enables more service quality and/or quantity to be available to end users.

This is where the focus is not just to the cheapest. The reason for this is seen with problems of reverse auctioning, where a problem may come with determining just where the Value for Money lies; this essentially giving an efficiency versus effectiveness debate, where the emphasis may be given to the way that services are obtained such as following processes and procedures, as opposed to, focusing upon what service is to be delivered.

The question is then, how can Value for Money be measured?

UK government policy states that it can be done in several ways. The problem here though is found with the nature of the service contract. For example, with PPPs, on whether the contract provides true VFM or not may be immediately be realised.

Another concern with VFM is, by what means is it measured or determined? This will undoubtedly depends on the context to which the notion is being applies.

VFM can therefore suffer from the length of time with which the budget is forecast, versus the length of time, the service provisions are expected to take place.

It has been argued that as market principles have been adopted by the public sector, satisfaction of the customer has become more important. This is debatable as due to the nature of public sector money spending, there has always been a requirement to spend tax payers' money responsibly. However perhaps the notion of what defines responsible spending has changed. Whereas before, it might have been deemed that the customer was satisfied with the government saving tax payer money on services and thus having more money to spend or to reduce taxes; there is a precedent with VFM that such savings must not come at the expense of service quality.

This is where the activity of reverse auctions can be used as an example of efficiency as opposed to effectiveness. Though reverse online auctions may have given the cheapest price, it may have done so at the compromise of quality. The following case study on e-auctions and the elderly illustrates this:

Case Study: Elderly Care Suffers After Reverse E-Auctions

On 9th April 2009 the BBC presented a Panorama investigation entitled 'Britain's Home Care Scandal'. The findings of the investigation led to MPs calling for an investigation into the standards in elderly care provision. What the Panorama investigation found was that four UK councils had run controversial schemes where the care for the elderly was auctioned off to private sector companies through the use of 'reverse e-auctions', resulting in substandard care.

It reported that local councils who deliver the care internally were doing so on average for £22 an hour. The auctions were returning bids as low as £9.95, such as that bid by Domiciliary Care for whom the investigator for the programme worked in an auction for the care of the elderly in South Lanarkshire Council. What resulted was that the services provided were not up to the requirements for the contract, with some care visits lasting four minutes instead of the required 30.

The UK homecare industry is a £1.5 billion organisation, and as such it attracts a variety of bidders ranging from charities to larger healthcare corporations. However, the problem lay with the way in which the competition was held. By awarding a contract through reverse e-auction and subsequently awarding the contract to the lowest bidder it was harder to guarantee that service delivery could be met with the amount of money being spend on personal and training by the private sector companies as a result of the contracts final value.

The investigator's training for example consisted of four 20 minute DVDs and a tutorial lasting 90 minutes. The investigator was also allowed to work 14 shifts before passing the required check by the Criminal Records Bureau.

Though such practices do not reflect all those who have successfully won contracts for the provision of services for the public sector through the use of reverse e-auctions, these have long been criticised by trade unions and suggests awareness that there are general issues which exist in the use of such practice contract awarding. The public visibility of the failing discussed here has brought such practices to the fore of discussion as noted with the MP's investigation called as a result.

What this highlights is that though public procurement policy for the provision of services states that contracts should be awarded on a basis of VfM, the pressure exists to conduct such procurements under practices more inline within the perceived inefficiencies of CCT. Though VfM states that such contracts must be valued based not solely on the lowest price but also on service delivery, this does not always happen, and suggests that failings in the system are occurring in relation to the adherence of public sector procurement policy.

There could be many reasons for such failings to properly apply policy direction to procurement at the council level. However, because several councils have found to have used such ineffective practices for service delivery, there exists a fault in the systems designed to govern the buying of services from the private sector.

Managing the contract through life

Organisations within the public sector often have a range of multiple goals, many of which are hard to measure. There is often a lack of uniformity between how such goals are measured between different organisations within the public sector, let alone in adoption of private sector models within a public sector context. As has been seen, the public sector in the procurement of services needs to measure success based not just whether the procurement is offering VFM whilst operating within the legal and policy framework provided, but also whether the procurements of relevant services are socially responsible.

It also means it is hard to measure the performance of employees and brings in the notion of accountability, which is generally more vague and harder to quantify than in the private sector, where (for example with PLCs) strict legality issues exist on accountability.

Unlike the procurement of tangible goods, the procurement of services is unlikely to be a one off activity and increasingly is likely to be delivered over a considerable length of time. Therefore the performance of the service provider over time is needed so as to access whether the service provision is effective. Great care needs to be taken in determining what measures are to be used and these are often about cost efficiency and effectiveness, this being more difficult to quantify but is crucial for customer satisfaction.

Visibility of EU and UK regulation and law

What has been outlined above is the requirement for public sector procurement practices relating to services in the UK to abide by EU and UK regulations. In outlining the requirements and some of the potential consequences for the success of the procurement, what was not touched upon were the issues relating to the visibility of not just these regulations and laws at the practitioner level, but also considerations which have to be given to areas such as contract law etc.

Due to the need to abide by the EU legislation, it is important to ensure that the directives and the changes that occur, such as to EU thresholds, are as transparent as possible. This is not always the case and is a reflection of the general inadequacy to properly vocalise the sources of information (such as the OGC).

Understanding is also hampered by the degree and frequency of change which occurs regarding laws and regulations. It is because of this, that much of the policy framework recommends consulting the legal profession before making definitive decisions. This consultation covers not only the overall procurement, but also the further policy issues in areas such as equality, skills etc. that were noted earlier.

What the case study below on the part nationalisation of East Coast Rail highlights the importance of understanding legal issues on contracting for public sector services:

Case Study: Part Nationalisation of the East Coast Rail from National Express

This case study highlights the responsibility held by the public sector for the delivery of services, and ensuring that such services are delivered even when the responsibility to do so falls to the private sector.

There are several effective examples of this happening during the 2008 financial down turn, not least with the examples of the nationalisation of the banks.

The Department of Transport had to take the London-to-Edinburgh East Coast Rail Route back into public ownership after National Express declared that it could no longer afford the £1.4 Billion franchise contract lasting seven and a half years. This is the second time in three years that the contract has been handed back to the Department of Transport with GNER giving up the franchise in 2006.

National Express defaulting on the franchise service contract highlights the legal complexity involved with the contracting for services. For example, Lord Adonis, Transport Secretary, warned that the government "may have grounds" to take back the remaining franchises and put National Express on notice that it will be banished from the franchise market.

As such the government is facing a legal battle over the nationalisation of its other two franchises, East Anglia and C2C.

This issue is complicated, with National express arguing that a clause existed within the contract that it does allow for a company to hand back a franchise in return for surrendering a performance bond, which in the case of East Coast was £32 million.

It is unclear whether the government will be able to cease all franchises at the handing back of one, but if it is the case then National Express could stand to lose up to £72 million from the collapse.

Another representative for the Department of Transport reflected a similar view stating that *"It is simply unacceptable to reap the benefits of contracts when times are good, only to walk away from them when times become more challenging."*

Sources:
http://www.guardian.co.uk/organisation/2009/jul/01/national-express-london-to-edinburgh

http://organisation.timesonline.co.uk/tol/organisation/industry_sectors/ transport/article6615184.ece?token=null&offset=12&page=2

It is also important to give consideration to legal and regulatory issues when services are being purchased outside the UK, and this requires a greater understanding of the differences that exist. This is even truer, when such a service is being purchased outside of the EU, where legal and regulatory differences may be even less visible or understood. An example would be the different 'value' with regards to legally binding aspects placed on a contract by different countries.

Hence those making decisions at a practitioner level need to be aware as to where such current legal and regulatory requirements can be found.

The need for probity

There are codes of ethical practice which can be referenced that give an understanding of the moral and ethical expectations to be expected from a professional operating in the contextual setting of the public sector. For example, the Chartered Institute of Purchasing and Supply (CIPS) have a Code of Professional Ethics which states:

Checklist: CIPS Code of Professional Ethics

- As a member of the Chartered Institute of Purchasing & Supply, I will maintain the highest standard of integrity in all my organisation relationships.
- reject any organisation practice which might reasonably be deemed improper.
- never use my authority or position for my own personal gain.

- enhance the proficiency and stature of the profession by acquiring and applying knowledge in the most appropriate way.
- foster the highest standards of professional competence amongst those for whom I am responsible.
- optimise the use of resources which I have influence over for the benefit of my organisation.
- comply with both the letter and the intent of:
  - the law of countries in which I practise
  - agreed contractual obligations
  - CIPS guidance on professional practice
- declare any personal interest that might affect, or be seen by others to affect, my impartiality or decision making.
- ensure that the information I give in the course of my work is accurate.
- respect the confidentiality of information I receive and never use it for personal gain.
- strive for genuine, fair and transparent competition.
- not accept inducements or gifts, other than items of small value such as organisation diaries or calendars.
- always to declare the offer or acceptance of hospitality and never allow hospitality to influence a organisation decision.
- remain impartial in all organisation dealing and not be influenced by those with vested interests.

Source: www.cips.org/aboutcips/whatwedo/codeofprofessionalethics/

There is value to be had in applying such codes of practice in order to gain or maintain probity. However, in doing so it is important to be aware that the code is outlined with a general purpose in mind and that ethical practices will need to be contextualised to reflect the requirements and expectations of those working specifically in the purchasing of services within the public sector.

The environment changes and this is reflected by CIPS updating their code of professional ethics from time to time.

Probity can be considered an important issue to consider when purchasing services for the public sector because, for as described at the start of this chapter, the main differential between the public and private sector is that the public sector is purchasing services for people using what are effectively public funds.

This is not to suggest that the private sector lacks a need for probity rather that in the public sector there should be a greater awareness of accountability to the stakeholders, particularly the general public as a whole. This is accountability on effectively two levels:

- Firstly it is important that the public feel that the service being procured is acceptable to provide for the requirement.
- Secondly that the public feels that the money spends are acceptable for the service being delivered.

These two points are reflective of the key policy requirements governing the nature of public sector procurement of services noted above, as the policy is designed to ensure responsible procurement of services, within its framework.

Policy reflects that the buying of services takes place in an environment where considerations have to be made other than the financial. Some of these have been reflected in the other policy considerations have been outlined above, such as environmental sustainability, social issues, creating opportunities for SMEs, etc.

It is because of this accountability that the public sector is in many respects leading the way in practices which can be deemed to reflect good corporate social responsibility (CSR). Challenges do exist however, as reflected in the earlier case study regarding the care of the elderly. These challenges stem from the balancing of public sector spending with the attainment of the best service for the public sector, both of which are the responsibility of the procurement professional.

When services are purchased for the public sector, the actions of the successful company represent those views of who issued the service contract. Thus the public sector organisation must make sure that it ensures that the company reflects the morally responsible practices of the public sector. It is easier to ensure that this will be the case during the planning and pre-contract award stages, and it must also be ensured that such moral working practices are maintained through life.

Identification of stakeholders

In order to achieve all of the principles governing the procurement of services in the public sector, it is necessary to be aware of all of the stakeholders involved. This is something which should be initially identified during the pre-procurement process.

In any public sector procurement activity, particularly that of purchasing services, it is important to be aware of who the stakeholders are, and the affects that the award may have on them, as well as ensuring their input into the purchase of the service. The stakeholders will differ for each purchase as the vested interests will change based on the nature of the service purchase. The varied nature of the stakeholders to be addressed is reflected in the number and variety of definitions which exist; for example:

- Any group or individual who can affect or is affected by the achievement of the organisation objectives. (Freeman, 1984)
- Those who have an interest in the company (so that the firm, in turn, may have an interest in satisfying their demands). (Argandona, 1998)
- Everyone in the community who has a stake in what the company does. (Frederick, 1998)
- Parties that have a stake in the corporation: something at risk, and therefore something to gain or lose, as a result of corporate activity. (Clarkson, 1999) (The sources above are from Moore, 2008.)

Stakeholders need to be managed as they have ability to impact upon the purchasing of the service. In order to effectively manage stakeholders there should be a degree of analysis to assess the potential of the stakeholder to impact upon the procurement, and a subsequent categorisation that is based on the severity of the potential stake or impact. One way to do this is to divide the stakeholders into internal and external, and then identify the key stakeholders in each area through stakeholder analysis conducted; for example:

- Internal stakeholders are those stakeholders within the organisation and also those who can be affected by wages and job stability, for example, employees, managers and owners/shareholders.
- External stakeholders are those who are involved with the organisation but are not employed by it, for example, customers, suppliers, government or society in general for example.

The case study on the part privatisation of the Royal Mail below provides a good example as to how the management of services within the public sector can go awry should stakeholders and their interests not adequately be identified and accounted for.

Case Study: Part Privatisation of the Royal Mail

In December 2008 it was being argued by ministers that in order to avoid financial disaster within the Royal Mail, the organisation should be part privatised. The arguments were primarily driven by the decline in demand for letter carrying, and the £7 billion deficit which existed in its pension scheme. Private companies would be brought in to offer expertise and capital in an attempt to replicate the schemes used in other countries such as Denmark.

Total privatisation was out of the question due to the commitment by Labour in its 2005 Manifesto to not privatise the organisation, but it was also viewed by Labour that something needed to be done to save the organisation. Proposed ways around this included partnerships with the private sector owning 30%.

The debate over Royal Mail part privatisation was particularly heated due to the 440,000 members of the organisation who are part of the pension scheme. It would also be difficult to find private sector organisations willing to foot the bill for the deficit within this scheme, leading to arguments that it would be the tax payer which would have to foot this bill, without effectively seeing an improvement in the company.

Part privatisation was likewise unpopular within staff of the organisation itself, with postal workers protesting in Westminster on a number of occasions over fears of job and pension losses in an already volatile financial climate. In the end there were only a few private sector companies demonstrating any serious interest in purchasing part of Royal Mail, such as the Dutch company TNT and the private equity company CVC. As such fears were raised over the effectiveness of the universal service with it being part owned by a non-British company.

The discussions over the part privatisation of the Royal Mail came to a head in early July 2009 with the government shelving plans, arguably amid the threat of back bencher rebellion. Any moves to part privatise the organisation have since been postponed, though it remains to be seen whether such plans will again be put forward in a more favourable economic climate.

This is an interesting case study for several reasons. One of these is the realisation of the degree of stakeholder consideration which has to be made in the outsourcing of public sector service delivery to the private sector.

Opposition to the proposed move came from a number of areas who perceived that they had significant investment in the direction Royal Mail should take; these included:

- General Public.
- Trade Unions e.g. CWU postal Union.
- Political parties.
- Royal Mail Staff generally.
- Customers with pre-existing contracts with Royal Mail.

Sources:
http://www.telegraph.co.uk/finance/financetopics/financialcrisis/3774743/Royal-Mail-should-be-part-privatised.html
http://news.bbc.co.uk/1/hi/uk_politics/7907179.stm
http://news.bbc.co.uk/1/hi/uk_politics/8129892.stm

As the case study suggests, stakeholders may be divided into many categories or groups, some more key than others, with some internal and others external.

However, by the fact that they can be categorised as stakeholders, their ability to affect and be affected by the action of any particular procurement means that they cannot be easily dismissed. This is why it is necessary to place weight on stakeholder management and because stakeholders change, then so do the ways they are managed. Thus the management of stakeholders should be should be considered on a procurement by procurement basis and in line with the direction of policies outlined above.

Bearing in mind the Kraljic portfolio and the recognition of high risk but also high potentially Value for Money of certain service procurement, it may be worth developing a Stakeholder Engagement Plan (SEP). This would result in an output that would enable identification of those who could have an influence on the procurement or those who would be affected by it and the way in which they should be managed. The following is an example of how such a SEP might appear.

Stage	Purpose of stakeholder involvement	Stakeholders involved	Methods of achieving involvement
1 Preparation	Notify interested parties	Indicate who will be involved	Indicate initial mode of communication: e.g. letters, press adverts/articles, newsletters, dedicated website, e-mail, stakeholder forums/workshops or other groups.
2 Information-gathering	Collect information	Identify anticipated sources of information, including that held by key stakeholders.	State how information will be gathered: questionnaires, public meetings, workshops/forums, groups, round-table dialogue, seminars, conferences, desk research, field research, email networks. State how data will be recorded, collated and used.
3 Data review	Review by stakeholders to validate data	Identify stakeholders able to offer informed views. Different approaches may be taken with different stakeholders	State how information will be disseminated: public meetings, workshops/forums, groups, round-table dialogue, seminars, conferences, email networks.
4 Agreement	Resolve any differences and agree draft plan	This should include all stakeholders. Different groups may be informed in different ways	State how stakeholders will be informed and how they can make their views known. State how representations will be recorded, collated (e.g. use of database) and subsequently dealt with.
5 Dissemination	Ensure that all persons and organisations needing to be aware of the plan know it has been published	This should include all stakeholders and, where necessary, the general public.	Establish where the SEP will be made available and how it will be publicised. Establish whether any specific interaction with particular stakeholder groups is required for plan implementation

6 Action	Ensure that plan is fully agreed, that the data are valid, that awareness has been properly raised, that the process and decisions are transparent.	This should include all stakeholders.	State how information will be disseminated. State how responses will be made, recorded, collated and used.

This is a guide to the action that can be taken to ensure that all stakeholders are identified and a strategy for engaging with them is (at the very least) considered. If undertaken it can smooth the way for an effective procurement project and ultimately its delivery of the required services.

Relationships

There is a spectrum of relationships going from adversarial to co-operative, and as many of the service contracts are of high value/high risk, if they are not delivered effectively they have considerable impact upon Value for Money. Therefore, out of necessity, relationships have to be at a co-operative end of the spectrum. Many will refer to this as 'partnership'. This is a much used word and without entering into semantic debate over the legal use of the word, it is arguably an overused word, even to the point of being put forward as a panacea for all ills in the public sector.

It should not be seen as so.

Like all procurement, especially in the procurement of services for the public sector, there is a need for co-operative and collaborative relationships that need careful consideration, clarity of requirements, careful planning and preparation with continual monitoring to ensure that all parties (including stakeholders) are gaining benefit from the resultant contract and delivery of the particular service.

This is not a process-only activity; it cannot just be a set of procedures that have to be followed; it requires competence and knowledge on the part of the procurement professional involved.

As mentioned, the books *Excellence in Supplier Management* and *The Relationship Driven Supply Chain* cover the relationship and collaboration topics fully.

Knowledge

The procurement professional responsible to such service procurement must be able to see the 'wider picture' and 'think outside the box'. These are rhetoric-style phrases, but they must be underpinned by a genuine ability to recognise opportunities and develop ideas in an entrepreneurial manner. This also needs a holistic perspective on the requirement for a particular service or services, understanding that in a public sector context, there are guidelines and legal aspects that must be taken into account, in reaching a proposed solution.

Such a person must be aware of the importance of relationships and understand the need for process and be able to balance these. The required knowledge is on one hand system or process led including the UK and EU law, public sector guidelines (especially OGC), and on the other hand, those issues to ensure that user of the service are well served through out the life time of the contract.

At this point it is essential to recall that there are three stages of undertaking the procurement of a service for the public sector environment.

Stage 1: Pre-procurement

This is an absolutely key part of the process, here much will be determined that may ultimately decide the efficiency and effectiveness of the procurement activity, that will only be seen at the delivery stage, which of course may well be some time away.

It is in this stage that the requirement will be discussed and generally confirmed. An organisational case will have to be developed to confirm that it is viable with a project plan to ensure that the necessary activities can take place to enable the whole process to be progressed.

Details of how performance of any resultant contract for service will be measured can be considered. Time and effort spent during this stage that is well in advance of the procurement activity will seldom be time wasted. In the past, little effort was expended on this stage, as typically a specification was received and processed as quickly as possible, often resulting in problems resulting later in unplanned time and effort during the actual delivery of a contract.

Much of the detail of what is noted here as pre-procurement activity will be internal, including discussion of whether the service is provided internally, whether it should continue to be so and criteria for internal and external supplier evaluation. However, for innovation to be encouraged and to seek optimal VFM, it will be necessary to engage with potential suppliers in the marketplace. The EU Procurement Directives permit this through the Competitive Dialogue Procedure or the Competitive Negotiated Procedure that have been detailed earlier.

It is possible also for communication to take place with potential suppliers through OGC recommended approaches such as Design Contests, Research and Development contracts that progress solutions and the Forward Commitment Procurement, which is based upon a pilot process, as was also noted earlier.

These will require knowledge, competence and confidence to navigate through the complexities that are inherent in the public sector procurement environment.

To assist in this important professional activity, there are some approaches that have been developed to ensure that opportunities are optimised whilst meeting all requirements and guidelines. Professor Christine Harland at Bath University has written on the aspects of 'Commissioning' that must take place to ensure effective communication between all interested parties and stakeholders. This is particularly applied in the National Health Service.

In a similar vein, another example is that of ROAD (Moore and McPherson, 2009). ROAD is an acronym for a technique which has been developed with the purpose of providing an approach to enhance pre-procurement planning and preparation where the final specification is not fixed, ultimately allowing the selection of a preferred procurement strategy to be better identified.

During this pre-procurement communication stage any aspects of the procurement project may be discussed and solutions developed. Those responsible for the public sector organisation continue the communication process until they identify one or more solution(s) which satisfy the requirement. It is a six stage process which can be summarised as:

Checklist: ROAD process

(1) **Research** the requirements of the project in order to define an Operational Statement of Requirement (OSR);

Match this OSR with (2) **Observing** and then (3) **Orientating** to what is achievable in the marketplace by benchmarking and evaluating the success, failure and overall affordability of other projects and gathering intelligence on potential bidders;

(4) **Adjust** the outline specification to align with the ability of the market to deliver those needs to time, budget and specification and then:

(5) **Define** and (6) **Decide** upon the system specification and routes to market which will ensure that this resultant Output Based Specification (OBS) will be both appropriate and achievable.

Effective planning is always reliant on crucial intelligence, both internal and external, enabling strategic decisions to be made. In the procurement context this is outlined below as:

- **Affordability:** does the likely cost of the project fall within budget constraints now that more is known about the service to be purchased?
- **Achievability:** is the outline specification achievable by the market and its available resources today?
- **Ability of the Market to Deliver:** do potential bidders for the work have the capacity to deliver within time bounds? Can potential bidders afford to even bid or deliver?
- **Timescale:** is the service achievable by the market within the timeframes desired by the contracting authority? Are those timeframes appropriate?
- **Output based specification (OBS)**, often known as performance based specifications: This will include achievable timescales, affordability to both contractor and authority and will enable a robust contract to be written. This final part is crucial to all complex procurements. Robust contracts are essential where outputs form the basis of the deliverables if the project is not to be 'de-railed' with cost overruns and disputes over final outputs.

The above is where the emphasis is needed, rather than merely following procedures or seeking the lowest price.

Stage 2: The Tender Process

This is process led and will be enhanced by the time spent and effort to ensure relevancy and accuracy of details communicated during the pre-procurement stage.

Adherence to guidelines and legal aspects is necessary. Pre-planning and preparation should have enabled clarity on the outgoing tender document. Nevertheless, again, knowledge and competence must be applied to determine and question all elements of the submitted tenders, in order to fully understand what is being proposed as the service solution. It should not be merely a section of the lowest priced tender.

Through-life costing and its underlying assumptions must be stated and then examined and validated to ensure that VFM is paramount.

Stage 3: Contract and Supplier Management.

This is an area that has not received the attention that it deserves and is also covered fully later in this book. If all of the elements discussed so far are to be taken into account to ensure effective delivery of service s to the public sector, then sound relationships must continue between the parties and stakeholders. If not, VFM will not be maintained and the users will not gain the services that they expected, plus taxpayer's money will not be continued to be spent efficiently.

A recent (December, 2008), report from the National Audit Office (NAO) on 'Central Government's management of service contracts' noted:

Case Study: NAO Report on Central Government's management of service contracts

In 2007-08 central government spent over £12 billion on service contracts primarily in the areas of information and communications technology, facilities management and organisation process outsourcing.

As well as providing routine support services, service contractors also deliver high profile, organisation-critical services, such as the IT system supporting the payment of social security benefits, the provision of security at court buildings, and the production and delivery of passports.

Service contractors also regularly handle large amounts of personal and security information.

The organisations surveyed estimated that they spent on average the equivalent of two percent of annual contract expenditure on managing their service contracts.

Applying this average indicates that central government spent an estimated £240 million in 2007-08 on managing service contracts. The delivery of public services, protection against service failure and achievement of Value for Money are all dependent on effective contract management.

The consequences of service failure can be serious and we have reported previously on the difficulties the Rural Payments Agency and its contractors experienced in implementing the IT systems for administering the single payment scheme for farmers.

The more recent delays in the marking of SATS tests have further highlighted the important role contractor's play and the impact service failure can have.

At the same time, this report identifies examples of good practice contract management, such as the Department for Work and Pensions' contract with BT to provide telecommunications services where there was good senior management engagement with the supplier. There has also been some effective joint working between government organisations and suppliers to improve services and reduce costs.

Key findings of the report (which focused upon contracts for information and communications technology, facilities management and organisation processing outsourcing) included central government organisations that:

- Are not always giving contract management the priority it deserves.
- Do not always allocate appropriate skills and resources to the management of their service contracts.
- Have weaknesses in key performance indicators and have limited use of financial incentives to drive supplier performance.

- Did not have in place some or all elements of good practice risk management processes.
- Have variable testing of the Value for Money on ongoing services and contract changes.

It also noted that in general both central government organisations and their suppliers, that whilst positive about working relationships, fewer than half of organisations had actually implemented a supplier relationship management programme, despite what appear to be clear benefits.

The NAO's conclusion was that whilst there were examples of good practice, central government's management of service contracts is not consistently delivering Value for Money as *"Nearly all the organisations we surveyed thought that Value for Money could be improved through better contract management, in terms of more or better services, and/or lower costs."*

It was also estimated that better contract management could potentially generate efficiency savings of up to £300 million a year through reduced contract expenditure and this figure being based only on the limited number of organisations surveyed.

It further indicated that as well as financial savings, better contract management could bring improvements in the quantity and/or quality of services, the avoidance of service failure, and better management of risk.

Part 4: Summary
- A timeline was utilised to illustrate how the procurement situation has changed.
- We have provided a general overview because:
  - the public sector often seeks to adopt or adapt commercial best practice to the environment in which it operates:
  - there are specific, contextual settings for the public sector and this chapter does not have the space to deal with each of these differing contexts
- We nevertheless, provided a number of case studies and examples from differing public sector based organisations in order to give a flavour of the approaches that can be taken.

- This was followed by insights into policy and then an overview of pertinent processes; including context/scope, complexity and challenges, with processes to be followed and with a strong legal rigour.
- In respect of environmental and sustainable issues, the public sector, with procurement professionals is to the fore.
- Issues to be recognised, include probity and the role of stakeholders.
- An overview of how all these can come together in a coherent manner to meet the challenges was given in the example of the 'ROAD' approach.
- Ultimately, success in procurement of services for the public sector will depend upon professionally trained, educated and experienced professionals and examples were provided on this critical aspect.

5: Services Contexts

We have covered the principles involved when outsourcing. We now look at some specific service activities and operations that are commonly outsourced and will examine for example:

- Why organisations specifically choose to outsource such services.
- Details of the service supplier market.
- Procurement specifics when selecting service providers.
- Additional skills and other aspects for managing such service suppliers.

Readers may also find it useful to review each of the specific service examples we look at, so that they can gain ideas and review best practices from the different service contexts.

Managing 3PL (Third Party Logistics) Contractors

Here we look specifically at the outsourcing and subsequent management of the logistics (transport/warehousing) contractors, or to give them a more correct alternative name, Third Party Logistics (3PL) Service Providers (3PLSP).

Defining 3PL

Typical logistics services considered for outsourcing to a third party include the following:

- Warehousing (facilities, MHE, racking, labour).
- Transport (inbound/outbound).
- Freight Consolidation/Distribution/Cross-Docking.
- Product Labelling/Packaging.
- Product Returns and Repairs.
- Stock reporting.

When any one of these services is transferred from in-house service to a separate logistics provider via an agreement for a specified period of time, outsourcing has occurred and a logistics contract with a third party is established.

Checklist: 10 Questions before outsourcing logistics operations

1. Is logistics a non-core activity? (Management control must however remain a core activity, as should, customer contact).

2. Can we release some capital? (Third party industries have reported low ROCE ratios, typically 10 percent).

3. Will we retain some operations in-house? (Maybe it will be useful to do this for cost comparisons and service benchmarking).

4. Will we retain Management expertise? (Yes, very important, never sub-contract control).

5. What increased monitoring will be needed? (Should be the same as currently done, but especially watch customer service standards).

6. What are the risks of committing to one contractor? (Flexibility in the contract maybe possible, alternatively, multi-sourcing is the answer).

7. Will flexibility be increased? (It should be flexible as, in theory, the 3PL operator can maybe divert non-specialised resources elsewhere, and after all, transport and warehousing is their core business).

8. Will costs be reduced as service is increased? (This is the ideal).

9. How will we account for future changes? (The same as without the contractor presumably however it is the contract term and 'get outs' that is the issue here).

10. Are there any The Transfer of Undertakings (Protection of Employment) Regulations (TUPE) legislation implications? (Probably not if fewer than 5 people, if some control of, for example, routing is retained and if relocated. Probably will, if assets and or the whole business are transferred, however legal advice will be needed).

Source: Emmett (2005) Logistics Freight Transport, updated as Emmett (2009) Excellence in Freight Transport

Why people outsource Logistics

Checklist: Reported reasons for using 3PLs

- Customer satisfaction.
- Financial benefit.
- Speed, focus, and fire power.

- Complex requirements with required flexibility.
- Insufficient internal competence.
- Need for unbiased expertise.
- Capitalize on efficiencies.
- Economic environment.
- Economies of scale.
- Planned/known/reduced costs.
- Logistics is non-core.
- ROCE as capital is released.
- Asset utilisation improves.
- Marginal size of operations.
- Flexibility in 'spreading' peaks/troughs in delivery times and in future changes.
- Use of better ICT.
- Geographic specificities.
- Management constraint.
- Globalization.

Source after: Schneider Electric Eye for Transport 4th European 3PL Summit, Brussels October 2006

The 3PL Market

There are literally hundreds of 3PLs and it is not possible to contact them all. Selection can be made from knowledge of who your competitors use or from trade sources, maybe using the following trade associations:

- Road Haulage Association (www.rha.uk.net/business/directory).
- United Kingdom Warehouse Association (www.ukwa.org.uk, and then click on finding logistics services).
- British International Freight Association (www.bifa.org, and then click on member directory).

Initial information gathering and informal meetings with logistics providers can be a good way to identify those 3PLs that have the promise of being a good match for you. Ask them, for example:

- What other customers have needs that are similar to ours?
- What is your experience with handling the unique and critical requirements of your organisation?
- What share of your customers is approximately similar to our organisation?
- How many of your other customers use the same combination of ICT, warehouse management and transportation systems that we have?
- What do you see as the keys to logistics success for organisations like us?

This involves being willing to share, openly, information about your situation and objectives. To effectively come up with a short-to-medium-size list of candidates requires asking some clear and direct questions early on. This will guard against having discussion sessions with 3PLs that focus too much on high level 3PL corporate capability presentations such as "we are global, so here is a map that shows how global we are." Whilst such Power Point presentations may be useful, they can sometimes have more of a marketing/selling focus rather than one of factual telling, for example, of the scale and size of such operations, people, equipments, owned facilities etc.

Meanwhile as a guide, 3PL industry performance can show the following:

Checklist: European Logistics Service Providers End User Survey

Survey of 700 senior managers in hi-tech, automotive, consumer goods, pharmaceutical and retail sectors in UK, Benelux, France, Germany, Italy, Spain.

- 3PLs have a weak performance in:
    - Price.
    - Tailored solutions.
    - Reliability (the most important requirement).
    - Customer service.

- 3PLs would lose business if:
    - Inferior Value for Money.
    - Lack of reliability.
    - Inferior service quality.

- Satisfied with 3PLs on:
    - Expertise.

- Size.
- Geographical coverage.

- 3PL "not a problem" areas are:
  - Lack of geographical coverage.
  - Specific industry knowledge.
  - Limited service range.

Source: SHD May 2004: Datamonitor "European Logistics Provider End User Survey"

Procurement considerations

This involves preparing a quality contract by considering the individual tasks required to be undertaken in the competitive tendering process and to the point of contract award.

The competitive tendering process includes the following standard procurement tasks, which must be planned and considered against the organisation's own needs and requirements:

1. Draft and agree the specification.
2. Plan contract strategy.
3. Agree evaluation criteria.
4. Enquire and research the marketplace.
5. Communicate with potential contractors.
6. Possibly use a pre-qualification document to select tenderers.
7. Request tenders and evaluate tenders.
8. Tender negotiations.
9. Recommend tender for award.
10. Award contract.
11. Debrief unsuccessful tenderers.

There is much to be done in the pre-contract award management. Doing this correctly means that the winning contractor has been already involved and is already perhaps seen as being a part of the organisation. This is very important for the subsequent 3PL management.

Regrettably the formal adherence to rigid tender procedure policies can present a major barrier for some organisations to do this. Thus, it is perhaps no surprise that the subsequent award and contract does not run smoothly.

Those organisations that find they are unable to share early with potential suppliers must also *"embark on a scheme of attitude and culture change, so that everyone with supplier contact, not just those in purchasing, understands the main implications of their behaviour and how their actions affect the way their suppliers respond and behave towards them."* *(Source: Supply Management 15 June 2000. Will Parsons)*

The methods used in 1 to 5 above (draft and agree the specification, plan contract strategy, agree evaluation criteria, research the marketplace and communicate with potential contractors), are amplified below, using, in part, the improvements model as follows:

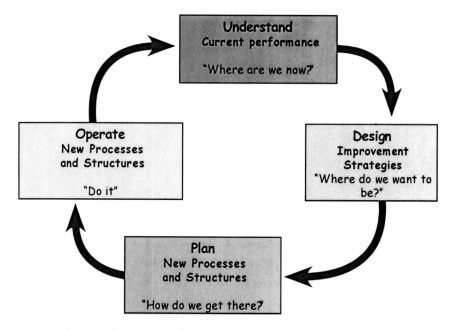

Source: Emmett (2008) Excellence in Supply Chain Management

1) Document and map product flows and requirements (where are we now?)
This includes the following:
- product characteristics.
- handling and packaging requirements.
- origin and destination points for today as well as future forecasts and sourcing changes.

- interplant flows of product.
- aggregate volumes today and over the next several years.
- manufacturing and distribution facility capacities and constraints.
- delivery cycle times.
- special customer or channel requirements.
- seasonality.
- procedures for returns, spares and service parts.
- hours of operation and related factors.

This process has significant benefit by itself, even if no outsourcing ever results, as it can be the first time such a comprehensive picture has been put together. The answers provide for both an ongoing internal use and to also brief potential 3PL candidates in conjunction with the steps below.

2) Know current levels costs and performance (where are we now?). At some time there is a need to document the impacts of outsourcing logistics, for example:
- Have costs actually gone down?
- Is performance equivalent to or better, than what you had before?
- Are we getting our money's worth?

The only way to answer such questions is to have available the current baseline of cost and performance to enable the "before" in the "before-and-after" comparison.

Many organisations do not actually have a good view on their own cost and performance levels. For a shipment routing, it's not just the truck rate per mile/KM or the rate per 1000 kilos/CBM; what is affecting the performance are many factors, for example, how much product was on the truck, how often was it delayed when loading /unloading, how frequently damage occurs, how fast the order was processed, how frequently backorders were involved, how much internal staff time was involved in fulfilling the customer requirements, etc.

3PLs also want and need this information so that they can evaluate what benefits they are expected to provide and what goals they're expected to hit, as well as to what extent they will share in gains or losses as part of any performance-based contract.

3) Develop the scope and objectives (where do we want to be). It is critical to take the time to specify what is in scope and what is not and why. Does, for example, transport management include all modes or just some; does it cover domestic or also international movements? Organisations need to clarify what they are trying to achieve through outsourcing, for example:

- Is it a reduction in costs?
- An improvement in service?
- A reduction in error rates?
- Shorter lead times?
- Use of more advanced IT systems to plan and optimise operations?
- On-the-ground expertise in new markets?

Different objectives point to not only needing to have different directions in evaluating and selecting the logistics provider, but also to initially arrive at the clear and agreed SORs/specifications. A healthy debate on this subject is therefore beneficial.

What is needed here is to avoid a situation where potential 3PLs say something like *"Thanks, but no thanks. You don't really know what you want, so we can't respond to you and won't participate in your selection process."* It takes time and effort and cost to respond to requests so this is not an unusual situation. After all the 3PL view here is *"if they do not know what they want, how can I give them something?"*

Having clear objectives from the beginning also makes it much easier to evaluate the 3PL success later on. The following shows some of the wide ranging evaluation criteria choices.

Checklist: Criteria used to select a 3PL

- Market Intelligence.
- Supply market and industry knowledge.
- Market share the 3PL holds.
- Background checks on the 3PL finance, equipment, facilities etc.
- RFQ Analysis.
- Quality of the solution.
- Customer focus.
- Operations involvement vs. Sales pitch.
- Ability to answer to terms and conditions.
- Ability to optimize operations.
- Clarity and measurability of the deliverables.

- Certifications (sustainable development, security, quality, ethics, environment).
- ICT capabilities.
- 3PL team background.
- Proven track record.
- Ability to become a key supplier or be a challenger.
- Global reach.
- Financial viability.
- People.
- Personal fit.
- Willingness to engage in a long term relationship.

Source after: Schneider Electric Eye for Transport 4th European 3PL Summit, Brussels October 2006

4) Build the right project team (how do we get there?). Logistics outsourcing of transport/warehousing can "knock on" and affect a wide range of activities such as manufacturing, purchasing, sales, customer service, finance, marketing, inventory, stock levels as well as the people involved in all of these. As already mentioned, it is therefore important, from the beginning, to involve each of these areas/departments. This is to establish requirements and objectives which will also help in the later selection and assessment of the "best fit" 3PL.

To get the benefits of outsourcing, all of these activities/stakeholders have to go along with the results of the selection process, so it is best to involve them early, rather than announce an outcome that may then be resisted and thus doomed to failure. There are two simple steps to use here:

Firstly, appoint a dedicated project manager who "owns" the project and has clear responsibility for the identification and selection process and directing the activities of the team.

Secondly, have clear and visible top management commitment to set the tone, make resources available and break through the inevitable delays and blockages that occur. Not only do these factors help the project proceed more smoothly, they will improve the attention and responsiveness from 3PLs as they have a "one stop shop" as they can detect whether there is commitment and discipline to engage and work with them. They will then react accordingly.

Meanwhile **strategic issues** to be considered by top management involve considering, after the decision to contract to a 3PL contractor, then what for example:

- Will be our ability to change to another contractor or take back the operation in-house?
- Are the internal implications?
- Are the risks involved?
- Will be our customer reactions (customer contact must remain a core activity and should not be subcontracted)
- Will it assist in any internal change/new strategies/expansion?

Checklist: "Extra" skills needed when managing 3PLs

- Analysis.
- Change management.
- Contract management.
- Back-up plans.
- Risk management.
- Relationship handling.
- 3PL Industry knowledge.

Source after: Schneider Electric Eye for Transport 4th European 3PL Summit, Brussels October 2006

How to buy Consultancy services

Spending on consultancy services is one of the fastest growing categories. Most organisations have struggled to procure consultancy services effectively. The category is broad and complex, including services from IT and strategy to HR, Marketing and outsourced services, and many organisations have not managed consultancy as a category until recently.

Purchasing professionals have often been excluded from the decision making process in the procurement of consultancy, and therefore the tools and process that are needed to track spends, have been limited.

Why use consultants?

According to a "Supply Management" poll, 57 percent of purchasers questioned believe consultants offer Value for Money. For example, *"consultants have skills, for example, in systems implementation works, that we will never have"*. They were also seen a bringing experience in managing strategic relationships, in addition, consultants can help *"gain quick wins on the board"*. To recruit staff as part of any transformation, involves time and *"with consultants, you get pace, agility and you can move quickly."*

Case study: Mobile network, O2

O2 has used consultants and outsourced procurement providers for a number of years for a range of projects and category areas. O2 Head of category management says *"Consultants bring a skill set in terms of benchmarking against what they have done with other organisations. This third party perspective lends some credibility to the recommendations they make."*

Too few clients properly consider their reasons for employing consultants, which is why they don't always get what they bargained for. "Do you want to achieve a transformation in the skill set of people, or is your real emphasis on driving cash savings into the business?" Once goals have been identified, it is then up to the client to ensure they have been met.

Case study: Purchasing Consultancy Certeza

Purchasing Consultancy Certeza, says it can help to sit down with one or two organisations of consultants when putting the brief together.

"Make it clear to them that they aren't necessarily going to win the work and don't give too much away, but do get their views on what you need to do, what sort of course of action may be open and what might be required in terms of consultancy input. Then start to develop a brief from there."

To manage the engagement, they suggest regular reviews and feedback sessions.

Management Consultants may be employed by a client for a number of reasons, over varying timescales, and in different ways. These may include:

- To provide a strategic overview of the position of the organisation in its marketplace or environment, and thence to recommend mid to long term strategic directions.
- To provide an independent review of a proposed alternative benchmarked again other organisations.
- To catalyse change by recommending alterations to management processes and organisation i.e. Business Process Re-Engineering (BPR).
- To strengthen a team.
- To achieve the implementation of a new system or process.

The Supplier's Market

Two key bodies provide best practice advice in the process of acquiring consultancy services are as follows:

1) Institute of Management Consultancy (IMC), now the Institute of Business Consulting (IBC) affiliated to the Chartered Management Institute (CMI). Members sign up to working professionally, complying with their code of practice and ethical standards.

2) Management Consultancies Association (MCA). Membership is open to organisations of consultants established in the UK, "of good reputation and capable of sustaining a high quality service", and practising management consultancy as a core activity over a least two of the defined key fields. Members must generally have been practising in the UK for at least five years, employ at least 15 full time consultants, with at least three seniors having a minimum of ten years consulting experience each. Additional rules, e.g. 25 percent of staff to have been with the organisation at least five years. 90 percent to hold degree or equivalent qualification demonstrate experience and stability and member organisations' qualification are verified annually.

The Institute of Management Consultancy (IMC), now the Institute of Business Consulting (IBC) working with a group of organisations which regularly buy significant amounts of consultancy support, has developed a range of behavioural requirements for successful consultancy projects. The following are recommended practices:

The consultancy should:
- Always bid with the team that will deliver.
- Have full knowledge of and understand the business of the client.

- Thoroughly understand the client's requirements.
- Ensure that the required expenditure has been understood by the client.
- Make sure that both client and consultancy have clear expectations about roles, responsibilities, costs and benefits before the assignment starts.
- Assist the client with economies of scale.

The client should:
- Define clear rules of engagement to govern the procurement process and communicate these to all parties.
- Ensure the consultants know about internal political barriers.
- Have a mechanism for allowing key influencers to engage with consultants during the procurement process.
- Identify and make available internal resource required to deliver the assignment successfully.
- Be clear and explicit about the need for the work and desired outcome.
- Have clear benefits and smart objectives.
- Consider a variety of resourcing and remuneration options to obtain best value.
- Be clear with the consultant about the true state of knowledge and understanding of the problem.
- Be open to alternative ways of looking at the problem and be prepared to change views.

Procurement's role

As mentioned above, procurement is often excluded when appointing consultants, however, innovative organisations are increasingly putting systems and processes in place including tight management of suppliers, rates and projects. This is to ensure they get Value for Money and control of their consultancy expenditure.

Putting agreed rates and terms in place is the first step; next, projects must also be tightly scoped and managed. This ensures that the best suppliers are considered for each project. The supplier must then complete a detailed scope of work document, which gets approved by both the customers departments and purchasing.

Many large organisations are implementing similar system programmes, all with four similar components:

1. Detailed supplier databases of rates, terms, past projects and capabilities. Buyers can search for approved suppliers, then compare and view capabilities, past internal ratings and past projects.

2. Benchmarked day rates and activity rates.

3. Internal processes to monitor all projects. Purchasing and the business buyers can view all current projects and see which ones are over budget.

4. Sign off and control of the scope of the work. Finance can sign off from a budget perspective, purchasing from a Value for Money perspective and the business from a scope perspective.

Risk Sharing

Nowadays partnership agreements are normally associated with the sharing of risk and reward. A contingent deal, where the consultant is paid according to savings or other tangible goals, is another way of ensuring targets are achieved.

Case Study: Accenture

Supply chain practice at Accenture comment that signing over 100 percent of fees against a financial target can lead to misaligned goals and short term behaviour. "Often the part about knowledge transfer goes out of the window because we are more focused on doing what we have been asked to, which is save money".

It is also hard to measure the success of knowledge transfer. *"You could link it to what the client's staff used the knowledge and training to achieve. However, that is very tenuous and if clients achieved great things with the training that the consultant provided, I am not sure they would want to share those savings because the consultants may not have been actively involved in implementing it."*

Clients can measure the success of knowledge transfer by looking at demonstrable improvement in the competence of their people and measuring that in terms of their ability to facilitate it in others.

Consultants should be used for specific projects and to a brief. Once they have delivered they should hand over that knowledge and move on.

The reality is often that the clients have the knowledge and ideas within the business. The problem is putting them into practice.

Consultants can be excellent at implementation in terms of providing the right resources in a timely manner, which are not often immediately available to the organisation in-house.

In addition, however, the authors are very familiar with the scenario in which a consultant comes up with a strategy but as the specification did not require implementation by their services, then the idea/strategy is either not executed, or poorly implemented.

Selection

If a consultant is required, the next issue is choosing the right one for the job. It is the quality of the people that is the greatest differentiator between organisations and therefore it is recommended to meet the team beforehand.

Spending time interviewing will give a real sense of how good they are. Consultancies will often be reluctant to let you meet real people until you have signed the deal, but you should demand this, even if you accept the people that you are meeting may not be exactly the same team.

Acquisition of consulting services

Purchasing and managing professional services in general, and management consulting services in particular, represent a complex task with high stakes both financially, given the often high prices of these services, and strategically, as consultants are generally hired in critical situations where the consequences of failure may be substantial. Purchasing management consulting, however, as mentioned earlier, has, and continues to take place, often without the involvement of purchasing professionals.

Managers generally believe they are experts in and need to be personally involved in the purchasing of consulting services where personal relationships between managers and consultants do play a central role. Recent studies also indicate that purchasing professionals may have a contribution to make in the purchasing of professional services.

Challenges

There are many specific challenges when it comes to management consulting services, which are said to be unique in terms of service characteristics, knowledge base and purchasing situation. The following are but a few examples of this:

- The first step in a rational procurement process, need definition, is complicated by the fact that client managers are often unable to properly define their problem and thus their detailed needs.
- When it comes to the search for alternative suppliers, this is made difficult by the intangible nature of the service and the difficulties of gaining information about alternative suppliers. Once managers have established a relationship with a consultant, the main tendency is to reuse this consultant.
- When it comes to evaluating alternative suppliers, most studies indicate the importance of "soft" judgemental variables that make the systematic and objective comparison difficult.
- Stressing the personal traits of the consultant-client relationship, for example, the buyer is less interested in the service itself and more in the individual service provided by the consultant. Personal contact, reputation and experience are central selection criteria. However, clients are more likely to stress factors such as their own or others' previous personal experience with a particular consultant or consultancy than more formal factors such as the consultants' proposal or price.
- The main challenge in the contracting phase is the definition of the task to be carried out. Many professional service agreements are executed without clear specifications Therefore in practice, contracting is generally rather informal and emergent, with the trust based psychological contract being far more important than the legal contract.
- With respect to execution, this emphasises the client manager's control in order to ensure that the agreed upon service is delivered at the agreed upon price. However, the co-production of results in management consulting requires close, trustful and ongoing interaction between consultant and client to ensure the results of the consultant's work.
- Finally, when it comes to evaluation, the effects of the consultant's work are hard to identify, as they may appear with a time lag. Identifying the specific contribution of the consultant may also be difficult, as effects are produced in interaction with client managers and their staff. Managers' subjective impressions of the consultant's work and their relationship with consultants consequently emerge as central and formal evaluations of consulting projects are rare.

The above discussion indicates that the management consulting services have traditionally been purchased in a rather different, less formalised manner. Rather than being controlled by rational procedures, administrative control and objective evaluations, the procurement of consultants seems to have been governed by the interpersonal, trust based relation between consultant and client.

We observe, therefore, a gap between what are generally regarded as rational and effective purchasing procedures, and the actual users emotional and subjective purchasing of management consultants.

The role of the procurement professional

The above review indicates a dominance of a relationship-orientated approach to purchasing, which gives the end user, i.e. the high level manager, a strong role and leaves little room for the involvement of procurement professionals.

It has, however, been argued that these informal practices may have a number of negative consequences, including:

- uncertain/mis-estimation of consulting demands.
- unsystematic selection of consultants.
- the reinterpretation of aim and scope to suit the consultant's business.
- assignment of inexperienced consultants in consulting projects.
- no utilisation of synergy potentials.
- no verification of consulting fees.
- no evaluation of consulting projects.

Consequently, arguments for more formal and systematic purchasing processes mediated by purchasing professionals have been proposed. Early involvement of purchasing professionals may push managers towards more concise formulation of assignment goals as well as specification of the kind of consultants needed to reach these goals. This promises a more efficient and well considered use of consultants.

Purchasing professionals may also assist client managers in identifying suppliers with a suitable competence profile, ensuring that the best available competence is used in solving the manager's problem.

Soliciting several proposals, systematically evaluating those proposals and comparing them to internal alternatives also both helps client managers gain new ideas and puts pressure on suppliers, leading to more favourable commercial deals.

There are four categories of strategies for organisations to manage suppliers of professional services:

- Relational (buying a bundle of services from the same supplier over time).
- Fractional (linking transactions with similar services over time).
- Serial (linking different services and changing suppliers for these over time).
- Transactional (no links between different services or over time).

The suitability of these strategies depends on the organisations need for outside services, the existence of internal alternatives, management capabilities and the nature of trust required by the service.

Procurement professionals may also implement increased control of billing, costs, and the performance of consultants, thereby reducing the risk of overbilling. They may also prevent undesired scope redefinition by the consultants, and help to hold them accountable for the results of their assignments.

Procurement professional's legal expertise may also help in underpinning assignments with necessary and commercially stable contracts. Throughout an assignment, purchasing professionals may act as neutral mediators in the case of conflict between client managers and consultants.

Procurement professionals should market their services to managers and demonstrate their value to them in order to build trust and a reputation of ability and benevolence. The level of involvement can be described as evolutionary, passing the levels of:

- Transactional orientation (focusing on the clerical tasks).
- Commercial orientation (requesting and comparing different tenders, negotiating).
- Coordination of purchasing (gaining control over and coordinating demand, managing the supply base).
- Internal integration (cross functional involvement, supplier development).
- External integration (focus on the entire supply chain).

- Value chain integration (working with the supply chain from the end customer's perspective).

The procurement process for management consultancy

The procurement of consultancy should follow the normal procurement cycle:

1. Preparation and project definition.
2. Identification of potential bidders, pre-qualification and either a formal invitation to ender, or negotiation with selected prospects and receipt of bids.
3. Tender assessment and contract award.
4. Project award and contract terms and conditions.
5. Subsequently there will be project review at regular intervals of the project management process.
6. Post-project review.

The project bid

A project brief (i.e. the specification) against which the consultants will tender, or the negotiations conducted, should be prepared. The brief should include:

- A background to the organisation and the project.
- The objectives of the project.
- Expected products and deliverables ; this is a statement of the required result.
- Project timetable; this should include any critical path dates relevant resources available within the client organisation.
- Reporting arrangements.
- Any limitations or constraints on the consultant.
- Procedures or practices that must be complied with.
- Any conditions on the use of sub-contractors.
- The form of contract and method of payment to be used; a fixed fee may be appropriate, especially for a well defined and short term task or incentive based.

Pre-qualification and tender

The client organisation will wish to pre-qualify, formally or informally, a shortlist of, probably between three and six organisations who will then be invited to respond to the formal ITT or to negotiate in a less structured manner as appropriate.

Criteria for short listing

The qualities to look for in drawing up the shortlist of consultants will include:

- Specific expertise.
- Evidence that they work to professional standards and ethical guidelines (for example, Membership of the IMC/IBA).
- Evidence that they are competent management consultants (for example, they have the Certificate in Management Consultancy (CMC)).
- Breadth and depth of resources adequate for the task; this includes not only consultants, but back office and support systems, and of course some evidence of financial stability and backing.
- Evidence that the organisation has experience, as well as expertise relevant to your situation, that they have operated successfully in organisations of similar size or complexity or industrial sector, with similar constraints. In some cases where overseas operations are involved, evidence of knowledge of the relevant countries should be sought.
- A complementary culture.

If an ITT is issued it must, as with any ITT, contain all the information that the bidder requires to make the bid. A private sector client will in fairness ensure that the results of any points of clarification are circulated to other bidders. The ITT should include an indication of the way in which bids are to be assessed, e.g. lowest cost, or on some more sophisticated assessment of value.

The latter may include, besides cost estimates, any of the following:

- Understanding and experience of the issues.
- Clarity of approach.
- Relevance of the proposed methodology.
- Commitment and enthusiasm.
- Evidence of innovation and creativity and realism.
- Calibre of the proposed team.
- Ability to meet proposed deadlines.

Elements against which each proposal will be judged include:

- The approach the consultant intends to take.

- The identity of the team.
- Qualifications and experience of the team (s) to be employed.
- The detailed work plan and timetable.
- The costs and fees.

Project award

Following the award of the contract, undue delay should be avoided. The team they have proposed (and which the client is expecting) will have put up on the assumption of particular start and finish dates. Excessive delay in appointing the consultancy may means that some of these individuals are no longer available.

Terms and conditions

Organisations that regularly employ consultants may develop a standard for of contract for this purpose.

Professional institutes have standard terms and conditions to which organisations may wish to refer when drawing up the contract.

Project management

Successful management of a consultancy project requires effort by staff at many levels in the organisation. This needs to be managed, to ensure that the consultants receive the help and the information they need promptly, while preventing undue disruption to normal business. All employees need to be made aware of what is expectation from then, what they are expected to provide to the consultants on demand. Other points are:

- The progress of the consultancy should be formally reviewed at appropriate intervals.
- The purpose of a review meeting is to review progress against the project brief and identify any areas where work is either falling behind or moving off track. In some contracts this will be linked to the release of staged payments.
- A review meeting also provides an opportunity to consider and, if appropriate, approve variations in the project specification.

Review

At the end of the project, reviews should be held to discuss the way forward, to ensure that the client understands the recommendations. Furthermore, post-project reviews can provide evidence of:

- Value for Money.
- Best practice/lessons learnt for the next project.
- Possible follow up projects.

Checklist: Risk reducing strategies for the Procurement of Consultants

- Prepare a detailed brief for the consultants.
- Using the consultants who are known to have done work in the subject area of interest.
- Ensuring constant communication between the client and consultant.
- Setting an upper financial limit for the project.
- Asking the consultant to prepare a detailed work plan for the job.
- Ensuring regular meetings of a steering group which would oversee the project.
- Asking to see similar pieces of work done by the consultants.
- Refusing to pay before submission of a fully satisfactory report.
- Using a consultant with whom you have worked before.
- Obtaining interim reports, if the project can be subdivided.
- Ensuring a reasonable commitment from a senior partner within the organisation.
- Specifying exact limits and costs of data provision by the consultant.
- Asking the consultants to deliver an oral presentation before choosing.
- Including a termination clause in the contract.
- Choosing a consultant to whom you can relate on a personal level.
- Asking for a specific consultant you know within a organisation.
- Choosing the consultant with the greatest knowledge of your areas.
- Producing a check list and score consultants on various factors.

Conclusions and implications

Management consulting services are among the most difficult for purchasing professionals to get involved in. In spite of the high financial and strategic value of management consulting services, they have traditionally been outside of purchasing involvement, even in organisations where other professional services have been under the control of purchasing professionals for many years.

The authors challenge the assumption in much of the literature, as well as among managers and consultants, that management–consultancy services have certain characteristics (e.g. difficulty in defining the task, assessing qualifications and evaluating outcomes) that make them difficult to deal with according to standard procurement procedures.

The difficulties, for example, of defining or evaluating the consulting service, are not inherent in the service but rather a consequence of the knowledge distribution between consultant and manager.

The better the managers' understanding of the services, the better their ability to handle them according to procedures and the greater the possibility for procurement involvement.

The current trend towards procurement involvement in management consulting services may thus be understood as a result of the maturing of the service, making it better understood by managers and procurement.

This "demystification" of consulting services, however, is not only a prerequisite but also a consequence of increased involvement of procurement professionals. In all cases of purchasing involvement, an important aspect of the buying process is the initial definition of the task to be performance and the required qualifications of consultants, as a basis for an RFP, a formal contract or an evaluation of alternative supplier.

An increased involvement of purchasing professionals is facilitated by a better understanding, among managers, and purchasing, of management consulting and its opportunities and limitations. In organisations where managers perceived their knowledge to be on par with the consultants' knowledge, the inclination to involve purchasing was higher than in organisations where managers perceived a strong knowledge deficit.

The above also implies that the involvement of procurement professionals may become less problematic as managers' general experience and knowledge about consultants continues to grow.

One important factor behind the challenges of involving procurement in the purchase of management consulting services is the difficulty of defining and evaluating the services, and the fact that their users were top management, who have a reputation of resisting purchasing procedures in this area.

Services that are difficult to specify and evaluate and used by top managers or strong specialist functions (e.g. advertising services, legal advice and financial advice) may show similar patterns to consultancy services.

An increased focus on formal criteria, for example, for the choice of consultants, may shift the focus towards measurable variables such as price and time, while more intangible aspects, such as the consultants' cultural fit, the manager's trust in the consultant or reputation, become downplayed. In regard to consulting services that are well understood and fairly standardised, such a shift may increase service quality and price/performance ratio.

Procurement of marketing services

Procurement's role in buying Marketing services

Best in class organisations report "significantly more involvement" of their procurement of all marketing areas, according to research from the Aberdeen Group

They categorised best in class organisations on savings across marketing spend, and showed that:

- 67 percent used competitive bidding for marketing.
- 64 percent have established standard policies on procurement for marketing services.
- 50% have aggregated spend on marketing materials.
- 57 % have a procurement expert focussed on the marketing category.
- 45% said spend on creative and marketing services, where procurement is rarely involved, had large opportunities for savings.

The report recommends that procurement departments engage with marketing during the budgeting phase to understand opportunities.

All sides need more clarity if relationships between buyers, marketers and marketing agencies are to be successful. One of the key problems is a lack of clarity of brief and of context for procurement. Marketing therefore needs to clarify the "confusing world" before procurement can really do their job properly.

The basic point here is that you have to make sure you have clarity about what you want. If you are unclear about what you want from the external marketplace then you will eventually fail and any relationships will also fail.

A related importance here is about role clarity. Marketing's role is to say, "That is what I want and I believe this the best thing for our business". Procurement's role has to be to understand why Marketing thinks that and then to go through a transparent procurement process which will add value and help Marketing understand some of the weaknesses in the submission and proposal.

There is no shortage of unproductive spend therefore offering both scope for measurable results and sustained cost improvement. For example, most procurement teams have no reliable understanding of current costs and processes in the often opaque area of advertising production fulfilment (the process after the creative side is complete), whether for the traditional media of TV, press and outdoor, or the growing category of digital/online.

It is now relatively straightforward to access reliable external cost benchmarks for all these activities against which a persuasive business case for change can be built. The typical outcome of such an approach shows potential savings averaging 25 – 40 percent.

There is still plenty of scope, however, for further centralisation not only of marketing print (point of sale materials including display stands near tills, etc.) but also by integrating across broader categories of print related activity including adaption or artwork, proofing and even storage and distribution.

Other areas of marketing spend, including marketing premiums (giveaways and promotional items) and merchandising equipment (whether for in store display or to support events and exhibitions). These can also be consolidated to create savings.

The Supplier's Market and Charges

Procurement will often find considerable upsides by exploring agency bonus schemes and performance-related remuneration. Achieving a well balanced relationship can result in these elements totalling upwards of 25 percent of the agency remuneration. Procurement is ideally placed to act as impartial negotiator and gatekeeper; as both the internal marketing team and the external agencies are hampered in such negotiations.

Whilst each has their own compelling vested interests, these are compounded by a lack of skill in creating transparent, fact-based incentive driven models. For marketers and their agencies, finding the next "big idea" is a constant preoccupation and in many ways, their reason for being. This single minded pursuit of the big picture may explain why inefficiency, opacity and casual third party relationships often exist within the marketing supply chain.

For purchasers the ability to segregate types of marketing spend and identify "non-productive" elements is crucial to achieving sustainable savings. They must therefore develop a detailed understanding of marketing processes within each major spend category. This understanding needs to be supported by analysis showing how the money flows through the supply chain.

It is only after the money flows have all been mapped and understood, that it is possible to benchmark key cost components, for example, most usefully against current market rates. When this benchmarking is complete it will be possible to both understand the issues and opportunities and then to assess a variety of strategic options.

On the one hand, a lack of understanding about the purpose and objectives of procurement means it is often kept at arm's length by marketers and their agencies. This is counter to the view that procurement must become more "engaged" and to "empathise" more with their marketing colleagues by attending meetings, visiting agencies and understanding the creative process. Sharing a common problem among procurement, marketing and agencies, such as "how to reduce spend by 4 percent without impacting activity, quality or response speeds", is far more likely to result in positive engagement.

It should be possible to be able to get an hourly rate for the creative agent suppliers account directors, right down to the cost of production assistants. Similarly the cost of a TV commercial can be broken down. An independent agency can be used to see (following a radio campaign) whether the message has become more noticed, reached more people (by knocking on the door or telephone) and if there is a say 50 percent increase in awareness of your message. If so, then the creative agency gets a bonus.

In addition, as agencies usually employ another agency that "buys the time "for an advert to be on radio or on TV, so you can ask for these rates to see if they are competitive or not. Another supplier to your supplier may have better buying time rates with another agency, this can help to decrease costs; at least procurement can at least see just how much of the cost is going to the buying time agency.

Best Practice Procurement of Marketing Services

Procurement's involvement in marketing has followed the path of many other service categories such as travel and HR; its progress has been slower but marketing is another one of those services in which procurement is increasingly having an influence.

The authors have found that there is often mistrust and scepticism about procurement's motives and agenda, and that this response is often reinforced as a result of inappropriate behaviour and/or misaligned objectives on the part of procurement.

In many instances, the typical performance objectives and targets for procurement (which tend to operate on a relatively short term time horizon), can cause conflict. The extreme example here is cost reduction targets versus, long term marketing objectives to build brand equity. Clearly it is essential to adopt a framework within which business needs can be objectively determined and used as the basis for developing a sourcing and contracting strategy.

To be effective, the sourcing methodology must involve the budget holder (marketing), procurement and other stakeholders. There will be a number of discrete phases to the methodology, including:

- Category profiling and needs definition; to understand the value and concentration of spend and past/future trends, market conditions, the sourcing history and, critically, business needs.
- Data gathering and analysis; to understand the impact and implications of cost and cost drivers, market structure, key players, market influence, technology trends and supplier selection criteria.
- Option generation and evaluation; to identify all options for sourcing, contracting and supplier management and then evaluate these against the defined business needs.
- Strategy implementation; to plan how to approach the market and the timing.
- Category/supplier governance; to plan how to ensure required performance levels are achieved and how changing business needs will be reflected in supplier performance.

Applying the above methodology and ensuring the customer is part of a category team will foster consensus and convergent thinking. In particular early and rigorous definition of business needs and associated agency capability will naturally develop a focus on a common agenda, but it is essential, following open challenge and debate, to understand the business needs clearly, for example:

- What we are buying.
- Why are we buying it.
- What its purpose is and what we want to achieve.

The answers to these questions will guide on sourcing and contracting options, supplier selection criteria and key performance indicators.

Another feature of procurement's involvement is the growing move towards more cost and performance based fee mechanisms, whereby the agency fees are linked to their costs and/or performance achieved against defined targets or outcomes, for example, the level of favourable media comment, brand awareness and cost per lead generated.

One area of concern remains with this shift towards payment by results. For such agreements to be effective, it is essential to achieve high levels of cost transparency. Interestingly, the survey mentioned above, suggested a 34 percent buyer satisfaction level with agency cost transparency, however this was virtually unchanged since 1997.

We suggest therefore, that this should be a prime area for the use of procurement's expertise; along with appropriate performance measurement and management.

Incorporating the above then a best practice approach is as follows:

1) Understand the need
- Understand the needs/priorities, learn the language and develop relationships.
- Identify marketing's "pain" and focus on it. For example, budget pressure, market pressure and agency performance.
- Define clear and appropriate objectives as a discussion document.

2) Assess existing relationships
- Assess agency performance against defined business needs.
- Develop joint key performance indicators.

- Secure agreement to a relationship management mechanism.
- Establish a two way review process.
- Identify and compare industry benchmarks and trends reflecting good practice and performance.

3) Category definition and expenditure analysis
- Budget analysis.
- Invoice sample analysis.
- Supplier provided data.
- Visit key agencies and ask them to define their scope and how it's delivered internally and externally.

Selection, negotiation and evaluation
Important parts of the buying process are agency selection, contract negotiation and the continuing evaluation of the agency's performance.

Agency selection involves two parallel assessments, creative and commercial. Short listed agencies that appear likely to have the appropriate skills and resources are asked to respond to an invitation to tender. It should include a detailed written brief.

This will outline the scope and purpose of the campaign, marketing messages and objectives, target audiences, timing and delivery, proposed methods for evaluating effectiveness and so on. The brief also needs to make clear whether the client is looking for a broad strategic proposal or a detailed creative "pitch"; bearing in mind that the latter is a costly and time consuming exercise.

When it comes to assessing an agency, a team combining marketing and procurement people should be involved. Clearly the marketers will take the lead in assessing creative and strategic issues, but procurement managers need a good enough understanding of these to be able to assess the commercial value of the proposals.

Creative issues cannot be rigidly commoditised to a tight specification, but production and delivery issues certainly can and here procurement can add significant value. Procurement's role also includes creating clear lines of accountability in a complex supply situation. When an agency is regularly employed on an account, a retainer may be suitable. A fixed fee may be paid for the delivery of a specific campaign. Alternatively, a percentage commission may be payable, based on their party and media costs, or a combination of these methods may be used.

A problematic issue is evaluation. In direct marketing, for example, and continuing or repetitive work in general, performance can be measured fairly rigorously, how many mail shots reach the agreed target market and the response rate, for example.

At the other end of the scale, the effectiveness of PR activity may be unquantifiable, except in a damage limitation crisis.

Overall, the message is that performance must be assessed where it can be, on cost control, response and delivery times, but there will generally be a large area of performance that can only be judged subjectively.

Checklist: Prerequisites for Success
- Choose the right agency: creativity and cost are important, but so is the ability to work with your marketing staff.
- Brief the agency well: tell it about the specific product or brand and the wider corporate strategy and culture.
- Work as a team: internally and with the agency and its key subcontractors.
- Go for a win-win deal: explore partnerships and methods of sharing risk and reward. The negotiations will affect the ability of the agency to attract and retain the staff you want on your account.
- Be proactive and creative: the agency doesn't have a monopoly on good ideas.
- Advertising and marketing are complex and fascinating supply chains and buyers can make a real difference.

"Get the confidence and trust of the marketing people; they may see buying as old school, but they need to recognise that purchasing has moved on. We can help marketing become better practitioners."
Source: Procurement Manager, major FMCG Organisation.

This quotation emphasises that Procurement has strengths that any business unit will welcome, including negotiation expertise, policy and compliance advice, project management experience, strategic sourcing/market knowledge, contract negotiation/ agreement, terms and conditions discussions and commercial relationship responsibility.

This in turn leads to better management information, clearer costs and improved campaign management performance.

Therefore, whilst Marketing and Advertising colleagues often perceive a threat of procurement involvement that will prolong negotiations and delay the reaching of contract agreements and therefore of service delivery; the opposite is in fact the case.

Mini Case Study: BA

Organisations such as BA have led the way in setting up specialised procurement teams to work with their marketing functions.

Their approach is that they are not buying a commodity but are paying for creativity, time and the desire of a client to work with this organisation. Obtaining the cheapest option will not produce the best value they cannot work hand in glove with a supplier.

Procurement's role is to facilitate this relationship by helping to identify critical suppliers and cementing partnerships

So why has marketing services remained outside procurement's remit for so long? Marketing people have tended to have a perception that what procurement does, is to buy things cheaper; yet, many will have no idea of the creative element of procurement's work.

The issue of cost versus value highlights one of the difficulties of exerting influence over marketing services: measuring effectiveness

Supplier relationships is another important area of potential added value procurement can bring.

Despite the increased pressure professional procurement can bring, suppliers generally welcome the benefits of improved processes, in terms of more definable specifications and performance targets, making disputes less likely. Suppliers want contracts which motivate them and incentivise them. They want to feel more involved in the business and have longer term relationships.

Checklist: "Pitch Guide"

The following is a "pitch guide" from the Incorporated Society of British Advertisers. It clearly demonstrates areas where procurement expertise will add value.

Where prospective agencies present to the client for a particular job this is in some ways similar to any other contracting process. However, there are important differences for procurement professionals.

- Prepare background information (outline brief, profile of type of agency required, research from trade press) and make informal approaches to agencies that match your criteria.
- Invite up to 3 agencies to pitch (4 if incumbent is included).
- Prepare a thorough brief, making clear all the judging criteria. It should be made clear whether strategic proposals alone are required or whether creative input is expected. Proposed remuneration and contract terms should also be outlined.
- Prepare an organisation timetable for responses. At least 4 weeks is suggested for work to a full creative pitch.
- Be prepared to share confidential data with agencies and allow their staff access to organisation people they would work with in the future.
- Establish an objective evaluation system for pitches. All decision makers should be fully briefed on the process and present at all pitches. Ensure that agency presentation teams include those who will actually work on the contract.

Procurement of Public Relations

What are Public Relations (PR)?
PR may include the following:
- Press releases and "advertorials".
- Features.
- Articles.
- Leaflets.
- In-house journals.

- Marketing literature.
- Financial presentations.
- Opinion polling.
- Sponsorships.
- Road shows.
- Videos/DVDs.
- Conferences.
- Exhibitions.
- Radio and television.
- Product launches.
- Lobbying.

To highlight the intangibleness of services and PR in particular, the following is the reality of what is being bought:

- Images and perceptions, therefore not necessarily reality.
- Improved corporate commercial positioning.
- Heightened public respectability.
- Damage limitation when needed.
- Potential influence with top decision makers.
- Access to powerful opinion forming groups.
- Mechanisms to best push your message.

Procurement specifics with PR

Let us look at a specific area here, the buying of in-house journals, leaflets and literature. Procurement is usually only needed in the external buying of such services when these are required to facilitate the production of in-house journals and general promotional literature.

When a buyer has to buy in directly the design and production of marketing literature and financial presentations, they should consider a range of key issues such as:

- Ability of PR outsourcers to successfully project up key business issues.
- Succinctness of presentation as demonstrated in existing work.
- Use of graphics, illustrations, aides-memoirs, colour.
- Impact of the artwork and creative concepts.
- Quality of the documentation, handouts, and card inserts.

- Quality of paper used (fine art papers used for image projection?).
- Clarity of arguments and logical development of themes.
- Effective motivating conclusions in other briefs prepared.
- Environmentally friendly production of the presentation material.

All of these will enable the buyer to set some benchmarks in evaluating the forward direction and the worth of a PR consultancy for projecting their organisations business.

The Public Relations Consultants Association (PRCA) and the four key trade and consultative bodies for the advertising and marketing industries (the Direct Marketing Association, Institute of Practitioners in Advertising, the Marketing Communications Consultants Association, the Incorporated Society of British Advertisers and its procurement directors group Compaq) have jointly collaborated on guidelines that provide direction for clients selecting consultancies. To examine this publication, called *"The Guide"*, visit the PRCA website at www.prca.org.uk

How to buy Legal Services

Legal services is an area of spend that has historically been outside the remit of procurement in most organisations; however, it is an area in which value can be added and procurement is gaining increased involvement.

So, where do you begin with the procurement of legal services and what does it encompass? How do you know if you have got a good deal? When and how can you make best use of this knowledge?

Definitions

"Legal services" is the use of solicitors, barristers, legal trainers and any other legal professionals across a huge scope of activities. These range from an impromptu phone call for a few minutes of advice, to years of representation during court proceedings.

In 1989, the Green Paper *"Work and Organisation of the Legal Profession"* pointed out that *"a comprehensive definition of what is meant by legal services is very difficult to frame but, broadly speaking, legal services are concerned with the advice, assistance and representation required by a person in connection with his rights, duties and liabilities".*

Part 1 of the Access to Justice Act 1999 describes the scope of legal services as comprising:

- The provision of general information about the law and legal system and the availability of legal services.
- The provision of help by the giving of advice as to how the law applies in particular circumstances.
- The provision of help in preventing or setting or otherwise resolving disputes about legal rights and duties.
- The provision of help on enforcing decisions by which such disputes are resolved.
- The provision of help in relation to legal proceedings not relating to disputes.

The Supplier's market

Legal services can be restricted to lawyers (such as litigation, estates, probate), although many legal services may be provided by non-lawyers such as;

- Accountants.
- Arbitrators.
- Organisation secretaries.
- Insolvency practitioners.
- Legal executives.
- Conveyancers.
- Loss adjusters.
- Patent agents.
- Tax specialists.

The procurement of legal services starts with identifying a problem. The team will look at the problem in the light of:

- The risk it poses to the organisation.
- The similarity to previous problems.
- How far the 'ideal' solution differs from the realistically likely outcome, whether it is likely to be a "one off" or a recurring difficulty.

Checklist: Five Pieces of Legal Advice

1. Functional managers are not expected to be legal experts, but they should be required to keep abreast of changes in those parts of the law that affect their operations.
2. It is always cheaper to seek and take legal advice before a problem arises than it is to brief lawyers afterwards.
3. See the most appropriate advisers for a given issue. They will not necessarily be solicitors and barristers.
4. Always explore non-litigious methods of dispute resolution, such as arbitration.
5. Legal costs can be controlled by accurate briefing, focused negotiation and structured monitoring.

Advisors specialise, and one recommended for their success in employment law, may not be ideal for example, on health and safety.

Selection could depend on many factors from geographical proximity to current clients, but costs, quality and personal relationships will be paramount. Quality may be indicated by the Lexcel mark, a voluntary, independent scheme awarded by the Law Society.

Supplier's charges

Costs consists of several elements, typically an hourly expense rate covering salaries and overheads plus a mark-up, sometimes called "care and conduct" or "uplift" which is commonly around 50 percent, and representing the solicitor's commercial profit.

In some areas, such as property transactions, there may be a third ad valorem element, based on the value of the property being transferred. There is no set scale of charges for commercial matters, so there is plenty of scope for negotiations. There could be a fixed fee or straightforward non-contentious work, and/or fixed costs per interview, phone call and so on. In many civil cases, conditional or contingency fees are now allowable.

Mini-case study: BT

BT treat their external legal provider in the same way that they would any other service provider, by producing a proper written brief and understanding what they are trying to achieve. In that way they ensure that they will get Value for Money.

Lawyers are used to interpret and offer advice on complex legislation, provide guidance and counsel on legal precedent, draft contract terms and conditions, evaluate tenders and hand disputes.

While larger organisations tend to have an in-house legal team, most organisations still require external legal services from time to time and procurement's role in securing these has grown as it has in securing other services mentioned in this book.

Legal services procurement is all about engaging with and influencing your in-house legal team (if they indeed exist at all).

As with other service categories, the in-house legal team is likely to be concerned that the involvement of procurement will destroy long standing relationships with suppliers by focusing on cost at the expense of other elements.

One procurement department known to the authors commented: *"We started small, which allowed us to demonstrate that procurement supports, rather than detracts from overall quality."*

Case study: Abbey

Abbey buyers worked alongside colleagues in the legal department to develop a supply strategy, which reduced the number of providers from about 80 to a dozen, divided by legal service type.

Buyers also helped to set up supplier management processes to manage both internal demands for third party legal services. Abbey subsequently retendered part of the work using an online auction for the rate card and further supplier rationalisation. It says this strategy has improved service quality and made considerable cost reductions, *"We now have governance in place to ensure all parts of the business engage through our in-house legal team first to enable this team to either self deliver, remove or place the business within our approved supplier panel".*

Case study : AXA

"Buyers need to understand what services lawyers provide and at what costs," says Head of Client Management and Technical Procurement at AXA. They believe it is the mismatch of expectations on what can be provided, and at what costs, is the most common area for dispute once a service has been introduced.

It is vital; therefore, these aspects are plainly covered in a written agreement. *"A solicitor can draft a contract for services but unless the services and payment obligations are clear to all parties and would be clear to the courts, there is little value in having a contract."*

So what do buyers need to be aware of when approaching this category; the following will be of assistance:

Both suppliers and buyers in this area place a great emphasis on moving away from a traditional client relationship to more of a partnership arrangement. After not buying on cost alone, developing a partnership approach is the second most common piece of advice stressed to buyers of legal services; for example:.

"A partnership approach completely changes the conversation compared to an adviser client relationship. Talking about clients as 'partners' tests the approach of law organisations like nothing else. It helps close the divide that law organisations are focused on process and in-house counsel on results".

Good relationships will result in added value, for example, you are less likely to be charged for advice over lunch or a brief phone call. Another benefit is the increased likelihood of having immediate access to the person you need, when you need them, for example, the night before you close a deal.

Fees

Most invoices continue to be based on hourly rates. If clients are unsure about hourly rates, one option is to provide incentives for the legal organisation to complete work efficiently and effectively. Buyers should check they are not employing the services of a large organisation with a large price tag but receiving the services of a junior legal adviser. The organisation should state in their engagement letter who will be doing the work for you, and if they do not, or you find yourself dealing with someone else who is likely to be more junior, you can raise the point and demand to have it resolved.

While more than 85 percent of legal services are still billed on an hourly basis, alternative fee arrangements (flat fees, contingent fees, for example) are used by an increasing number of progressive legal departments.

There is usually the option to pay a fixed rate or flat fee for repetitive work that can be more easily commoditised. Caps can also be applied to ensure an invoice for a piece of work does not exceed a given amount. In some cases buyers can negotiate to pay for a service only if they achieve success. However, the legal sector is traditionally risk adverse, and is generally not keen to enter a risk share arrangement. Here again, a partnership approach can help buyers to achieve the aim of shared risk and shared reward. Many organisations are now rationalising the number of providers and set up framework agreements with the remaining handful of suppliers providing different services and varying levels of expertise.

So while buyers may be able to negotiate a set rate on standard contract work, for example, for more complicated propositions, such as mergers, it can pay off to spend more to assure a certain level of know how. It is essential to recognise when you need a specialised or routine service and pay accordingly.

Checklist: Dos and Don'ts

Do
- Build a strong relationship with in-house lawyers and engage them in the process.
- Consider forming a partnership with your supplier.
- Ensure you know which individuals will provide you with particular services.
- Ensure the contract has a service level agreement with meaningful and measurable key performance indicators (KPIs).

Don't
- Focus purely on suppliers' rates.
- Use the most expensive suppliers for routine work.
- Focus on cost alone with complicated situations.

The procurement process for legal services is no different from the typical process of need, specification, sourcing, selection, award, contract management and review.

Selecting the legal provider

The selection of a provider of legal services depends on many factors such as:

- Professional and technical skills.
- Partner accessibility.
- Range of services provided by the supplier.
- Geographic proximity to the supplier.
- Organisation's proposal and fee.
- Specialisation or type of service.
- Legal reputation.
- Industry specialisation.
- National standing.
- Word of mouth recommendations.
- Third party referral.
- International network.
- Current client list.
- Specific aspects to consider.

There are three factors to which purchasers of legal services need to pay particular attention to:

- Cost.
- Quality.
- Personal relationships.

Costs mean the amount of money charged in a solicitor's bill, including, where appropriate, fees, VAT and disbursements. The general principle is that a solicitor's costs shall be a sum as is fair and reasonable to both the solicitor and client, having regard to all the circumstances – "circumstances" relating to:

- Complexity of the matter in which it arises.
- The skill, specialised knowledge/responsibility required of/the time expended by the solicitor.
- The number and importance of the documents prepared.

- The place.
- The amount or value of any money or property involved.

Costs are defined as:
- The expense rate (i.e. the hourly rate).
- The mark up (i.e. profit, commonly around 50%).

Other methods of charging and alternatives to or variations on the hourly rate may include:
- Fixed fees; these can only apply to non contentious matters where the work is fairly routine and reasonably straightforward.
- Conditional fees; in contentious work the client agrees with the solicitor that, if the case is lost, the client is liable only for the opponent's costs and the solicitor's disbursements, but not fees. If the case is won, the client pays the solicitor's basic costs, disbursements and a success fee.

Quality, not price, should be the main consideration when buying legal services. There are of course, numerous definitions of quality:
- ISO 8402 defines quality as the totality of features and characteristics of a product that bears on the ability to satisfy stated or implied needs. In this definition, features and characteristics of a product implies the ability to identify what quality aspects can be measures or controlled, or constitute an Acceptable Quality Level or AQL;
- Ability to satisfy given needs, relates to the value of the product or service to the customer, including economic value as well as reliability and other features. Freeman has pointed out that quality in the context of legal means two things:
  - The degree to which the legal work conforms to an agreed and written specification of work
  - The degree to which the legal work satisfies identified client needs and expectations.

Freeman states that the first of the above criteria conformity to specification involves three things:
- The standard of work in the case must be legally correct.
- Legal knowledge, procedures, forms, precedents, time limits, expertise and the written work must be correct and conform to established practice.

- Clients know precisely what work will be done and have some input into discussing and agreeing the work stages and can be confident that the services provided will meet their requirements.

Two further points may be made regarding the quality aspect of legal services.

- Quality is defined by Crosby as *"conformity to requirements not goodness"*. This means that quality is based on exactly what the customer wants such as a service is a quality service only when it conforms to the client's requirements as jointly identified by the client and provider.
- Quality should also not be sacrificed to cheapness. The costs of non-conformance to standards include:
  - The time and expense of remedial work.
  - Trouble shooting of defect/failure analysis.
  - Client complaints.
  - Loss of client confidence and good will.
- That the service provider should be "right first time" is a basic quality requirement.

Personal Relationships; apart from the cost and quality, a third criterion in the selection process is that of "can we work together?" This implies:
- The client knows the person or persons who will actually provide the services.
- The client is confident in the ability of the designated person to provide services to the agreed specification.
- The client is satisfied that the providers will be approachable, easily contactable, courteous, and willing to give full consideration to the client's viewpoints and suggestions.

Good relationships depend to a large extent not only on the provider knowing the expectations of the client but the client knowing the expectations of the provider. These include:

- Clear instructions.
- Prompt provision of additional information, evidence of changes in requirements.
- Prompt settlement of bills.

Checklist: Best practice procurement management for legal services.

- An agreed strategy across the whole organisation buying legal services.
- Visibility of spend across the whole organisation.
- Strategic relationships with key suppliers, enabling joint working to deliver service improvements, innovation and greater efficiency.
- Established contract terms and conditions.
- Use of alternative fee structures such as
  - Fixed fees, most commonly used for routine, predictable legal work
  - Blended rates where a standard rate is charged regardless of the level of the lawyer
  - Volume discounts
  - Discounted rates in return for a performance bonus
- Reduced cycle times
- Reduced costs
- Improved communications and transactional capability through use of e-procurement

How to buy Business Travel

There are still many organisations not running a disciplined travel programme that has a travel policy to direct travellers towards preferred suppliers. This suggests that there is significant room for improvement in the procedures for the procurement of business travel.

Automation and other good practices can help target not only processing costs of travel but purchasing costs as well.

Research has shown that, in many organisations, the Travel and Entertainment (T & E) expenditure is the second or third largest item of 'controllable' expense.

If looking at the total cost of travel (100 percent), the cost of the Travel Management Organisation (TMC) is around 5 percent, the internal process costs (authorisation, booking, payment) is around 3%, which leaves 92 percent as the cost of the air tickets, the room charges etc. This is the area of maximum opportunity to save cost, whilst obtaining value.

It is therefore vitally important that organisations improve value from money spent on travel and a travel policy is the cornerstone on which good procurement can achieve that objective.

Travel and Procurement

British travel buyers were recently asked in the Air Plus International Travel Management Study to agree or disagree that procurement will increase its role in travel management. It is perhaps no great surprise that 68 percent agreed and a further 18 percent somewhat agreed.

More procurement departments are therefore assuming direct responsibility for managing travel spends.

Perhaps because of a desire for control and transparency, travel buyers are beginning to see their processes and systems integrate more closely with those of the finance department. In particular, both travel and finance have a stake in expense management, a process that is increasingly being automated.

Expense management systems are also being integrated with an online booking tool, the domain of the travel manager, and the expense data is flowing through to an enterprise resource planning (ERP) application.

Survey: The role of procurement in travel.

Do you expect the role of procurement in travel management to increase?
Worldwide, the results were:

Agree	53%
Somewhat agree	24%
Disagree	23%

In the UK, the results were:

Agree	68%
Somewhat agree	18%
Disagree	14%

A survey of more than 1000 decision makers from global organisations found that over two-thirds of respondents expected procurement's role in travel management to increase in the near future. Despite this prediction the study also established that only one in 11 organisations dealt with travel management purely as a services procurement issue.

So is procurement beginning to play a far more active role in driving compliance in a cost area that has traditionally lacked visibility? The following case study provides some answers, as according to Aberdeen Group this is definitely the case.

Case Study: Research by the Aberdeen Group

"Procurement is really now taking a hands-on approach to managing the relationship with suppliers to ensure that the costs are driven down and, crucially, that staff within the business are beginning to comply with organisation policy."

Compliance is still one of the most important issues facing most enterprises.

Easy access to data and reports was essential or important to achieve the Travel cost savings that the business demanded.

With this in mind, its small wonder that procurement is becoming increasingly essential is ensuring that data is captured and subsequently used to drive compliance and leverage the best deal possible from vendors.

"One of the major challenges facing many organisations in this area is a lack of compliance. And if you're monitoring the process it becomes increasingly difficult if data is coming from a wide range of areas."

Of those organisations deemed best in class, average compliance to corporate travel policies was 89 percent, with a further 85 percent adopting preferred travel management organisations (TMC) or online booking tools. These figures compare with an industry average of 70 percent compliance and 50-85 percent adoption rates. Those at the bottom of the pile recorded compliance rates of 55 percent and adoption rates of just 20-50 percent.

The study concluded that:

"Organisations are attaching increasing importance to travel and the need to control it. That is leading to growing centralization and consolidation, with procurement and finance taking the lead in applying more discipline to the buying and management of travel."

The survey indicated many organisations are adopting analytical tools to better manage travel spending, with more than 40% of respondents claiming they now used "special electronic tools to analyse their expenses".

The number of organisations that had eliminated paper backups had also doubled over the past 12 months, and nearly half of respondents now said that they received payment card invoicing electronically.

When looking towards future savings, respondents from high-spending organisations were looking for reductions from electronic invoicing, automated expense reporting and reclaimed VAT.

Case Study: Intel

Technology giant Intel has told its US travellers they are now permitted to book domestic flights directly through airlines booking websites, as well as via the organisation's chosen Travel Management Organisation or corporate booking tool.

The results showed than on average travellers booking independently paid approximately 30 percent more for hotels and 50 percent more for car hire, but 10 percent less for domestic flights.

Travellers will have to continue booking hotels and car hire through official channels because these proved so much cheaper.

Travel at SMEs (which is defined as organisations with 10 to 250 employees) goes unmanaged. Is generally the case that 48 percent do not set an accommodation budget and stick to it, while 53 percent cannot hazard even a rough guess at the size of their hotel charges.

A large number of SMEs are not therefore following best practice procurement when buying and booking overnight accommodation, meetings and events; a fact that is likely to be causing them to waste significant time and money. The numbers can still be significant, especially as this is a controllable cost.

Although there is a growing involvement at SME level by procurement professionals in buying travel (and although they are very professional), they rarely have specific travel procurement experience or of buying services of any category generally.

Procurement specifics when buying travel

There are two steps all travel buyers should take.

1) Hire a Travel Management Organisation (TMC).

Those organisations with travel budgets above £1.5 million will often pay their TMC a management fee, which bundles all the services into a single price. Below £1.5 million, more commonly it would be more beneficial to use a transaction fee instead.

2) Implement and communicate a travel policy.

What is clear is that smaller organisations have more options for bringing their travels expenditure under control then they originally realised.

When procurement professionals start tackling their travel costs, they naturally look first at air and hotel deals and other forms of direct expenditure. What tends to receive less attention, are the indirect process costs borne by a travel programme, items such as expense handling and trip planning and booking.

According to a report from American Express and AT Kearney, entitled European Expense Management, these indirect costs account for 4.6 percent of the average organisations total travel spend. This may be more than buyers realise, given that the figure does not include another indirect cost, the fees to travel management organisations. TMC fees are generally reckoned to eat up another 3 to 6 percent of travel bills.

Checklist: Indirect spend; Cost breakdown

Expense claims processing	=52%
Trip planning	=23%
Trip booking	=17%
IT costs	=5%
Cash advances	=2%
Central billing	=1%

The study claims organisations that introduce a comprehensive range of best practices can reduce their process costs to 2.1 percent. For a business spending £4 million per year on travel, that equates to a saving of £100,000.

More efficient processing leads to better visibility of costs and empowered decision making for travellers.

Common behaviour among Best Practice organisations

An Amex/AT Kearney study identifies the following six characteristics among organisations following best practice in indirect travel cost management.

1) Implement a clearly defined travel policy and enforcement processes that are communicated frequently.
2) Collaborate with suppliers and intermediaries (e.g. card providers, travel agents).
3) Invest in automation and have a high adoption rate of tools and system usage.
4) Centralise back office activities through a shared service centre and/or outsource non-core activities to a third party, achieving economies of scale and access to specialised skills.
5) Focus on user satisfaction as well as on cost reduction.
6) Leverage management information to refine and improve processes, optimise spend visibility and use for supplier negotiation.

The Travel Supplier's Market

Checklist: TMCs - the major multinational players

- Carlson Wagonlit Travel; claims to have overtaken American Express as the world's largest TMC. Ownership or joint ventures in 35 countries and partnership in 114 additional countries. Sales volume in 2007, $25.5 billion.
- American Express; presence in 140 countries (ownership undisclosed). Sales volume in 2007, $20.5 billion.
- BCD Travel; presence in more than 90 countries, with whole/majority ownership in 2007.
- HRG; ownership in 25 countries and partnerships in a further 81 countries. More than 200 clients are served in more than one country.
- Egencia (formerly Expedia Corporate Travel); Ownership in 15 countries.

Claims to be the fifth largest TMC in the world. 2000 clients in the US and 1000 clients in Europe.

- Global TMC networks of independent TMCs include: Radius, Global Star, and International Travel Partners.

Case Study: Philips

Until recently, Philips had worldwide umbrella agreements with three TMCs. Each national Philips business had historically been allowed to pick any of the trio to handle its travel. That changed when the organisation decided to appoint American Express as its sole TMC worldwide.

Philips made the decision after concluding that multiple TMC relationships meant more work but less control. *"It was very difficult to manage,"* commented the organisation's travel manager for Europe, the Middle East and Africa. *"Each TMC had different processes and ways of working, which was very time consuming".*

Phillips found it hard to standardise crucial tasks, such as collecting management information. *"Phillips defined a standard, but it was only after 18 months of challenges that we achieved a satisfactory level in the majority of markets and a less satisfactory level in smaller markets where they didn't want to make the effort."*

When the three year umbrella agreements ended, Philips examined numerous options, including retaining the same structure, but concluded a single TMC was most suitable for its business needs. The reasons cited included tighter control, optimum data consolidation, improved internal efficiency, consistency, an improved financial offer and strategic alignment between client and the TMC.

Phillips understands but rejects the criticism that a single TMC cannot be the best in every market. *"I agree they cannot be the best, but strong regional players will have weaknesses in some parts of that market too. We didn't find enough differentiation to make it worth going for the regional option."*

Successful travel management

Travel buyers should communicate what they do and why they do it. "I am seeing a misconnect between the people who procure travel and their travellers," commented one of the many contacts made by the authors when writing this book. "They don't always communicate their contracts to the end users."

Failure to communicate can easily result in the failure of the programme. An additional complication is that the content and mode of the messages that need to be communicated to different stakeholders vary enormously.

It is recommended that buyers create a travel user group involving as many stakeholders as possible. These might include senior travellers, bookers, representatives from procurement, human resources and security departments and ideally a board member.

The user groups is ideal for two way communication, both to explain the principles of the travel programme and in providing feedback on what is and what is not working.

Travellers

Principal messages to be given to travellers include explaining the policy rules, especially the need to use preferred suppliers and booking channels, to save money and keep them safe. It is also vital to clear up traveller's common perception that they will find better deals when booking independently. For instance, the following are true:

- Travellers are usually unaware of all the discounts the organisation is obtaining.
- The conditions attached to their own bookings, constrain their flexibility.
- They may be wasting hours of their valuable time trying to save a few pounds.

Budget holders

A stakeholder for whom the primary means of communication is data. This has become easier in recent years because management information systems are now flexible enough to show budget holders real time data of travel spend by employees who report to them.

Case Study: Estee Lauder

"Take time to plan," says the Director of travel services for Estee Lauder, who recently persuaded the board to back investment in building a strategic meetings

and events management programme. *"Your presentation should be simple and straightforward, and be prepared to show you are smart when asked to substantiate your claims"*.

Suppliers

Hold quarterly review meetings and be prepared to reveal factors that could make your organisation's travel programme either contract or expand over the coming months. If you can show why changing business needs mean you will fail to meet volume commitments, it could save the deal. "Make sure there are no surprises."

Case Study: Air Conditioning Engineering Organisation Trane

"Communication is the most important part of my job, both to vendors and to stakeholders in 40 countries. It is nice to have a good contract, but if no one knows about it, it won't be successful. We carry out regular surveys asking travellers what they think of the programme. The results are an important tool for communicating with vendors and help with negotiations".

Source: A Global Travel & Meeting Services Director.

Case Study: Cost Reduction

A multinational organisation has told employees it intends to reduce its travel budget by almost 20 percent in one year through reducing trip numbers by 10 percent and average trip costs by 10 percent.

It has laid out a five point plan to achieve this goal. Steps one and two are to insist all flights are booked through the organisations travel management organisation (TMC) and online booking tool, the latter to be used for all simple point to point (there and back) trips. Using the TMC ensures greater use of preferred airlines, while the booking tool provides additional savings through lower TMC transaction fees and a greater likelihood of accepting the lowest available fare.

The third step is telling travellers they must book flights more than two weeks in advance unless they have a good reason for doing otherwise. The fourth is ordering them to use preferred hotels, unless there are exceptional circumstances. Finally, travellers need to obtain pre-approval for a trip from a senior manager; a trend that evidence suggests is growing.

Travel procurement is now more organisationally in the spotlight of senior management.

Monitoring policy

The travel buyer should be responsible for monitoring their organisations travel policy, but all the statistics should come from suppliers, such as Travel Management Organisations (TMCs), charge cards and airlines.

Quarterly reviews, allied to regular exception reporting (on non compliance) should be sufficient.

Management information provides several functions:

- It provides material for future negotiation and existing deal reconciliation, i.e. demand management.
- It shows compliance levels to policy.

Hotel Accommodation

Accommodation is now often the largest slice of expenditure for trips within Europe. *"Air travel is a fraction of what it was. Air is probably only 25 percent of the whole trip cost, while the hotel can be as much as 70 percent,"* says travel training organisation Talking Travel.

Case Study: General Electric (GE)

General Electric (GE) reckons its European travellers spend 2 Euros on accommodation for every 3 Euros they spend on air.

Case Study: BCD Travel

BCD Travel's consultancy wing, Advito, says air typically accounts for 45 to 50 percent of travel spend and hotels for 17 to 20 percent.

So if one accepts as a working hypothesis that hotel costs often exceed air costs on overnight short haul trips, it may be time to reconsider the travel programme to reflect the shifting priorities.

Late bookings

The most obvious change would be to encourage travellers to book their hotels before their flight. Now that hotels have yield management systems similar to those deployed by airlines, the price differential between popular and less popular nights is growing.

Travellers could think more about the normally used UK peak nights of Monday and Thursday and use those either side of the peak nights, but it does need some planning. A different solution proposed by another, is for organisations to create standard air and hotel packages for the destinations they visit most frequently.

Case Study: General Electric and tackling high hotel rates

The biggest challenge in hotel procurement continues to be excessive demand pushing up rates in key business cities such as London, New York and Moscow. General Electric travel manager acknowledges that the supplier has the upper hand in such cases, but has devised a two headed strategy to redress the balance.

1) Set a rate cap

Tell hotels there is a maximum rate you are prepared to pay in a city. "It is amazing how many hotels come in at 50 pence below your cap because they don't want to fall off your programme."

2) Revise your hotel selection

GE has negotiated rates with 36 different hotels in London, and has removed a couple of properties from the top of the price range and added a couple at the bottom. "We have taken one or two hotels out of Mayfair and replaced them with some in Gloucester Road."

Hotel spend policies

Figures from BCD show that typical compliance with air policy is 70 to 80 percent, while with hotels policy it is 60 to 70 percent. Only 12 percent of organisations mandate hotel policy.

Organisations with a heavy hotel spend should employ a hotel booking agency. *"You can't commoditise hotels in the same way as airlines, you have to accept standard and location come into it as well as price."*

Buying accommodation looks set to remain a semi-unconquerable process that will continue to frustrate purchasers even if it does account for a rising proportion of their total cost of travel.

Case Study: Airbus

Airbus has invested heavily in an extensive reporting programme aimed at controlling and reducing its £150 million travel budget.

In use since spring 2007, the reporting is divided into two sets of KPIs. One is described as a set of "bottom-up" KPIs for the organisation's travel managers, aimed at reducing the unit cost of travel.

The other is a set of "top-down" budget tracking KPIs for senior management, intended to reduce the number of trips made by employees.

The KPI programme was conceived by Airbus in 2005 as one of three strategic priorities to cut its travel bill. The other two were the introduction of an online booking tool and adoption of a consistent expense reporting tool across the business.

The full list of bottom-up KPIs chosen by Airbus is shown below:

1. Number of trips.
2. Percentage of trips booked online; some organisations prefer to make this calculation as a percentage of bookings capable of being made online.
3. Percentage of trips within Europe booked online; Airbus policy mandates that all point to point (there and back) trips within Europe are booked online.
4. Percentage of trips compliant with policy.
5. Percentage of 'best buy' purchases; did the traveller choose the cheapest available fare within the business rules of policy? For example, passengers are expected to select the cheapest fare within 90 minutes of their chosen departure time for short haul travel and four hours for long haul travel.

6. Percentage of bookings made by the traveller; Airbus encourages travellers to make their own arrangements instead of their secretaries. This is to minimise duplication of effort and because travellers are more prepared than their assistants to choose low cost alternatives.

7. Average number of days travel is booked in advance of departure; generally the earlier a flight is booked, the cheaper. The Airbus benchmark is 14 days.

8. Average booked cost per trip.

9. Average booked cost per trip to Europe.

10. Average missed savings online.

11. Average missed savings – off line; Measure the efficiency of bookings via the online tool versus those made by the TMC.

12. Average number of modifications and cancellations per trip; making changes attracts a TMC transaction fee and the price of the re-booked ticket is often higher than the one it is replacing.

13. Percentage of trips booked with pre-trip approval.

14. Average fare booked online versus average fare booked online; Measures the return on investment in our online booking tool.

These KPIs all relate to the various factors likely to affect the cost of a trip. In addition to the average cost per journey, other relevant variables include whether the trip is booked offline (i.e. by telephone) or online.

Airbus: Best Practice

Ensure you understand your business requirements, especially the datasets required by your internal stakeholders, and make these the basis of your KPIs. Set the expectations of stakeholders. Once the information starts flowing, some assume the data bank can provide any figures they like.

Make all parties involved in-sourcing data aware of the importance of accuracy. One error in booking or cost centre code can create severe problems further down the chain, but travel agents and others do not always understand these consequences.

Ensure the person responsible for managing the data system also has some responsibility for analysing it.

Allow time. It took Airbus two years to get its KPI project fully up and running.

Siemens: Case Study

Siemens, one of the world's largest buyers of travel, is urging the rest of the travel purchasing community to join it in establishing a universal KPI that calculates travel and entertainment costs as a percentage of increased revenue from new orders and sales. It believes this would enable organisations to understand if their investment in travel helps to boost revenue.

It already uses the KPI within its organisation but says if more organisations made the same calculations, it would help everyone to compare the efficiency of their travel programmes. It spends £1.35 billion per year on travel and has 280,000 travellers but claims its KPI is relevant to all businesses.

Case Study: Institute of Travel Management

Business travel impacts directly on personal experience and people take it personally. *"It's not like buying widgets,"* says Executive director of the Institute of Travel Management. *"It's all about getting people from A to B in way that they're reasonably happy with and that enables them to do their job effectively. You've got to take people's emotions into account and that is not a simple matter."*

People have their own preferences when it comes to airlines, hotels and cars and getting control over maverick spending is notoriously difficult in this area, especially with the arrival of online booking offering cheap deals. It's axiomatic that any attempt to bring travel spending under control should tackle this problem. But an element of flexibility should be built into an organisation's travel policy; so that people feel they have some control over their own experience.

"It's all about giving individuals a certain element of choice while working within a corporate policy. You don't want to mandate everything. People feel better about things if they have some choice over how they are going to travel. And there are local

differences to take into account. What works in Basildon will not necessarily work in Japan or the US. Sound purchasing principles still apply, but you can't be too rigid."

Travel is in itself a complicated business: there are multiple suppliers, dozens of airlines, ticketing deals, routes to choose from and so on. Juggling these to come up with the right solution for every business trip demands specialised knowledge.

Managing travel in-house is quite likely to be effective for smaller organisations with relatively simple travel requirements over regular routes. Online booking means anyone can reserve a flight, hotel or car at the touch of a button through a preferred supplier. There are more sophisticated systems available - aimed principally at smaller organisations - through which an entire travel policy can be managed.

For larger organisations, the services of a travel management organisation or TMC are likely to be required. Travel procurement can be handed over totally to the TMC so that the parent organisation takes no day-to-day responsibility for it. A TMC not only has specialist knowledge of the travel business but will also provide detailed management information on all the trips undertaken over a given period. Alternatively, in what is generally thought to be a preferable arrangement, an in-house manager, or team of managers, depending on the size of the organisation, can be appointed to look after the business relationship with the TMC.

Case Study: ICI

Manager of global procurement at ICI describes how the organisation moved from a situation where more than 100 travel agents were being used by people throughout the organisation to one where all bookings are made through a TMC. This, he says, has clear benefits to ICI in terms of savings and of ensuring organisation policy is followed. "If you have a travel policy that says you must go business class here and economy class there, you only need to say that once to your TMC. Previously we had more than 100 travel agents, so it was much more difficult to get those kinds of messages out."

Whether to outsource or not, he says, is as usual a question of core competence. *"Our core competence is not the travel industry so we don't have links into booking systems and so on. We regard that as a very specific area of expertise that we don't have in-house, so we prefer to outsource it.*

"The big question for many organisations is whether they can implement that kind of approach. Travel is a very emotive subject. Quite a few people may need to change from their existing travel agent to another one and that's not always an easy thing to do."

Case Study: Nottingham University

Purchasing adviser for business travel at Nottingham University is planning to reduce the number of preferred suppliers from three to one by the end of this year, from a total of six as recently as three years ago. *"The arguments for consolidating all travel procurement through a single supplier are unassailable,"* she says. *"We're here to make sure we get the best Value for Money both for the individual traveller and for the university. The best way to do that is through a single TMC."* Either way, it is crucial to ensure that the total cost of travel is being monitored carefully. It is estimated that fees paid to airlines and other providers usually amount to about five percent of total spending, while the cost of internal processes, the time it takes to deal with procurement of travel plus overheads, is likely to be about a further three percent.

This means that by far the biggest area of spend is on the products bought,- airline tickets, hotel bookings, car hire and incidental expenses, so this is the area offering the best opportunities for savings, or making sure maximum Value for Money is achieved. That could mean persuading people to use cheaper airlines and less luxurious hotels. Or it could mean negotiating with suppliers for upgrades, better quality cars or other benefits at no extra cost.

In an attempt to establish an effective travel policy, the first challenge, as in any procurement exercise, is to identify what spending is taking place and by whom. Fairly obviously, if you can't identify it, you can't manage it. Secondly, the policy must be clear and easily understood, and communicated effectively to all those who will be affected by it. Excellent communication in such a sensitive area is essential. Listen to feedback and address people's concerns.

Gaining the support of top management is crucial as there is very likely to be some resistance to change. Persuasion is, of course, by far the best route, but there may be some need to enforce the policy. Doing this without support from the top is likely to be ineffective.

The good news is that most people understand the need to control spending if it is put organisationally in the context of the business's objectives. Again, effective communication is the key.

Buying Facilities Management

Definitions
"The term has been coined to describe the management of buildings, infrastructure and support services."

"It is the co-ordination of buildings, work and people into an interactive system."

"The professional management of all physical resources which underpin the ability of organisations to do business."

But to complicate matters further, the boundaries of facilities management are notoriously fluid, ranging from the general (health and safety, cleaning, catering and security) to the highly specialised (property strategy and estate management, IT infrastructure).

The driving force behind the growth in FM as a discipline has been technological change, as much competition and this has focused attention on the physical resources used by organisations. For example:

- The rise of the "intelligent building".
- The increasingly complex office technology.
- The growing recognition that working environments have an effect on productivity and operating costs.
- Staff recruitment and retention.

Relatively few organisations are large enough to establish in-house functions with the skills to coordinate the kinds of activities in the box below, although some organisations, including Sainsbury's, have established large FM functions. Others outsource their FM to a consultancy which provides an on-site facilities manager.

The term facilities management has been used to define all kinds of support services outside the main core business. Traditionally it can include:

- Property strategy.
- Building services.
- Engineering maintenance.
- Project management.
- Space management.
- Cleaning and security.
- Catering.
- Office services.
- Budgets and cost control.
- IT voice and data.
- Fleet management.
- Graphics services and reprographics.

Procurement of facilities

Decisions must be made before even considering outsourcing: Consultant Arthur Andersen says *"Closely examine which support and maintenance services add the greatest value; what services can be dispensed with; what services can be outsourced to gain the best results and technology as well as reduce costs; how organisation property can provide flexibility during times of rapid change."*

Contracts have to be written in terms of the performance required by the end users, not in terms of the technology to be employed.

Arthur Andersen observes, *"In-house functions are monopolies…focused on maintaining their own dominance rather than fulfilling customer needs. An outsourcing advantage is its explicit introduction of market discipline."*

As organisations seek continual process improvement, they are increasingly recognising the important role support services play. Facilities management essentially means ensuring that buildings, equipment and services are used effectively to meet all business objectives.

The resources which can fall under the heading of facilities management can account for as much as 13 percent of total purchasing costs in commercial organisations. This requires particular skills in service procurement.

Case Study: Hewlett Packard

At information technology organisation Hewlett-Packard, the onus is on the facilities manager to show the optimum ratio of costs to service in a rapidly changing business.

Four levels of customer requirements need to be considered:
1. Shareholders.
2. Business managers.
3. Employees.
4. Customers.

All of these have different expectations. The organisation develops a number of key objectives for the year distilled from the perceptions of its customers, the direction of the business and the overall role of facilities. The different expectations of each group of customers have to be aligned with overall objectives through negotiation.

Value lies in the eyes of the customer, and a particular product or service will have varying value depending on individual user needs. Adopting a value management approach, measuring and showing the value added by effective FM, will help to focus attention on providing facilities at the best cost to an organisation, rather than pursuing the least cost and ignoring other benefits.

Facilities management is a cyclical process of planning, delivering and monitoring from service need to service result, measuring user response and satisfaction. The sourcing process is only one step towards customer satisfaction with the services delivered. The prerequisite to the sourcing process is a complete understanding of the ways in which facilities support the business operation and the reporting structures of the operation. Evidence that outsourcing is delivering better results, improved quality, lower life cycle costs and effective risk transfer is still as difficult as ever to validate.

Checklist: Outsourcing Facilities Management

- The key is to get the quality management right.
- During the compilation of the service level agreement both the client and outsourcing management contractor should study the detail of how the contractor will manage the individual services; cleaning, security, reception, and maintenance.
- They should also establish how the client will then manage and audit the outsourcing contract.
- The biggest single failure by clients is to continue to exercise the detailed management control they exercised before outsourcing was put in place.
- The client's role should be one of hands off auditing at intervals established as optimum at the start of the contract.
- Also established should be the deliverables; what standards are required of the various services and how they will be measured.
- The resources which can fall under the heading of premises and facilities management can account for 13 percent of total purchasing costs in commercial organisations.

Case Study: Facilities Management at National Power

Understanding client needs is not the only pre-requisite for building a successful facilities management relationship. The ramification and consequences of transferring in-house service provision to external organisations must be considered. An organisation can transfer the control of its internal services to whomever it sees fit, but the law ensures that changes are not detrimental to employees previously employed by the client organisation.

The Transfer of Undertakings (Protection of Employment) Regulations 1981, commonly known as TUPE, usually obliges FM organisations to take direct responsibility for the employment or redundancy of employees, involved in the transfer of service control.

Facilities management works best when FM organisations develop long term mutually beneficial contracts with their clients. As a result, FM solutions can be shaped to match the client's culture, thus creating a contrast to the old adversarial stance.

By identifying the needs of the client and forming working relationships to complement the client's core activities, an experienced facilities management contractor can achieve the dual goals of cost reduction and improving service standards.

Case Study: BBC Wales

BBC Wales outsourced Facilities Management and Broadcasting House, Cardiff, operates a total facilities management contract which provides for the management of all premises support services on site. Services include catering, security, PABX, reception, building and grounds maintenance, printing and office and window cleaning. The market testing exercise succeeded in achieving substantial savings on overhead costs.

Case Study: Shell UK

Close collaboration also avoids any procurement/FM conflict at Shell UK. Here the purchasing split is 75 percent services and 25 percent goods and materials. Shell's spokesperson explains, *"All the businesses in Shell, including FM, have their own procurement departments embedded in their organisation. So FM is procured by a professional procurement department inside the FM organisation, and the functional reporting line is to the group executive vice president for procurement. This structure allows procurement to operate day to day in co-operation with its business stakeholders while maintaining functional integrity across the group."*

Rather than buying on price, Shell says it buys on a total cost of ownership or a maximum Value for Money basis. Price plays a significant role but other factors such as security of supply, quality, experience, global spread are weighed in. If there are any differences of opinion between business stakeholders and procurement, these are resolved by the contract board, senior staff from business procurement and finance who judge the various aspects of a sourcing event.

Procurement of Catering Contracts

The Supplier's Market

As the name implies, these are organisations which specialise in providing catering at a client's premises in exchange for an agreed length of contract.

The UK contract catering industry is a typical oligopoly, that is to say, it is dominated by four organisations. The two largest organisations operate over 7,000 and 3,000 contracts nationwide, respectively. Whereas a medium sized contractor operates up to 300 contracts. The majority of contractors operate under 50 sites each.

The Buyer's View

Supply Managements (SM) survey on purchasing managers' opinions of catering contracts attracted a varied response from the manufacturing, service and retail sectors. All respondents agreed that purchasing professionals should be involved at all stages in the buying of catering services, from pre-qualification to monitoring of the contract once in place, but actual practice varied widely.

Although more than 80 percent of the sample was responsible for authorising activity up to and including the appointment of the contractor, less than half were involved in drawing up the specification and only a minority had responsibility for performance monitoring of the contract once in place.

In the majority of cases, therefore, purchasing is providing a contracting and negotiating service for other departments, who retain responsibility for the catering services. These are typically the personnel department (27 percent of replies), or a specialised office or estate services department (another 27 percent). In only one of the respondent organisations was the cost and responsibility for catering services allocated to the relevant production cost centres rather than being treated as a general overhead.

SM reported claims by consultancy Catering Price Index that catering buying clients were not fully benefiting from discounts negotiated by their contractors with suppliers. 36 percent of respondents claimed to be unaware of caterers' contractual agreements on discounts. Significantly, most of these cases seem to be in organisations where the purchasing department has "authorised" the contract, but has not been involved in the specification.

Only about half currently benchmarked catering contractors' prices against market prices. Many of these organisations also benchmark in other areas, such as stationery supplies (several respondents), small tools and consumables, security services, energy management services and building supplies. These maps closely to areas, other than catering services, where respondents stated they were unaware of discounting issues, although additions to the list here include cleaning, computer and IT equipment, telephone services and office furniture.

While it is dangerous to draw organisation conclusions from a small samples, it would appear that, in many organisations, the purchasing department's involvement in catering contracts (and presumably other business services), is little more than cosmetic. Here purchasing seems to merely append its signature to decisions that have been made (for better or for worse) by others.

Often the service specification is performed outside the purchasing department; specifications of course, largely pre-create the majority of the resultant contract.

Types of catering contracts

The catering services market poses some peculiar difficulties for the buyer, largely because it is, in effect, a complex oligopoly. A few large groups, each running several thousand contracts, dominate the market, although this is obscured by their use of multiple brand names.

Contract catering was one of the major outsourcing growth areas and successes in the last twenty years as now, most organisations do outsource catering (and cleaning and security). Accordingly, most procurement activity on catering today will be renewing or reviewing catering contracts, they are not starting afresh. Reviewing is therefore vital nowadays, because many contracts will offer less than the best value.

It is important to understand how the contractors make their profits, because not all the sources are obvious, and if affects the type of contract the buyer should look for. Traditionally, the industry operated on **'cost-plus' contracts**, the plus being a management fee, either as a fixed rate or as a percentage of turnover. This has a disadvantage of providing little or no incentive to improve efficiency.

With a percentage based fee, it can be argued that it is the suppliers' interest to inflate costs and the client accepts all the risk. Whilst, in theory, the buying client is able to examine and check the costs being charged, the reality is that few do this. Admittedly, the client still controls service levels and menu tariffs, but one reason for outsourcing is to be freed from that sort of micro management.

With cost-plus contracts; therefore, the client pays all the operating costs such as food, labour, and sundries plus, as the name suggests, a management fee to the contractor to supply and process these materials/skills. Any cash received is processed by the contractor and credited against the costs.

This is illustrated below.

- Cost of food
- Cost of labour
- Cost of sundry items
- Cost of fee
- Total cost

- Less sales of food
- Difference = subsidy

Some organisations will free issue the food to their staff. If this were the case in the illustration above, the subsidy would the total cost.

An alternative is a **fixed price contract**. At its most basic, the client and the contractor agree what the annual cost of catering should be, and it is up to the contractor to find ways of making a profit within this figure. The contractor bears the risk but also controls service and quality, which may suffer if profits become hard to find.

A fixed price contract is at the other end of the spectrum to a "cost plus" contract. Its most basic form is where an annual cost of catering is agreed between parties at the commencement of the contract. The client pays equal monthly instalments to the contractor for the term of the contract. It is then up to the contractor to provide the service and generate an element of profit within the total cost agreed; for example:

- Cost of food
- Cost of labour
- Cost of sundry items

- Total

- Less sales of food
- Difference = profit to contractor

The element of risk rests with the contractor and as such they may retain a high degree of control over the menu range, tariff, service levels and opening times after they have been awarded the contract.

Commonly, a **hybrid form of contract** is found. This is based on cost plus, but up to 50 percent of the management fee is at risk and is adjusted according to an agreed formula based on financial factors, such as labour costs and sales, and qualitative elements including menu range, service levels, health and safety standards, and, in some more adventurous contracts, the opinions of the people who actually eat in the canteen.

A management fee is the most common way for the contractor to earn income. Usually a sum is agreed annually between the client and contractor and charged on the monthly catering trading account.

Contractors can also earn revenue from supplier discounts. Catering contractors negotiate with suppliers to deliver goods to their contract sites. The price will be based on the cost of the goods to the supplier plus the cost of delivery, associated administration, and profit. In addition, there will be a mark up on this to cover "discounts" returned to the catering contractors. They are variously known as:

- Drop discounts.
- Volume related discounts.
- Royalties.
- Loyalty bonus.
- Overriding discounts.

However, as client organisations have become more aware of this practice, there has been a trend towards sharing some, if not all, of the income with clients or moving to "net into unit" purchasing. As the name suggests, net into unit purchasing is when produce is invoiced at catering site level at the lowest price, without any margin for return to the catering contractor.

The structure of the hybrid contract is based on the "cost plus" model. The earning potential of the contractor can increase or decrease based on their performance in both financial elements such as:

- Sales volumes.
- Gross profit margins.
- Labour and sundry costs.

And on qualitative elements such as:

- Menu range.
- Service levels.
- Staff appearance.
- Health and safety standards.

An agreed percentage of the base management fee is "put at risk". This is usually between 25% and 50%. Each of the elements listed above is weighted according to the importance attached to that element. Each is scored and the result is then reconciled, usually once a quarter, and the fee adjusted upwards or downwards accordingly.

Pre-qualification of catering suppliers

The difference between two contractors can begin to emerge by applying the following general questions to each of the contractors.

- How do the catering staffs manage a particular situation?
- What is the service delivery like?
- How can one distinguish between the quality of one service and another?
- Who provides better support and why?
- Which organisation is better Value for Money when the proposed costs for the service are different?
- Specifying the catering services.

It is recommended that the document be in the form of an output rather than an input specification. The reason for this is twofold, namely:

- It specifies each service required.

- It elicits bespoke responses from the contractors which identify how they would approach the contract.

Ultimately, this arrangement will help to differentiate between the contractors and facilitate a decision as to who should be awarded the contract. The detail for each service should include points such as:

- Name of service (e.g. lunch).
- Times required.
- Potential customer numbers.
- Menu range.
- Service standard required.
- Tariff policy (e.g. cost plus).

Evaluation could include:
- Food
  - Restaurants
  - Vending machines
- Labour
  - Number of hours
  - Costs
- Miscellaneous (e.g. laundry)
- Fee

Output specification

Price, though, is only one aspect of the contract. Contractors should be asked to tender against a specification based on outputs; what services are needed, when and where, for how many people. There may be several specifications, from vending machines to the directors' dining room.

The client has to debate the thorny question of subsidy. Contract catering's promise was that it could reduce the subsidy required to provide the service, or in some cases, eliminate it completely. "No subsidy", however, is a rather flexible term and it implies that the cost of food, labour, sundries and contractor fees is recovered from gross profit on sales.

Depending on the terms of the contract, it may include heating, light and water, contribution to rent and rates, the client's residual management costs and, particularly, the capital costs of new or upgraded facilities in kitchen and eating areas. The client must be clear in the specification what is meant by no subsidy or the level of subsidy on offer, or competing tenders may turn out to be based on quite different premises.

Comparing written tenders is not enough on its own. The buying team must visit one, preferably several, comparable sites run by each contractor, concentrating on the transferable elements; menu choice, food presentation, and customer service. They can ask about the contractor's management style and find out how many staff could use the facilities but choose not to, and whether this proportion has changed.

Checklist: 6 Steps to Managing Catering

1. Decide what level of subsidy, if any, you can tolerate.
2. Specify by outputs; tell potential contractors what sort of service you want and let them devise how to meet your needs.
3. Check supplier invoices; benchmark them against an independent source, and tell the contractor that this is what you will do. Even in a fixed price contract, you need to know this for next year's negotiation.
4. When visiting contractor operated sites, find out what users think of the service.
5. For a smaller contractor, ensure that the contract guarantees continuity in the event of the contractor being bought up.
6. Specialist consultancies can help; but make sure that they are truly independent.

Part 5: Summary

We have looked at some specific service activities and operations that are commonly outsourced and have examined for example:

- Why organisations specifically choose to outsource such services.
- Details of the service supplier market.
- Procurement specifics when selecting service providers.
- Additional skills and other aspects for managing such service suppliers.

Typical logistics services considered for outsourcing to a third party include the following:

- Warehousing (facilities, MHE, racking, labour).
- Transport (inbound/outbound).
- Freight Consolidation/Distribution/Cross-Docking.
- Product Labelling/Packaging.
- Product Returns and Repairs.
- Stock reporting.

When any one of these services is transferred from in-house service to a separate logistics provider via an agreement for a specified period of time, then outsourcing has occurred and a logistics contract with a third party is established. Key questions to ask before outsourcings were:

- Is logistics a non-core activity? (Management control must however remain a core activity, as should, customer contact).
- Can we release some capital? (Third party industries have reported low ROCE ratios, typically 10 percent).
- Will we retain some operations in-house? (Maybe it will be useful to do this for cost comparisons and service benchmarking).
- Will we retain Management expertise? (Yes, very important, never sub-contract control).
- What increased monitoring will be needed? (Should be the same as currently done, but especially watch customer service standards.
- What are the risks of committing to one contractor? (Flexibility in the contract maybe possible, alternatively, multi sourcing is the answer).
- Will flexibility be increased? (It should be flexible as in theory, the 3PL operator can maybe divert non-specialised resources elsewhere, and after all, transport and warehousing is their core business).
- Will costs be reduced, whilst service increased? (This is the ideal).
- How will we account for future changes? (The same as without the contractor presumably however it is the contract term and 'get outs' that is the issue here).
- Are there any The Transfer of Undertakings (Protection of Employment) Regulations (TUPE) legislation implications? (Probably will not be if fewer than 5 people, if retain some control of say routing and if relocated. Probably

will, if assets and or the whole business are transferred, however legal advice will be needed).

How to buy Consultancy services

Key points were that the consultancy should:

- Always bid with the team that will deliver.
- Have full knowledge of and understand the business of the client.
- Thoroughly understand the client's requirements.
- Ensure that the required expenditure has been understood by the client.
- Make sure that both client and consultancy have clear expectations about roles, responsibilities, costs and benefits before the assignment starts.
- Assist the client with economies of scale.

Meanwhile the client should:

- Define clear rules of engagement to govern the procurement process and communicate these to all parties.
- Ensure the consultants know about internal political barriers.
- Have a mechanism for allowing key influencers to engage with consultants during the procurement process.
- Identify and make available internal resource required to deliver the assignment successfully.
- Be clear and explicit about the need for the work and desired outcome.
- Have clear benefits and smart objectives.
- Consider a variety of resourcing and remuneration options to obtain best value.
- Be clear with the consultant about the true state of knowledge and understanding of the problem.
- Be open to alternative ways of looking at the problem and be prepared to change views.

Conclusions and implications

Management consulting services are among the most difficult for purchasing professionals to get involved in. In spite of the high financial and strategic value of management consulting services, they have traditionally been except from purchasing involvement, even in organisations where other professional services have been under the control of purchasing professionals for many years.

The authors challenge the assumption in much of the literature, as well as among managers and consultants, that management consultancy services have certain characteristics (e.g. difficulty in defining the task, assessing qualifications and evaluating outcomes) that make them difficult to deal with according to standard procurement procedures. The difficulties, for example, of defining or evaluating the consulting service, are not inherent in the service but rather a consequence of the knowledge distribution between consultant and manager.

The better the managers' understanding of the services, the better their ability to handle them according to procedures and the greater the possibility for procurement involvement.

The current trend towards procurement involvement in management consulting services may thus be understood as a result of the maturing of the service, making it better understood by managers and procurement.

This "demystification" of consulting services, however, is not only a prerequisite but also a consequence of increased involvement of procurement professionals. In all cases of purchasing involvement, an important aspect of the buying process is the initial definition of the task to be performance and the required qualifications of consultants, as a basis for an RFP, a formal contract or an evaluation of alternative supplier.

An increased involvement of purchasing professionals is facilitated by a better understanding, among managers, and purchasing, of management consulting and its opportunities and limitations. In organisations where managers perceived their knowledge to be on par with the consultants' knowledge, the inclination to involve purchasing was higher than in organisations where managers perceived a strong knowledge deficit.

The above also implies that the involvement of procurement professionals may become less problematic as managers' general experience and knowledge about consultants continues to grow.

One important factor behind the challenges of involving procurement in the purchase of management consulting services is the difficulty of defining and evaluating the services, and the fact that their users were top management, who have a reputation of resisting purchasing procedures in this area.

Services that are difficult to specify and evaluate and used by top managers or strong specialist functions (e.g. advertising services, legal advice and financial advice) may show similar patterns to consultancy services.

An increased focus on formal criteria, for example, for the choice of consultants, may shift the focus towards measurable variables such as price and time, while more intangible aspects, such as the consultants' cultural fit, the manager's trust in the consultant or reputation, become downplayed. In regard to consulting services that are well understood and fairly standardised, such a shift may increase service quality and price/performance ratio.

Procurement of marketing services

All sides need more clarity if relationships between buyers, marketers and marketing agencies are to be successful. One of the key problems is a lack of clarity of brief and of context for procurement. Marketing therefore needs to clarify the "confusing world" before procurement can really do their job properly.

The basic point here is that you have to make sure you have clarity about what you want. If you are unclear about what you want from the external marketplace then you will eventually fail and any relationships will also fail.

Key prerequisites for success were seen as:

- Choose the right agency: creativity and cost are important, but so is the ability to work with your marketing staff.
- Brief the agency well: tell it about the specific product or brand and the wider corporate strategy and culture.
- Work as a team: internally and with the agency and its key subcontractors.
- Go for a win-win deal: explore partnerships and methods of sharing risk and reward. The negotiations will affect the ability of the agency to attract and retain the staff you want on your account.
- Be proactive and creative: the agency doesn't have a monopoly on good ideas.
- Advertising and marketing are complex and fascinating supply chains and buyers can make a real difference.

We noted that Procurement has strengths that any business unit will welcome, including negotiation expertise, policy and compliance advice, project management experience, strategic sourcing/market knowledge, contract negotiation/agreement, terms and conditions discussions and commercial relationship responsibility. This in turn leads to better management information, clearer costs and improved campaign management performance.

How to buy Legal Services

Legal services is an area of spend that has historically been outside the remit of procurement in most organisations; however, it is an area in which value can be added and procurement is gaining increased involvement.

Key aspects identified were:

Do

- Build a strong relationship with in-house lawyers and engage them in the process.
- Consider forming a partnership with your supplier.
- Ensure you know which individuals will provide you with particular services.
- Ensure the contract has a service level agreement with meaningful and measurable key performance indicators (KPIs).

Don't

- Focus purely on supplier's rates.
- Use the most expensive suppliers for routine work.
- Focus on cost alone with complicated situations.

How to buy Business Travel

There are still many organisations not running a disciplined travel programme that has a travel policy to direct travellers towards preferred suppliers. This suggests that there is significant room for improvement in the procedures for the procurement of business travel.

Automation and other good practices can help target not only processing costs of travel but purchasing costs as well. Research has shown that, in many organisations, the Travel and Entertainment (T & E) expenditure is the second or third largest item of 'controllable' expense.

An Amex/AT Kearney study identifies the following six characteristics among organisations following best practice in indirect travel cost management.

1. Implement a clearly defined travel policy and enforcement processes that are communicated frequently.

2. Collaborate with suppliers and intermediaries (e.g. card providers, travel agents).

3. Invest in automation and have a high adoption rate of tools and system usage.

4. Centralise back office activities through a shared service centre and/or outsource non-core activities to a third party, achieving economies of scale and access to specialised skills.

5. Focus on user satisfaction as well as on cost reduction.

6. Leverage management information to refine and improve processes, optimise spend visibility and use for supplier negotiation.

Buying Facilities Management

Key aspects identified when outsourcing facilities management were:

- The key is to get the quality management right.
- During the compilation of the service level agreement both the client and outsourcing management contractor should study the detail of how the contractor will manage the individual services; cleaning, security, reception, and maintenance.
- They should also establish how the client will then manage and audit the outsourcing contract.
- The biggest single failure by clients is to continue to exercise the detailed management control they exercised before outsourcing was put in place.
- The client's role should be one of hands off auditing at intervals established as optimum at the start of the contract.
- Also established should be the deliverables; what standards are required of the various services and how they will be measured.
- The resources which can fall under the heading of premises and facilities management can account for 13 percent of total purchasing costs in commercial organisations.

6: Supplier Relationship Management

Introduction

As noted throughout the book, supplier relationship management (SRM) skills will need to be learnt, developed and will grow in importance, as organisations became more reliant on external and increasingly global deals. Additionally, in part 4 on public sector procurement, we commented in detail on the reported failure to comprehensively undertake post-award contract and supplier relationship management.

Definition

SRM can be defined as:

Supplier Relationship Management (SRM) is the management of the whole interface between supply and buying organisations through the whole life of the contract. The aim is to achieve maximum long term contribution from the supplier that works towards achieving the buying organisation's strategic goals.
(Source: Excellence in Supplier Management, Emmett and Crocker, 2009)

The key differentiator of SRM from conventional contract management is the focus on the whole interface with the supplier. This may cut across many contracts, and SRM therefore concentrates on the supplier contributing towards the buyer's long term strategic goals.

Benefits of SRM

Developments such as outsourcing and strategic partnering have increased the size and the importance of the contribution that suppliers can make. Upfront or pre-contracting activities are still very important but the initial signed contract is only one part of the whole. As a supplier's operation becomes more and more integral to the organisation, then all of the activities around the management of the contract and the management of the supplier become critical. It is also the positive supplier relationships that will produce any sustainable competitive advantage.

Indeed, the authors suggest that, for complex purchases, most of the value obtained from the supplier is actually driven by post-contract management, rather than from the upfront negotiated contractual terms.

Additionally, as procurement rationalises the supply base and reduces supplier numbers, then those suppliers who remain become more powerful. Therefore, if the relationships with these fewer, stronger suppliers are not managed properly, this may present a risk to the business.

As earlier pointed out, being the "customer of choice" is increasingly important, and the better the relations, the more likely they will be that customer of choice. This becomes particularly important if is a seller's market.

"You have to be attractive otherwise if there's a bigger partner, the supplier will go with them."

One of the most persuasive arguments for SRM comes from Henke (J. Henke, Oakland University) who believes that he and his team are on the edge of directly correlating strong supplier relations to a percentage difference in prices, so that if organisations go about SRM correctly, they can insist on more from their suppliers.

"If they do it the right way you can put more price cut and improvement demands on suppliers. If organisations can guarantee business and suppliers know you will support them when things go wrong, and work with them to improve things until you can't anymore, then suppliers will stick with you, not just switch allegiances."

An example of this is Phillips:

Case Study: Philips Electronics

The organisation has selected 30 strategic suppliers, a move which has reduced the time to market of some goods by 50 percent, i.e. twice as fast.

They had two suppliers of a particular product, one of which was running out of capacity so needed a third but they didn't really want to do because of intellectual property rights issues.

So they sat down with their two suppliers, each from different backgrounds and agreed to work together to improve productivity.

SRM can therefore lead to cheaper prices, give faster time to market, has more flexibility and brings in innovation.

Procurement to lead SRM

Many commentators see that it is actually up to the procurement department to determine the nature of the supplier relationship. The argument used here takes the view, that suppliers may not always decide what sort of relationship they will have with buyers/customers, and that suppliers will only be able to react to the way buyers/procurement behaves towards them. This point of view is also reinforced by our assertion that it is the buyer's demands that actually result in and create the type of supply chain.

After accepting the need to do this leading, then the "two coming together" are now able to blend better later in the relationship, learn from each other and synergise; consider the example of L'Oreal below:

Case Study: L'Oreal

L'Oreal procurement has been building long term relationships with suppliers for the past few years to support growth. Their approach is based on mutual respect, transparency and sharing information.

How are the existing relationships?

Once buyers have identified who to work with using SRM principles, then measuring the health of the existing relationship is the next stage. It will be necessary here to identify:

- Where the supplier relations are.
- Where you want the supplier relations to be.
- The status of your supplier relations, in absolute terms, across different sectors, sizes, countries.
- How your perception compares to that of your suppliers.

Starting out

The key components that drive SRM are trust, communication, whether you can help the supplier (e.g. to improve cost and quality), whether you hinder the supplier (e.g. by making late and excessive changes) and finally for a supplier, what opportunity they have to make a profit.

Checklist: Critical success factors for starting SRM

A management mandate to make sure your organisation wants to do SRM

- Build SRM approaches into sourcing methodologies by not only creating SRM manager roles but also by educating and training staff on SRM approaches.
- Supplier relationship managers need adequate skills and passion.
- Establish the required behavioural norms.
- Manage the stakeholders.
- Look for increased and incremental value over the duration of contracts and relationships.
- Build joint working forums focused on identifying and delivering joint improvement programmes.
- Incentivise and reward suppliers to deliver demonstrated value.
- Focus on total cost of ownership (TCO) and life cycle costs where any increased price can be evidenced and supported as a positive outcome as the TCO costs are reduced.
- Realise quick wins to motivate and work towards creating long term value.
- Establish mutual interest and relation targets.
- Performance needs to be measured, as only what is measured gets done. So have joint targets for the relationship that will, for example, increase productivity or mitigate risk.
- Don't wait for the right time to start; this will never happen, so just start.

At least once a year the major stakeholders of the two buying and selling organisations should meet. At these sessions they should seek to understand each other's intentions, priorities, exploit common ground and deal with any problems. They conclude by agreeing common goals and setting an action plan.

Checklist: Critical success factors to consider when managing SRM

- Remember you buy from individuals, not organisations.
- Be open and fast in your communication with suppliers, there's nothing worse than trying to hide bad news.

- Building trust takes time and effort.
- Try to maintain a "full reservoir of goodwill" because you never know when you might need to call in a favour.
- Procurement managers/directors would be better to see themselves as Relationship managers/directors.

SRM Case Study approaches

There are many examples of successful SRM approaches, we present a few of these over the next few pages:

Case Study: BP

BP believes SRM programmes require about 70 percent behavioural change and 30 percent process adjustment.

First the organisation segmented its suppliers to decide where to concentrate its efforts. It examined assurance and compliance to check if it was getting what it should from current deals, looked at spend volume and the value of the deals it had in place, and also examined what suppliers thought. It did this with the help of Honda, Toyota and an independent survey.

Of BP's 51,000 suppliers, it discovered it had just 6 to 8 key strategic suppliers. The next tier "sector critical relationships", had around 170 suppliers, and there are around 800 with whom BP has sector and/or local relationships.

Its SRM and supplier performance management programme – aimed at these groups – is expected to net savings of $200 million.

Start slowly with process based decisions around supplier performance until trust is established. *"If you have been beating them up for the past few years, it will take you at least 24 to 36 months to get them to talk about relationship management."*

Buyers had to send clear and consistent messages to suppliers and set KPIs appropriate to the relationship. For example, with top targets around innovation measurement for only the tier one supplier.

KPIs should support the organisation's overall objectives and performance management. Clear strategic goals, the right contracts, effective planning and capable managers should all be in place.

Case study: AVIVA Financial Services

"It reduces total cost of ownership and creates competitive advantage through deeper relationships with suppliers. For example, it means you may get privileged access to innovation, the best people, products and services within the supplier organisation."

Case Study: McDonalds

SRM helped the organisation focus on long term relationship needs and that it enhanced communication and helped to prevent "relationship value degradation". It also creates greater visibility, access to supplier capabilities and fosters innovation.

Case Study: British Airways

"You need to get the supplier to internalise you so that you become their 'customer of choice.' The world is currently moving into a world of scarcity, particularly because of the growth of India and China. The biggest challenge is competing with other buyers, not necessarily getting suppliers to compete."

Case Study: Philips' Procurement Strategy

The initial selection of suppliers is an important strategic decision and an essential stage in the procurement process. Both the supplier selection process and the assessment criteria have been defined. The selection process consists of:

- Identifying the strategic products.

- Identifying potential suppliers.
- Assessing and selecting suppliers.
- Defining the relationship with selected suppliers.

After following this selection process it becomes possible to define the type of supplier relationship, identifying those that have a strategic impact on the overall business. Assessment criteria are:

- Business capability (technological, manufacturing, commercial, logistics.
- Availability of products and services.
- Avoidance of conflict of interest.
- Management structure and organisation culture.
- Required confidentiality.
- Financial position.

In addition, the supplier's quality assurance system must be in compliance with the relevant standard of the ISO 9000 series and be certified by an accredited third party.

Relationships with Suppliers

As a leading electronics organisation, Philips is very involved in developments in electronic technology. Such developments have a considerable impact on the design of products, which require increasingly tougher specifications.

Success in these fields depends on close working relationships with suppliers. These require the development of supplier-partners on a 1:1 basis, the strategic importance of the relationship being underlined by top management involvement in the procurement process.

While good relationships are sought with all suppliers, intense working relationships can only be maintained with a limited number of suppliers. In order to identify the optimal supplier base, suppliers are classified into categories which determine the level of relationship.

The three categories, in increasing level of involvement are:

- Commercial suppliers.
- Preferred suppliers.
- Supplier-partners.

Commercial suppliers

Philips seeks to maintain and continuously improve product quality, delivery conditions and cost without specific initiatives from Philips' side.

Preferred suppliers

Mutual objectives have been identified and acknowledged by both parties. The preferred status is reciprocal. Philips has a preferred customer status with the supplier. The supplier introduces and implements TQM principles with Philips' support (if needed). Both strive for improved performance in quality, logistics and price.

Supplier-partners

In this closer relationship, in addition to sharing present expertise, supplier-partners co-operate in building new expertise and developing new business opportunities. The supplier-partner has, for example, fundamental proprietary knowledge which Philips must draw upon in order to launch a new range of products. The number of supplier-partners will always be quite small because this mutual dependency only exists for a small number of products. The strategic importance of the supplier-partner relationship is underlined by the involvement of top management.

It is to Philips' advantage to involve suppliers with a specific expertise in the product creation process from the start. Such expertise must, of course, been demonstrated by the quality of the supplier's previous products and processes.

Early cooperation makes it possible to utilise suppliers' knowledge and skills optimally and forms the basis for a short development time and timely introduction in the market. Sharing expertise is also the best way to control costs, both in the development stage and in the manufacturing process.

To reinforce the alliance with a supplier-partner, a senior manager (not necessarily from procurement) is assigned to act as the supplier's advocate. It is the task of this advocate to facilitate communication between the two organisations, remove managerial barriers, and make it possible, for example, to exchange planned developments in technology.

The boundaries for procurement processes are, to a great extent, determined during the product creation process. To reach a balanced decision on the specification of materials and the required supplier capabilities, the voice of all primary functions must be heard at the earliest possible stage.

A multi-disciplinary team comprising representatives from procurement, development, product management, and manufacturing brings together the competence for making the best decisions on product quality, logistic aspects, costs and supplier selection. Such teams provide the interface for early supplier involvement. Subsequently these teams provide the context in which supplier partnership can flourish and become the base for continued cooperation across functional boundaries.

It would be short sighted to evaluate a supplier (and thus the performance of a purchaser) on the basis of negotiated invoice prices along. Other cost factors, such as transport, product quality, lead time and stock obviously determine the cost as well. Total cost of ownership takes all these factors into account.

Open calculations and ship-to-line programmes can help to eliminate avoidable costs of ownership. Philips will support improvement programmes aimed at controlling processes at the supplier's end. This will cut down on avoidable costs and thus crate a "win-win" situation for both the supplier and Philips alike.

An integral requirement of every improvement programme is to upgrade the performance of the supplier in product specification, product quality, timely delivery and total costs. In each area targets are set and actual supplier performance is rated against mutually agreed upon targets. This systematic rating brings objectivity and focus for improvement. Minimum parameters on which suppliers are systematically rated are quality, logistics, price and responsiveness.

The basics of the rating system remain the same, notwithstanding differences between division and business units. The objectives of supplier ratings are to:

- Check the supplier's performance against the mutual target.
- Foster a continuously improvement process.
- Acquire the basic information for supplier assessment.
- Evaluate the relationship with a supplier.

Case Study: Chrysler

Car manufacturer Daimler-Chrysler is to spend an extra £2.5 billion on sourcing from low cost countries. The organisation also plans to reduce the cost of the materials it uses by £773 million.

The organisation will rely "more heavily on leveraging partnerships to manage costs", including working closely with suppliers to develop more cost effective products.

Case Study: Research into SRM

Organisations across a variety of industries are reporting difficulty in managing their suppliers, according to a study by Archstone Consulting.

While many organisations have conducted strategic sourcing and outsourcing to reduce costs, few have mastered SRM as a critical part of enhancing their supply chain and reducing overall costs.

Organisations that lack SRM elements such as supplier governance, performance management and supplier development, are often unable to realise the full value of their supply base.

A total 58% of respondents reported an inability to hold suppliers accountable and ineffective use of incentives and penalties. Fewer than 10% said current systems can effectively support SRM.

The research found that while most SRM initiatives are in their early stages, organisations have achieved or expect to achieve significant benefits. These include a 7 – 11 percent reduction in cost of delivery and a 10 – 14 percent reduction in procurement headcount.

Case Study: Research into SRM Leaders

Organisations that invest in supplier relationship management achieve greater savings and respond more quickly to changes in the marketplace.

The study by Accenture found that leaders in SRM achieve savings of 3 percent on their annual procurement spend, whereas other organisations achieved only 1 percent.

The study classed organisations that achieved more than 50 percent of procurement benefits from post-contract award activities as "SRM Leaders".

Most leaders were found in the media/entertainment, car and pharmaceutical/health industries, with property/facilities management, banking/insurance and manufacturing having fewest.

Whiles the majority of organisations expect the future focus on SRM to increase; there is a shortage of staff with relevant expertise.

Case Study: Automotive Industry

Attempts by Ford and General Motors to improve supplier relationships "may be starting to work" research has found.

The Original equipment manufacturer (OEM) – Tier 1 supplier working relations annual study found that while Toyota and Honda still have the lead in good supplier relations and are the preferred carmakers in the US to do business with, efforts by Ford and General Motors seem to be working.

The principal reason for this is that both Ford and General Motors are providing more timely and adequate information to suppliers than had been done in previous years.

The improved communication leads to greater trust, both of which are important components of strong working relations

Case Study: Asda

"Drilling down" appears to be a vital aspect of successful SRM and supplier collaboration and integration was an area that Asda was quick to home in on when it turned its attention to sourcing from local suppliers .

The supermarket now has a dedicated local sourcing team whose sole aim is to identify local products and work with small suppliers to enable their products to reach the stores. The team enlists the support of regional food groups, customers and colleagues to discover essential local brands in each area and decides which stores they would sell in. If there is large demand for a product, they ensure the supplier is not overwhelmed and work together to reach supply agreements.

"Local products often come from very small suppliers," an Asda spokesperson says. *"Therefore it is important for us to make it as cheap, easy and risk free as possible for these suppliers to do business with us. This means we have had to change the way work."*

Reduced payment terms have been introduced to help ease cash flow problems and no costly technology is needed. Unlike other supplier, local vendors do not need an electronic information system that processes and receives orders and payments. A simple fax will do the job.

Each local supplier is given a glossary and guide on how to complete necessary paperwork, which has been simplified with the jargon stripped out. Goods can also be delivered direct to the store.

A food hygiene accreditation system has been created between Asda's technical team and an independent lab. *"It is just as effective but simpler, quicker and cheaper to implement than the current industry standard,"* the spokesperson says.

Closer Connections

In addition, supplier days are regularly held to bring all Asda's local suppliers together. This not only fixes teething problems, but ensures they have access to as many members of Asda's local sourcing team as possible. The supermarket has also drawn up a commitment to the supplier. This includes selling products for between three and six months regardless of sales figures to give the product every opportunity to succeed.

SRM needs a new skill set and outlook

British Airways and others have observed that the skills buyers are traditionally trained in are not the same, as those skills required for traditional procurement activities. SRM requires a longer term perspective and the use of a range of soft skills; this is not always easy for logical minded numbers driven people; for as has been said, it is the soft skills that are actually the hard skills in business.

The following checklist indicates more on the SRM skills and approaches needed:

Checklist: The SRM Skill set for Managers

Supplier relationship management demands an intricate blend of hard and soft skills.

Traditional procurement is focused on "doing the deal", whereas SRM has a broader remit on the long term health and value of the supply relationship. To be effective, SRM requires an intricate blend of the following soft and hard skills.

- **Communication.** The ability to communicate effectively through a variety of channels, internally and externally.
- **Interpersonal sensitivity**. The ability to understand the other party's point of view.

- **Negotiation.** The ability to influence internal stakeholders and the supplier in relation to objectives, and to manage conflict.
- **Project management.** The ability to manage the processes and promises of delivery by both the supplier and the buying organisation.
- **Technical.** The ability to measure, monitor and cultivate the relationship through tools such as balanced score cards and continuous improvement programmes.

Case Study: Research into leaders in SRM

SRM leaders have done the following:

- Supplier segmentation; identifying the right buyer-supplier relationship to form part of the strategic sourcing process.
- Contract management; enabling comparative analysis and the monitoring of contract compliance.
- Supplier performance management; the monitoring of suppliers' operational, administrative and cost management performance.
- Integration and collaboration; integration relates to systems integration with key suppliers, allowing for more streamlined planning and fulfilment.
- Collaboration relates to joint improvement planning.
- Correct organisational structure: where SRM is a critical function and the cross-functional team efforts are institutionalised and encouraged.
- The right people whose skills are developed and deployed: with a focus on working more closely with key suppliers to deliver value over time, for both the supplier and their own organisations.
- The right technology to capture and assimilate supplier specific information and data.

Case Study: Centrica

Centrica has brought together the two functions of Procurement and Supplier Relationship Management into one department in recognition of the importance of laying the groundwork for effective long-term contracts.

Case Study: BA

BA developed a three pronged SRM strategy because many of its supplier relationships are complex and long term. The strategy involves a "Category Management planning process" where BA works out which suppliers it can "relationship manage" – the airline spends on average, UKP 3.80 billion a year and aims to actively manage 80 percent of that total.

Of the cost benefits they report, 60 percent comes from supplier management activity.

Once it has identified who to manage, an account plan is drawn up outlining what BA wants to achieve with the supplier. It states:

- who is in control of the relationship.
- potential risks.
- details the supplier's interests.

The airline researches how well the supplier is performing via online surveys and looks at buyer satisfaction and supplier responsiveness. The final aspect is an internet based systems tool for buyers. It provides answers to problems they are trying to solve, suggests what path they should take, who should be involved and how they can get to where they want to be.

BA believes that contracts are very important but they do not describe the whole trading relationship. Procurement departments tend to focus on doing deals. This is important, but misses the point. A big part of what procurement should be doing is managing the supplier, to bring in more sustainable advantages.

Procurement once thought information translated into power, but, today realise that the power is in the sharing of information, which in this context, provides an opportunity to reduce costs that can be shared by all the constituents within the supply chain.

As we have mentioned many times, too many organisations believe that the management of the procurement process actuality stops at the placing order stage and then the procurement department moves on to the next negotiation/the next deal, leaving the contract to manage itself.

This is an area that needs to be addressed, particularly as organisations are becoming more global and where souring and outsourcing has become increasingly reliant on an extended supply chains. As this trend continues, the need to actively manage suppliers and performance becomes even greater.

"Global procurement functions are doing well in terms of their visibility and cost cutting efforts, but poorly on contract management."
(Source: Ariba Live Conference 2005)

"Major barriers are the lack of internal competency to manage partners".
(Source: PTRM 2007; Global Supply Chain Trends 2008-2010)

With increased competition in the market, organisations will need to their suppliers to provide sources of value and differentiation. If an organisation fails to manage its supplier relationships, it is then leaving to chance the realisation of any potential and/or latent value in the relationship.

Effective Supplier Relationship Management

Effective SRM can deliver value for the organisation through a solid sourcing process and supplier management approach that will lock in the value from sourcing, this being so often lost in the post-contract interactions. It can then extend the value delivered from suppliers through an ongoing focus on collaboration and integration.

The need for the management of a supplier after the "deal", it has been concluded, is therefore fundamental, so that organisations are able to achieve the real benefits from their procurement strategies.

It is not good enough for organisations to draft a first class agreement with a top supplier, and then simply sit back and expect the medium to long term benefits to roll in. In a world where expectations and performance standards are always getting higher, organisations need to be able to build and maintain relationships with their major suppliers if they are to capture the maximum long term value from the supply chain links and connections.

Supplier management provides this catalyst for organisations to acquire products or services that will meet or exceed their expectations and to give them competitive advantage.

However, it need not be restricted to the post-contractual phase of supplier relationships. Effective management of suppliers during the sourcing and contracting process will normally produce a much better result, as here the buyer can then better and more clearly communicate their expectations, and in turn require and demand a greater insight into a supplier's infrastructure and capabilities. Indeed, we have already examined this service provision selection aspect with 3PL (third party logistics) in part 5 of this book.

Relationship segmentation is a critical element in planning a supplier management programme. As discussed earlier, approaches to supplier relationships will differ depending on the difficulty of the market in which the buyer is operating, the anticipated duration of the relationship or, the perceived probability of further engagement between the parties. This is shown below in the Supplier Management Behaviours diagram:

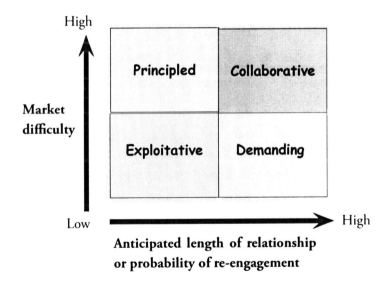

(Source: Johnson, R, 2003)

Many organisations do actually remain too "deal-focused" and are not good at all in managing relationships. Effective supplier relationship management will provides an integrated communication and information driven management process and one that is clear to all those who have the contact with suppliers.

To put supplier relationship management in context, the following diagram provides an overview of the whole Supply Management process, which illustrates how the objectives of any supplier management policy can be derived from the sourcing strategy.

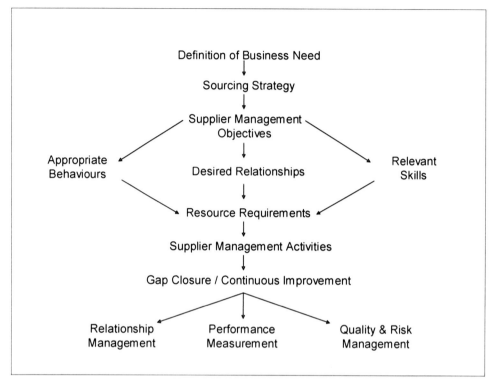

As with any process, and procurement and supplier management are no exception, they need to have an iterative element. Such a review process will then result in regular feedback, enabling the organisation to better determine their continuing business needs and supplier management objectives.

In an effective supplier management process, suppliers will come to expect a higher level of meaningful feedback to help them improve their operations at all levels. Feedback from their customers will typically include regular reviews and analyses of areas for improvement.

Effective supplier relationship management can then provide suppliers with the necessary opportunities for improvement through a process of regular measurement, review and feedback. Where necessary, it can also help suppliers to develop the capabilities to meet current and potential customer needs, enabling them to drive out costs and inefficiencies throughout their own supply chain that will benefit both parties.

Contract Management by Non-Procurement people

Sometimes non-buyers in organisations have to get involved with the ongoing contract management; the best approach to use is the following three step process:

1. Educate non-buyers so they know what it means to manage a contract. This is the most empowering step as it gives them the insight to understand the ramifications of their contract management decisions.

2. Enable the non-buyer with tools and processes and support their knowledge by offering a framework in which they can apply this new found knowledge.

3. Support requirements, this is the most strategic step and there are two options here. Procurement people agree to serve as an adviser or they become the lead contract manager. Either of these options will strengthen the relationship between buyers and the non buyer as by leading contract management activities, procurement will free up the non buyer to concentrate on their direct responsibilities. By agreeing to serve as an advisor on contract management activities, this then leaves buyers more time to develop value adding procurement initiatives.

Good contract management does not necessarily rely solely and only on procurement experience, but rather on having effective managerial, negotiation and interpersonal skills.

It is important to clearly define the scope of the respective roles, for example, who handles contract reviews, performance management, cost reduction activity and contingency planning.

Training should be provided on these and other basic principles, and ongoing advice and support for specific contract issues including relationship management, risk management and terms and conditions. Procurement support should also be given for key review meetings, negotiations and dispute resolutions utilising contract review templates.

Case Study: Bank of England

Non-buyers should take charge of contract management, according to the former head of procurement at the Bank of England.

Deals that perform well are often neglected, for example one healthcare contract, had not been looked at for seven years because it delivered good service. However by then working more closely with the supplier, significant savings were made and the level of service also was increased.

One way of tackling this neglect, was to devolve the management of contracts and suppliers to those departments that have the expertise in that specific area. HR staff could then manage the healthcare deals or the executive team could be given responsibility for existing consultancy contracts because they know what is expected of suppliers.

Case Study: Research

Most purchasers believe non-buyers are capable of handling contract management.

According to a "Supplier Management" poll of 100 buyers, 78 percent agreed ongoing contract management should, at least sometimes, be handled by non buyers.

It was agreed that it is procurement's role to equip non practitioners with the training, tools and support that allows them to manage contracts more effectively.

Procurement KPIs

As is well known, "if you cannot measure it then you cannot manage it." We therefore present below, for references purposes, a range of key performance indicators for procurement, in an approximate order of priority:

- Negotiated cost reduction savings per annum.
- Implemented cost reduction savings per annum.
- Cost avoidance.
- Procurement ROI (savings/operating costs).
- Percentage of suppliers accounting for 80% of spending.

- Supplier performance (price, delivery, quality, service).
- Contract compliance.
- Requisition, PO, or invoice transaction volume.
- Subjective feedback (structured, survey based).

The important thing is to select a few appropriate measures from each procurement category and then to look at them as a set, not individually. Also, it is better to try to measure by process rather than by function. Using the 5 Rights can assist on this.

The 5 Rights and Key Performance Indicators

Key performance indicators (KPIs) can be used to ensure control of all procurement activity and highlight any deviation from the standards expected.

The actual KPIs used will depend on the product or service being purchased and they can then be monitored to ensure supplier interest is maintained in the contract and also to build historical data for reference.

In general terms, the KPIs will cover those Five Rights of quality, quantity, price, place and time aspects, related to the goods being purchased; examples follow:

Quality includes:
- Re-work.
- Rejects.
- Warranties.
- Procedures.
- Complaints.
- Control.

Quantity includes:
- Full or Part Order receipts.
- Discounts.
- Minimum order levels.

Price includes:
- Consumables.
- Tooling.
- Overtime.

- Re-work.
- Materials.
- Labour.
- Downtime.
- Absenteeism.

Place includes:
- Accuracy of delivery to location.
- Tracking availability whilst in transit.

Time includes:
- Lead times.
- Emergency response.
- Set-up.

Below is an example of a supplier rating scorecard from Phillips:

SUPPLIER TOTAL QUALITY PERFORMANCE MEASUREMENT

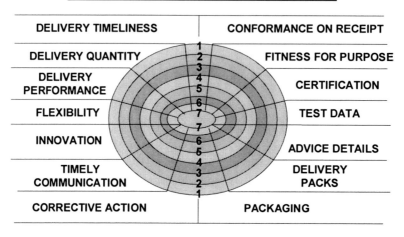

PHILLIPS

Here, the metrics are developed based on the priorities of the strategic plan, and with the supply chain metrics in particular, for managing suppliers to allow for effective SRM. Processes are then designed to collect information relevant to these Supply Chain key performance indicators (KPIs).

KPIs allow measurability, and therefore are objective criteria. They highlight areas for further improvement. Subjective criteria may also be involved based on the buyer's perception, for example to commitment, attitudes and mannerisms including:

- Motivation toward individual contract commitments, future business etc.
- Response to constructive criticism, problem solving.
- Input into problem solving, innovation.

Recent studies have shown that if buyers communicate as openly as possible with their suppliers about what they expect, they will be given more information on such areas as stock levels, lead times and quality problems.

Additionally surveys can be used to collate subjective opinions; for example the supplier survey mentioned below. Here the entire supply chain performance can be measured and the following Supply Chain KPIs can be used.

Supply Chain key performance indicators
KPIs reporting structures

Description	Measurement tool	Definition	Units
Customer orders fulfilment	On time/in Full rate (OTIF)	% orders OTIF	%
	Lead time	Receipt of order to despatched/delivered	Hours/Days
Customer satisfaction	Customer Survey	A sampling survey to ask for customers experiences, for example: -Support available -Product availability -Flexibility -Reliability -Consistency -Comparison to the competition	% satisfied
Supply management	On time/in full (OTIF).	As above	%
	Supplier Survey.	A sampling survey to ask for suppliers experiences, for example: as in the above customer survey	% satisfied
	Effectiveness.	Year over year improvements	%

	Lead Time	Time placed order- time available for use	Hours/Days
Inventory (measure for each holding place of raw materials, work in progress and finished goods)	Forecast accuracy.	Actual/Forecast sales per SKU.	%
	Availability.	Ordered / Delivered Per SKU.	%
	On hand.	Value on hand/daily delivered value.	Days
Cash flow	Cash to cash.	Time from paying suppliers, to time paid by customers	Days
Quality	Quality.	Non-conformances, as appropriate	Per 100 or 1000 or million
Operations	Utilisations.	Used/Available.	} Units
	Productivity.	Actual/Standard.	} Hours
	Costs.	Actual/Standard.	} Costs
	Lead times.	Time start/time completed per operation.	Hours or Days
People Relationships	Internal.	Absence rates	%
	External.	Sampling Survey, as customers / suppliers above.	% satisfied
Costs	Total supply chain or per operation cost.	Cost per time period/ Units.	£ per unit

The reporting structure should ensure that deviations from the KPIs are clearly and easily communicated both in a cost efficient manner and in an acceptable timeframe. The reporting structure should link the supplier, buyer and customer in a horizontal visible frame. Meanwhile, the operational, tactical and strategic levels should be linked in the vertical hierarchy.

Software can meet this need whilst a simple visual system can give adequate information in an appropriate format. For example, the 'Traffic High Light System' uses colour codes to report performance:

Green   = Acceptable

Amber = Cautionary

Red = Unacceptable

This simple system can be implemented quickly and easily as a basis for more comprehensive performance measurement:

Supplier "A"

	Jan	Feb	March	April	May	June
Quality	Green	Green	Amber	Green	Green	Green
Delivery	Red	Amber	Red	Green	Green	Green
Quantity	Green	Green	Green	Green	Amber	Green
Price	Green	Amber	Green	Green	Green	Green
Communication	Green	Amber	Red	Green	Amber	Green

KPIs and Suppliers

Once key performance indicators (KPIs) have been established and a system created, the relevant parties will need to adhere to the process. If a significant change is involved, this should include a timed plan for the introduction and induction of individuals with identified responsibilities within the process. Responsibility levels, lines of communication and reporting should also be included.

The supplier will need to commit to the programme and to recognise its advantages, for example, the performance measurements should also be of benefit to them.

The customer and any other interested parties must provide the required information expediently and recognise the benefits they will gain in terms of improved performance, reduced costs and greater co-operation. Without the co-operation of the customer and the other links in the supply chain, it can be impossible to collect the necessary data.

Supplier rating schemes also rely on the participation of the supplier and the buyer's internal activities (which both include goods in and despatch), along with the customer. Overleaf is an example of a supplier rating scorecard:

SUN MICROSOFT – SUPPLIER PERFORMANCE

	ACTUAL	MAX PTS
QUALITY PERFORMANCE (30)		
TOTAL FAILURE RATE (DPM)		25.0
FAILURE ANALYSIS		5.0
FIELD ISSUE/PURGE/STOP SHIP		(15.0)
DELIVERY PERFORMANCE (30)		
LEAD TIME		10.0
ON TIME DELIVERY		15.0
FLEXIBILITY		5.0
TECHNOLOGY PERFORMANCE (25)		
CAPABILITIES		6.0
CORRECTIVE ACTION/FAILURE ANALYSIS		10.0
CONTINUOUS IMPROVEMENT		9.0
SUPPORT PERFORMANCE (15)		
PURCHASING/MATERIALS SUPPORT		10.00
SUSTAINING TECHNICAL SUPPORT		5.0
PERFORMANCE MATRIX TOTAL		**100**

Source: Sun Microsoft

KPI's Effects on Suppliers

Suppliers must be given a thorough introduction to the supplier rating programme and understand their role. They must be encouraged to ask questions and be given thorough answers, so that, they can implement the process with little or no delays/errors.

The buyer, in turn, will need to understand the supplier's strategies and objectives in order to apply the performance measurements and improvements effectively; of course, this information may have already been learnt when sourcing the supplier.

The supplier must be able to trust the buyer where the cost of commitment is substantial. For small to medium enterprises, the amount of effort and resources required for monitoring and maintaining performance measurement might be overwhelming; buyers should take this into account.

KPI's Effects on Customers

Customers/users must also understand the value of performance measurement and recognise their role. Customers and other activities must interact with procurement as part of the responsibilities of an internally integrative supply chain.

Customers will need to be shown the benefits and cost savings and added value should be demonstrated. Equally the customer should be made aware that poor supplier performance that is not reported; would result in continued poor service.

The buyer can prioritise the customer's needs in order to maximise the benefits for them. Therefore, in addition to understanding the suppliers' viewpoint, they will have to understand the customer.

Monitoring Supplier Performance

Supplier performance should be measured over a period that is sufficient to capture any trends or fluctuations, such as seasonality. This however may not be necessary for projects to be completed within a specific timeframe.

Performance monitoring must be a set objective, for which individual buyers must take responsibility. Each buyer can be given the responsibility of monitoring individual agreements or suppliers. Alternatively, the responsibility for monitoring, as an activity, may be given to an individual or specialist team.

Information must be gathered, stored and distributed in an acceptable format. It should be available to management and suppliers on a regular basis.

Quantitative information on time and costs must be distributed to both suppliers and customers. This information should also take into account the quality expected from the supplier in terms of commitment and attitude.

Measurement should be made against historical data and projected improvements. The supplier should be driven toward continuous improvement to remain competitive; they should not be driven towards bankruptcy by making increasing and unrealistic demands.

Comparisons can be made against similar suppliers to create a league table of performance, this information being controlled for confidentiality reasons.

Downgrading Supplier Ratings

Suppliers who fail to keep within the set tolerances, must be notified within an agreed timescale. They should be given details of the non-compliance including dates and times.

The supplier must also be informed of their reviewed grade and the records updated. This can be used to trigger a closer analysis of the supplier's performance to ensure the situation does not deteriorate.

The supplier needs to be given the opportunity to explain why they have failed to perform and where the deviation is severe, a meeting should be arranged to resolve the problem.

The buyer should give the supplier guidance on how to achieve the required standard; this could include advice, co-operation, and the sharing of knowledge.

Where the supplier has to improve then a time scale should be set; additionally regular meetings may be necessary until the problem has been corrected, and the supplier can assure adherence to the expected performance requirements. Contingency plans may need to be drawn up in case of any recurrence.

Upgrading Supplier Ratings

Suppliers who have maintained or improved their performance should always be informed and thanked, for example:

'A' class suppliers should be commended.
'B' class suppliers should be upgraded.
'C' class suppliers should be upgraded.

Good suppliers can be encouraged to sustain their efforts and similar suppliers gauged against the improvements attained by others. This information can be discussed with these improved suppliers to try to identify improvement opportunities. This important concept of supplier development is considered in greater detail in part 4 of this book.

Increased performance should be rewarded and rewards used as an incentive for suppliers to maintain and exceed the performance expected. Acknowledging suppliers' efforts is important in building relationships. The rewards may be intrinsic in value, such as a certificate of achievement or other publicity. Buying organisations can create promotional contests to highlight the importance of performance improvement.

Substantial improvements or innovations may justify longer contracts, or other business opportunities. The buyer should always be looking for suppliers who can compete in tomorrow's marketplace. This will assist the buyer's organisation in staying ahead of the competition.

Longer term contracts and repeat business reflects the aims of modern procurement practice, such as reducing the supplier base for critical items, and forging closer working relationships where both the supplier and buyer are committed to continuous improvement.

Reviewing Supplier Performance

Supplier performance measurement methods should be regularly reviewed, to ensure that it is still in line with organisational strategy and organisation policy. Review meetings should be agreed with suppliers and customers/users and form part of the contract. For critical items regular reviews will be necessary.

The performance information collated will create a "performance profile" which will be invaluable to the buyer when analysing potential and existing buyers and for determining standards.

The supplier's opinion of their own performance, as well as that of the buyer's organisation, should be taken into account. Where suppliers are undertaking identical measurement themselves, then the comparisons should present no surprises, thus removing any conflicts of the "you did/I did not" nature. This can assist the buyer in making improvements to their internal supply chain, so also demonstrating a good working relationship with suppliers and assisting in the promotion of their organisation to other suppliers, as a quality client.

Supplier performance needs to be monitored in a positive manner to motivate better results; indeed any preferred long-term relationships will only succeed where both parties are committed to continuous improvement.

The determination therefore of the performance required from suppliers and the related supply chain activity is important for the whole business and must therefore be something that is agreed with all parties and departments involved. This of course also includes agreement with suppliers and internal users /customers.

Objective measurement will then enable accurate reporting and correction of deviations from expected standards. They will remove subjective opinion and any "you did, I did not" game plays and works towards achieving joint agreements on any variations with subsequent joint improvements.

The Relationship Positioning Tool

As mentioned earlier, in order to improve the supply chain more effectively, we must have a two way measurement which is an honest appraisal of each partner's performance in a no-blame culture. A very useful tool for this purpose is the Relationship Positioning Tool (RPT). *(Source: Douglas and Macbeth 1993).*

Organisations can only increase their own competitiveness and performance by continuously improving the performance of the other members of their supply chains. Whilst the focus of competitiveness has understandably been more traditionally directed downstream towards customers, many have failed and still fail to recognise the considerable advantages to be gained from a closer involvement with suppliers.

The aim should be to have all of the organisations in a supply chain performing to the highest levels, for example, 100 percent quality and delivery and at a reducing overall cost. Such a chain would also operate with minimum lead time and give maximum response to meet the customer demand.

The Relationship Positioning Tool is a technique which measures the relationship between an organisation and its suppliers. It identifies the strengths and weaknesses in the customer supplier relationship and encourages discussion between customer and supplier personnel in a way that avoids making "it personal" and blaming individuals.

RPT enables the customer and supplier organisations to create a joint agenda for improvement activities, including supplier development and buying organisation development. Whilst a 100% management effectiveness of parties that are not owned, can never be absolute or be dictated, it can be e gained through a willingness to collaborate. Attitudes of collaboration, sharing and open communication will then need to replace traditional adversarial practices, which tend to assume that product, services, suppliers and employees, are interchangeable and are therefore easily discarded when times are difficult.

Managers can have difficulties in understanding the full range of issues inherent in managing their supply chains. Additionally they can have difficulty in knowing where to start to make those needed changes that will increase the effectiveness of their supply chains. RPT addresses both these difficulties, by analysing the current situation between an organisation and a supplier and pin points aspects of the relationship that needs to be improved.

Where there are adverse variations from pre determined targets for quality, delivery and cost of supplied goods, then this represents waste and weaknesses in the relationship between suppliers and customers. Similarly, the relationship has to be effective in a way which ensures continuous improvement, through innovation, is undertaken.

The potential of the relationship to continuously improve to achieve present and future demands with respect to quality, delivery, cost and innovation is dependent upon the following:

- The strategy developed by the customer. This can be measured in terms of the attitude adopted towards the supplier, how the customer's requirements are specified and how these are supported through systems and people.

- The capability of the supplier to provide goods/services at the right quality, the right time and at the lowest overall cost. This is measured in terms of the overall organisation profile, people skills and organisation, process capability and supplier management

The customer's and suppliers ability to create a flow of information to the supplier provides the basis for the effective transfer of goods/services and for the sharing of knowledge and ideas. Aspects of these information flows are technical, involvement with the supplier, business and the people who make the contacts

The major contributory factors are made up of major roots, such as organisation profile, people, process, and supplier management, and the elements of the RPT "Tree" model divide into minor roots. For example, under the supplier capability, the following processes are examined.

- Design.
- Plant capability.
- Plant capacity.
- Systems.
- Process range.

- Flexibility.
- Lead times.

Generating and using the RPT scores

As with any analysis procedure, data has to be gathered to provide a base of information on which the identification of strengths and weaknesses can take place. Two questionnaires, one for the customer and one for the supplier, gather over 300 pieces of data. Each response to a question is then scored against "best practice" by a third party.

From these collected scores, the strengths and weaknesses of the relationship can be identified and areas for improvement identified for both sides.

By opening up the possibility of a free and open interchange of views on the results; to which both have contributed, the exercise rapidly develops into a mutual self help process in which both sides see value, since they have already recognised that each must change to some degree to effect the best possible improvements.

Review and Control of Long Term Contracts

One of the most challenging tasks for procurement is the management of long term service contracts, including outsourcing agreements. These types of contracts can last for up to five or ten years, during which time the business needs and risks may change significantly.

Therefore, one of the most important controls that a purchaser can put in place is a robust contract management structure. This will provide a framework for regular communication between the parties. It should provide a mechanism for regular reviews of the service, price and strategy, with a facility to agree any necessary adjustments to meet these new challenges. It should also provide an escalation structure for managing any disputes.

To ensure the correct type and level of service delivery, it is vital that the product, the services and their relevant service levels are clearly detailed.

The supplier/provider should also be required to provide regular performance reports for the buyer/purchaser. It is relatively easy to set demanding service levels, but it is also most important to monitor them regularly.

It is also essential that the contract contains a tailored mechanism that incentivises a supplier's performance. The most successful long term service contracts contain not only disincentives against poor performance but also incentives to improve it. The following questions may therefore be asked:

- What types of performance do we require?
- Does the contract incentivise these?
- What do we want to pay?
- Does the contract reflect this and protect us against unexpected price increases?
- Does the contract easily allow us to source our services elsewhere and/or terminate the contract?
- Does the contract contain exit provisions?
- How will the relationship be managed?

Measurement and Review Process

Both parties must put in a great deal of work to make a contract relationship work. The following diagram depicts one continuum of relationship types:

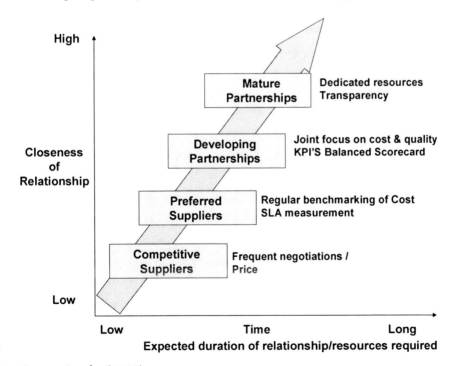

Source: Searles (2003)

Key steps in supplier relationships

The key steps that can be applied to supplier relationships are as follows:

1) Define the target and desired results.
2) The goal measurement.
3) Developing the measures.
4) Agree the reporting methods.
5) Review the process agreement.
6) Issue the report.
7) Refine and review the process.

Let us now look at these in turn.

1) Define the target and desired results. This first step is to establish clearly defined targets, as they lay the foundation for the relationship and ensure that both organisations are aware of their responsibilities. Goals should be set for the short, medium and long terms. The buyer and supplier should come to a joint decision and prevent unrealistic targets.

2) The goal measurement. Procurement relies on other functions for this measurement. Achieving each goal may require several initiatives running in parallel across different functions in both organisations.

3) Developing the measures. All those involved must agree the basic aspects of the process and what aspects of hard and soft measurement form they should take:

- Hard, objective measures will typically be quantitative, for example, percentage of deliveries received on time, delivery quality in parts per million, the value of annual cost improvements.

- Soft measures may require more subjective judgement and can be used to measure how the overall nature of the relationships is developing. Examples are management attitude, flexibility to changing business needs and a proactive approach to problem solving and resolution. One feature of many measurement and review processes that is often overlooked is the supplier's commitment and effort to making the relationship work.

To check each measure, then the following questions can be asked:
- The Measure, is it clear with a clear title?
- Purpose, why is it being measured?
- Relates to, to which business objective does this measure relate to?
- Target, what is to be achieved, and by when?
- Formula, what is the formula or rationale used?
- Frequency, how often should the measure be used?
- Who measures, who is responsible for collection and reporting, and who is the source?
- Who acts, who is responsible for taking action?
- What to do, what action should be taken?

4) Agreeing the reporting methods. Unfortunately, all too often, the contract manager is usually appointed when the contract has been placed, having had no, or at best, little pre-contract involvement. They will frequently therefore not have any real experiences of effective contract management. Consequently here, the contract management structure is inadequate and the contract manager is then at a disadvantage with their opposite number on the supplier's team in terms of experience and training. As a result there is often no agreement as to reporting methods and many of the following questions are not agreed.

- Who does what?
- For whom?
- When and where?
- At what cost and for what price?
- To what quality?
- For how long?
- Against what performance measures?
- Under what monitoring arrangements?

5) Review the process agreement. Within a typical strategic relationship, there will often need to be two types of review, strategic and operational.

Strategic reviews which are usually held once or twice a year, involving senior management from both parties with a wide ranging agenda focusing on future goals and direction, but also dealing with any consistent failures.

Operational reviews are typically held every month or quarter. The focus of the meetings here should be the performance against targets set for the year and actions to improve any areas of weakness. This will be discussed in further detail later in this section.

6) Issue the report. A successful review meeting should focus on looking at how previous processes and practices can be improved for the future.

7) Refine and review the process. An effective process has to be reviewed regularly, no less than once a year, to ensure that objectives continue to accurately reflect the business needs. Targets on continuing objectives should be increased in line with improvements in performance.

Case Study: BP Supplier Performance Management process

Category Management of Business Support Services for BP uses a Supplier Performance Management (SPM) process and upon implementation for one category of indirect support services, one business unit recorded a 30% improvement in efficiency, costs and lead-times. BP's SPM is comprised of the following stages:

1. Supplier Prioritisation
Using Kraljic, they highlight the key suppliers for immediate attention for the process.

2. Competent organisation
This ensures the procurement function for the category, have the required skills and competences for effective supplier management and full knowledge of the principles of Supplier Relationship Management.

3. Measures and Targets
Measures and Targets are clearly identified and agreed with the supplier base so that realistic KPIs can be established.

4. Performance Review Process.
Regular reviews and meetings are built into the process, so that both sides have regular feedback on performance, in order that the appropriate action plans for improvement can be implemented.

5. Drive and Sustain Value.
This recognises that monitoring of performance and continuous improvement activities should be on-going despite inevitable changes in processes and personnel, additionally, value-added needs to be managed through the SPM process.

Best in class organisations have formal criteria for the evaluation of existing suppliers as part of a structured SRM approach, and continually compare them to the performance of alternative suppliers.

Part 6: Summary

Supplier Relationship Management (SRM) is the management of the whole interface between supply and buying organisations through the whole life of the contract. The aim is to achieve maximum long term contribution from the supplier that works towards achieving the buying organisation's strategic goals.

Key performance indicators (KPIs) can be used to ensure control of all procurement activity and highlight any deviation from the standards expected.

The actual KPIs used will depend on the product or service being purchased and they can then be monitored to ensure supplier interest is maintained in the contract and also to build historical data for reference.

The Relationship Positioning Tool is a technique which measures the relationship between an organisation and its suppliers. It identifies the strengths and weaknesses in the customer supplier relationship and encourages discussion between customer and supplier personnel in a way that avoids making "it personal" and blaming individuals.

Bibliography

Aberdeen Group. **The Contract Management Benchmark Report-Procurement Contracts**. March 2006.

Air Plus International. (2008). **Travel Management Study.**

Alexander, K. (1996). *Tools for All Trades* in **Supply Management**, March 1996.

Arminas, D. (2003). *Contracts renewed on price, not performance* in **Supply Management**, May 2003.

Bailey, P., Farmer, D., Crocker, B., Jessop, D., and Jones, D. (2008). **Procurement Principles and Management.** Financial Times/Prentice Hall.

Barry, A. (1996). *Sorting out outsourcing* in **Procurement Weekly**, January 1996.

Bedford, R. (1996). *Outsourcing - A Supplier's view* in **Purchasing & Supply Management**, February 1996.

Beauchamp.M. (1995). *Procuring Persuasive PR* in **Purchasing & Supply Management**, January 1995.

Casey, T. (2005). *Influence Over Sales and Marketing* in **Supply Management,** September 2005.

CIPS Knowledge Works. (2008). **How to buy catering services**. www.cips.org.

CIPS Knowledge Works. (2008). **How to buy legal services**. www.cips.org

Clarke, E. (2007). *Consultants – Perfect Partners* in **Supply Management**, March 2007.

Cohen, A. (2008). *Business Travel* in **Supply Management Supplement**, October 2008.

Cohen, A. (2008). *Flying Low* in **Supply Management**, November 2008.

Communications. (2008). **Supply Management Travel Supplement**, April 2008.

Datamonitor. (May 2004). **European Logistics Provider End User Survey in Storage Handling and Distribution.**

Department for Business Enterprise and Regulatory Reform. www.berr.gsi.gov.uk.

Davies, J.P. (2009). **Research Summary: Procurement Project Innovation**, Cranfield University.

Ellram, L.M., Tate, W.L., Billington, C. (2004). *Understanding and managing the services supply chain* in **The Journal of Supply Chain Management 40 (4)**, and in **Knowledge Works** (2008), *How to buy consultancy.* www.cips.org.

Emmett, S. (2005). **Logistics Freight Transport**, republished with updates as **Excellence in Freight Transport** (2009). Cambridge Academic.

Emmett, S. (2005). **Excellence in Warehouse Management.** Cambridge Academic.

Emmett, S. (2008). **Excellence in Supply Chain Management.** Cambridge Academic.

Emmett, S. and Crocker, B. (2006). **The Relationship Driven Supply Chain.** Gower.

Emmett, S. and Crocker, B. (2008). **Excellence in Procurement.** Cambridge Academic.

Emmett, S. and Crocker, B. (2009). **Excellence in Supplier Management.** Cambridge Academic.

Emmett, S. and Granville, D. (2007). **Excellence in Inventory Management.** Cambridge Academic.

Emmett, S. (2000.) **Supply Chain in 90 Minutes.** Management Books.

Finance Section in **Supply Management Supplement**, April 2008.

Golder, A. (2004). *Outsourcing – Organisations unhappy with results in 50% of IT deals*, News, **Supply Management**, May 2004.

Golder, A. (2004). *Boots set to sign indirect buying deal*, **Supply Management**, June 2004.

Goolsby, K. (2001). *A guide for establishing service level specifications for outsourcing relationships*. Everest Outsourcing Center.com

Hotels. (2008) **Supply Management Supplement**, April 2008.

Hunt, M. (2004). *Teaming with Talent* in **Supply Management**, August 2004.

Insight Guide. (2008). *How to buy business travel*. www.cips.org.

Johnson, R. (2003). *Supplier Management: A deal of time and effort* in **Supply Management,** April 2003.

Kirchner, C. (2008). *All for one* in **Supply Management**, October 2008.

Kraljic, P. (1983). *Purchasing must become Supply Management* in **Harvard Business Review 50 (5)**.

Lankford, W.M. and Parsa, F. (1999). *Outsourcing: a primer management decision* in **Management Decision, 37/4 p 310-316**.

Lonsdale, C. and Cox, A. (1997). *Outsourcing: the risks and the rewards* in **Supply Management**, July 1997.

Lindberg, N. and Nordin, F. (2008). *From products to service and back again: towards a new service procurement logic* in **Science Direct, Industrial Marketing Management**.

Lancaster. G. (2003). *How to buy public relations services* in **Supply Management** October 2003.

Macbeth, D.K. and Fergusson, N. (1993). **Partnership Sourcing: An Integrated Approach.** Financial Times/Prentice Hall.

McPherson, I. A. and Moore, D. M. (2006). *CRISP - Challenger Innovative Spares Programme.* IDEA Conference.

Moody, M. (2005). *Facilities Management* in **Supply Management**, September 2005.

Moore, D. M. (2004). **Knowledge as the Basis of Professionalism in the Defence Acquisition Community: A Nascent Professional Project?** Ed D. Dissertation.

Moore, D. M. (2008). *Public Sector Stakeholders and Governance.* **CIPS Study Guide**.

Moore, D. M. and McPherson, I. A. (2009). *The 'ROAD' to Success in Competitive Dialogue in the Public Sector?* IPSERA Conference.

National Audit Office. (December 2008). **Central Government's Management of Service Contracts.**

News. (2008). *Buyers need marketing clarity* in **Supply Management**, July 2008.

News. (2008). *EMI to expand buying function* in **Supply Management**, July 2008.

News. (2006). **Supply Management.** November 2006.

News. (2004). *Outsourcing: RMC brings logistics back in house* in **Supply Management**, June 2004.

O'Brien, L,. (2004). *Outsourcing: Indirect savings need organisation direction* (News Focus) in **Supply Management**, April 2004.

O'Brien, L. (2000). *Outsourcing: Working It Out* in **Supply Management**, June 2000.

Office of Government Commerce (OGC). (2002). **Contract Management Guidelines - principles for service contracts**.

OGC. (March 2008). **EU Procurement Guidance.**

OGC. (2009). **Tendering for Public Contracts: A Guide for Small Organisations.**

Parsons, W. (2000). **Supply Management**, 15 July 2000.

PA Consulting Group. (1996). **Outsourcing: Best Practice** in *International Survey on Outsourcing.*

Schneider. (October 2006). **Electric Eye for Transport.** 4th European 3PL Summit, Brussels.

Searles, R. (2003). *Supplier Management: The Goal Standard* in **Supply Management**, April 2003.

Shaer, S.E. (2008). **Skills Assessment Model**. Project – BP Egypt CIPS Corporate Award.

Smeltzer, L.R. and Ogden, J.A. (2002). *Purchasing professionals' perceived differences between purchasing materials and purchasing services* in **The Journal of Supply Chain Management 38. (1).**

Supply Management, 15 June 2000.

Survey. (2007). *Best organisations involve buyers in marketing* (Aberdeen Group) in **Supply Management**, September 2007.

Trebilcock, B. (2004). *Modern Materials Handling.* IN WHAT???? , January 2004.

Tulip, S. (2001). *How to buy catering services* in **Supply Management**, June 2001.

Tulip, S. (1997). Facilities Management/Outsourcing: Classic FM? **Supply Management**, March

Tulip, S. (2001). *How to buy advertising and marketing services* in **Supply Management**, April 2001.

Tulip, S. (2001). *How to buy legal services* in **Supply Management**, August 2001.

Tyler, G. (1996). *Facilities Management: Building Relationships* in **Supply Management**, March 1996.

Tyler, G. (1997). *Outsourcing Premises* in **Supply Management**, October 1997.

Index